Racial Healing
for the Sake of the Gospel

MORE
Than
EQUALS

Revised & Expanded

SPENCER PERKINS
& CHRIS RICE

InterVarsity Press
Downers Grove, Illinois

InterVarsity Press
P.O. Box 1400, Downers Grove, IL 60515
World Wide Web: www.ivpress.com
E-mail: mail@ivpress.com

Revised Edition ©2000 by Nancy Perkins and Chris Rice

First Edition ©1993 by Spencer Perkins and Chris Rice

InterVarsity Press® is the book-publishing division of InterVarsity Christian Fellowship/USA®, a student movement active on campus at hundreds of universities, colleges and schools of nursing in the United States of America, and a member movement of the International Fellowship of Evangelical Students. For information about local and regional activities, write Public Relations Dept., InterVarsity Christian Fellowship/USA, 6400 Schroeder Rd., P.O. Box 7895, Madison, WI 53707-7895.

All Scripture quotations, unless otherwise indicated, are taken from the Holy Bible, New International Version®. NIV®. Copyright ©1973, 1978, 1984 by International Bible Society. Used by permission of Zondervan Publishing House. All rights reserved.

Cover photograph: Michele Stapleton

ISBN 0-8308-2256-9

Printed in the United States of America ∞

Library of Congress Cataloging-in-Publication Data

Perkins, Spencer, 1954-1998.
    More than equals: racial healing for the sake of the gospel/Spencer Perkins & Chris
  Rice.—Rev. & expanded.
      p. cm.
    Includes bibliographical references
    ISBN 0-8308-2256-9 (pbk.: alk. paper)
      1. United States—Race relations. 2. Race relations—Religious aspects—Christianity. I.
  Rice, Chris, 1960 II. Title.
  E185.615.P43 2000
    305.8'00973—dc21
                                                                                    99-086863

| P | 21 | 20 | 19 | 18 | 17 | 16 | 15 | 14 | 13 | 12 | 11 | 10 | 9 | 8 | 7 | 6 |
| Y | 18 | 17 | 16 | 15 | 14 | 13 | 12 | 11 | 10 | 09 | 08 | 07 | 06 | 05 | | |

Contents

Part 3: Commit

Acknowledgments

More Than Equals would not have been possible without some special people in our lives.

Spencer:
It took a very insightful God to give me my wife, Nancy. Her insight continually helps me crystallize ideas and concepts that I am able to write down later. She is my equal in every way, and she is willing to go with me wherever God leads. I'm also grateful to my father, who taught me how to see and understand more clearly the world around me and who demonstrated to me a nononsense gospel; and to my mother, who has loved me unconditionally over the years and has been patient with my slow understanding of God's call on my life.

Chris:
A Chinese proverb says, "When drinking water, don't forget the source." God put into my life three extraordinary people whose examples I have sipped deeply from along the stream of reconciliation: Mom and Dad, who pioneered for me what it means to love God through a life of risky faith; then my wife, Donna, my coseeker, who walked the path before me, who is our better half in servanthood, and whose steady perseverance and integrity before Jesus have continually inspired me to reach higher. God has knit us as one in heart and soul.

There are others who have helped us both.

The comrades of Antioch, our community and strength, without whom we would have had neither the passion nor the will to attempt this work. Their names deserve to be on the cover.

The "die-hards" of Voice of Calvary Fellowship, who, though sometimes battle-weary, are attempting to live out the vision of this book, and whose constant dialogue and confrontations have articulated and shaped these principles.

We can't imagine God giving us a better editor than Rodney Clapp, who has been a true servant in bringing the vision of this book into reality.

We also want to thank Lowell and Dixie Noble, two special people who have encouraged us not only in word but also in deed.

Finally, we have gained strength from struggling believers and bodies of believers all over America, especially our comrades in the Christian Community Development Association, who have the courage and commitment to swim against the currents of our time and wrestle with their own prejudices and insecurities in order to demonstrate to the world a gospel in which Jew and Greek, slave and free, male and female, all drink from the same cup.

Introduction to the New Edition

When Spencer and I walked across the fall-colored campus of a prominent private university and arrived at the black student center to lead a discussion on racial reconciliation, I expected sparks to fly. I was familiar with the cynicism of college students toward Christians.

So I wasn't surprised when not long into the dialogue, in a room crowded with both blacks and whites, a well-informed black senior admitted his misgivings. "When I heard it was going to be Christian speakers, I thought, *Oh, no. Some religious garbage.* I mean, what do *Christians* have to say about race with their record on justice?"

To him, Spencer and I were a strange new species. Our Christian convictions had led us across racial lines into a lifestyle focused on black-white reconciliation.

But what *should* he make of the Christian record on race, of those who claim allegiance to a Master who said, "By this all men will know that you are my disciples, if you love one another" (Jn 13:35)?

The student brought up South Africa. What was he to make of the fact that in the late 1980s, when racial apartheid was alive and well, one poll showed that over 80 percent of white South Africans identified themselves as born-again Christians?

I hoped he didn't know what I knew: that Rwanda, where black-on-black killing fields were soaked with the blood of one million people of the Tutsi tribe in the 1990s, was the most evangelized, Christianized country in central Africa; that eight of every ten Rwandans belonged to a church; and that church-going Hutus murdered many Tutsis, even brutally killing fellow Christians. The daunting task, said the chairman of the Rwandan Bible Society, was to "evangelize Rwanda anew."

In the book *God's Long Summer* author Charles Marsh tells the civil rights movement stories of both rabid segregationists and devoted freedom strugglers who believed they were taking orders from Jesus. It is well-documented that, as a group, white evangelical Christians were either silent or on the wrong side of that movement.

Our witness as Christians labors under the burden of a great historical contradiction: *that it is possible to be reconciled to God without being reconciled to your neighbor.* Whenever Christians make peace with that fallacy, it spells disaster for the world.

Truth Proof

To address this scar in Christian race relations in America, Spencer and I set out in the early 1990s to write a book not only grounded in biblical truth but in a story that "proved" that truth. From experience we knew there *was* an alternative, that racial redemption is possible *here and now.*

More Than Equals was the outcome of a long give-and-take between black and white Christians that continues today. The two of us lived in a rare American setting where the color line was broken in the most intimate arenas of friendship, family, social life, neighborhood and church. This unlikely laboratory for reconciliation was in Mississippi's capital city, in the black community known as West Jackson, home of Voice of Calvary Fellowship Church. There a congregation of friends has determined to stay together through tough times, "in sickness and in health." Within this crucible Spencer's and my relationship and partnership were formed.

For Spencer, taking on the yoke of reconciliation proved to be a life-long struggle in the trenches—from the 1960s fight for racial justice in rural Mississippi to the dream of racial harmony in our inner-city neighborhood in the 1990s. For me, it was nearly twenty years of living in a black community, working on relationships that didn't come easily and discovering the greatest joys possible on this earth.

Twelve years of our partnership were spent living in a small group with our wives and children, several other families, a host of youth, volunteers, guests and people in crisis, in an intentional Christian community we called "Antioch." We shared a common life of Christian discipleship and practical ministry. There—gathered around a dinner table with twenty-plus people, caring for each other, working together, fighting, forgiving, even washing the dishes—our individual stories were knit into the common story that we believed God was writing among us.

The years since the 1993 publication of *More Than Equals* saw Spencer and me enter new territory of learning and growth. (Our most important experience, a crisis in our relationship, is the subject of a new chapter added to this edition, "Playing the Grace Card.") Extensive travels in reconciliation work stretched us in new ways. Compelling national developments included a rising tide of attention to racial reconciliation within the Christian church.

Over these years four new convictions have emerged for me about race relations in America at the dawn of the twenty-first century. I call them "the paradigm shift," "the paradox," "the continuing perversion" and "the overlooked partners." They are important to introducing *More Than Equals*.

Conviction 1: The Paradigm Shift

"It makes no sense that the race problem is getting worse instead of better," Spencer and I wrote in the original edition of this book. "It seems that for every step forward, we take two steps back."

America's racial debate perennially errs on either side of "we've come so far" versus "not yet." Either progress is praised to the point of declaring the "end of racism" or divisions and gaps are so lamented that we often hear "things are worse than ever."

Who is right? My new conclusions from the growing evidence caught me by surprise.

After enduring two and a half centuries of brutal slavery, followed by another hundred years of violently enforced segregation and just three decades since the end of the civil rights movement, *ancestors of African slaves have become an integral part of American civilization, with an impact completely disproportionate to 13 percent of the population.* That they endured and transcended this oppression (carried out with an explicit "Christian" justification) with their belief in God intact and with a religious fervor unmatched in the nation is nothing short of an inexplicable miracle.

"Viewed from the perspective of comparative history and sociology," writes Harvard sociologist Orlando Patterson in *The Ordeal of Integration*, "it can be said, unconditionally, that *the changes that have taken place in the United States over the past fifty years are unparalleled in the history of minority-majority relations.* . . . There does not exist a single case in modern or earlier history that comes anywhere near the record of America in changing majority attitudes, in guaranteeing legal and political rights, and in expanding socioeconomic opportunities for its disadvantaged minorities."[1]

Whites had a 350-year head start, yet by 1995 the income of black married families reached 87 percent of white married families' income. A large, visible black middle class exploded—36 percent of African-Americans by that same year. Coupling that group with the large black working class equals *70 percent of African-Americans who have benefited from the enormous progress.* As of 1993 black women with a college degree or higher earned more than white women with the same education. And polls indicate that most blacks were very optimistic about their economic future.

African-American influence pervades the nation's life and thought. Culturally—in music, literature, entertainment and athletics—blacks are a highly visible force. What is American culture without jazz, blues and the foundational harmonies of gospel music and the black church? Politically, African-Americans and their interests are represented beyond tokenism. They have served as mayors of nearly all of America's largest cities, including Los Angeles, New York, Philadelphia and Chicago, and even largely white cities such as Seattle, Denver, Minneapolis and San Francisco. Nationally, the number of black elected officials nearly sextupled since 1970. Their opinions matter— half a dozen black columnists appear regularly in major city newspapers across America. The greatest national success story in race relations is the United States military: analysts now regard its culture as "Afro-European"; 30 percent of the nation's soldiers and 10 percent of its officers are black.

Who were arguably America's three most admired people at the end of the twentieth century? African-Americans Colin Powell, Michael Jordan and Oprah Winfrey. Were Powell to run for office, polls showed America could elect its first African-American president. Whose white son didn't want to "be like Mike"? Or his heir apparent, Tiger Woods, whose multiethnic heritage symbolized the emerging America of the new millennium?

This astounding progress embraces contact between blacks and whites. A 1997 Gallup poll found that the oldest children in over 60 percent of African-American families attended schools that were half or nearly all European American. And half of African-Americans lived in neighborhoods that were half or nearly all European American. Numerous polls and surveys indicate that friendship and contact between blacks and whites is much more frequent than acknowledged in the media.

Indisputable evidence of progress is summed up in that Gallup survey's startling conclusion: *"A portrait of a separate America for blacks is no longer valid.* Blacks in America today have relatively high levels of daily contact with whites across a variety of settings. Blacks live with, work with, send their kids to schools with, and have close friends who are white."[2]

A June 1999 cover story of *Newsweek* boldly proclaimed "the good news about black America": "By a wide array of measures, now is a great time—the best time ever—to be black in America." Inside, black journalist Ellis Cose (not a political conservative, author of *The Rage of a Privileged Class*, who declares the outrage of the black middle class) and a team of correspondents concluded that "the good news on black America is too clear to deny. In the past few decades, blacks' fortunes and prospects have soared toward the heavens. Blacks have entered virtually every sector of American society and breathed life into Martin Luther King's extraordinary fantasy. It's too late to put the racial-justice genie back in the bottle. It's time to acknowledge what America and African Americans together have accomplished and become."[3]

So is the racially tense world of *More Than Equals* an abandoned ghost town? Well, there's more to the story. But first, let the facts of hope and progress sink in. They represent a deeply significant paradigm shift for racial discussion in America.

Conviction 2: The Paradox

"Even after all the progress . . . our tired, embattled relationship has reached an impasse, and we are all suffering from race fatigue," we wrote in the first edition of *More Than Equals*. Truly, if America has "come so far," why does it feel so "not yet"?

Take that college Spencer and I were visiting. Nowhere did we find more talk about the value of diversity and tolerance than at universities like this one. Nowhere was there more evidence of progress: second-generation middle-class black students rubbing shoulders with the best and brightest. And yet nowhere did we see more visible, voluntary racial separation than on those same campuses. Black, Latino, Asian and de facto white dorms. Cafeterias divided into ethnic enclaves. The organized Christian groups on campus were mostly divided into separate ethnic fellowships with little if any contact with each other. Beneath the surface of correct language were distrustful, resentful and fearful hearts. Asking an honest question branded one "militant," "racist" or "Uncle Tom." Nowhere did we hear stronger calls for "separate and equal," a shrill new cry from black professionals and students who had seemingly "made it."

Instead of sending future leaders out with more cross-racial understanding and experiences, most students graduated as further casualties of the "race fatigue" that Spencer and I discuss in *More Than Equals*.

Other disturbing signs of conflict and dissonance have assaulted the national consciousness: Rodney King's 1991 videotaped beating, the police officers' acquittal, and Los Angeles's devastation by violence and looting. Another "not guilty" in the 1995 O. J. Simpson trial, leaving blacks mostly jubilant and whites mostly dismayed. Public division over affirmative action. Racially motivated violence and arson. Intractable inner-city crime and poverty, concentrated in black communities. The paradox of an exploding black middle class voicing less and less interest in racial integration. And media images of a white middle class fed up with special favors for minorities.

Whites and blacks reach completely different conclusions from the same events and evidence. One mostly contends "we've come so far," the other "not yet." Wrote *Newsweek*, "Blacks remain, in substantial measure, a race apart in America: a race admired, even emulated, yet held at arms' length. It reflects a particular American schizophrenia. We embrace equality and yet struggle with it in reality. We have come so far, and yet we have not escaped the past."[4]

The facts of both discord and progress cry out.

The Ordeal of Progress

The most convincing explanation of this dissonance, simple and yet profound, has been given by sociologist Patterson: "Things appear to get worse, and are perceived as getting worse, because they are getting better. *If the integration of two groups legally and socially separated for more than 350 years does not produce friction, it is the surest sign that no meaningful change has taken place.*" Patterson continues, "These experiences [of integration], it cannot be too strongly emphasized, are real—often vicious—and, for the African-Americans as well as many aggrieved European-Americans, traumatic. . . . *But they are side effects of progress, not signs of failure.*"[5]

The "paradox of progress" resonates with Spencer's and my experience. Often people have asked me, "How do I know when I'm on the road to reconciliation?" My answer: "When you start to feel pain." In this book you will read of a racial crisis that rocked our Jackson congregation in 1983. Many members left the church. But the lasting result of that conflict was to bring our black members into full empowerment within the life of the church. Great gains were made—but not without casualties, agony and a pile of clean-up work in forgiveness and reconciliation.

Racial progress is a great *ordeal*. It is uncomfortable and comes at a great cost—with friction, conflict, misunderstanding, grievances.

Everybody is not only gaining something but giving up something. For African-Americans especially, that is unfair, undeserved, agonizing. It is the "no pain, no gain" price of the remarkable breakthrough into the mainstream. But it is a side effect of progress, not failure.

As racial progress moves forward, resistance to it increases. Top Texaco executives were captured on audiotape in 1994 using racial slurs against African-Americans and apparently plotting to destroy documents related to a racial discrimination lawsuit. (Texaco settled the case for $176 million, the largest racial discrimination suit in history. It's nice to see the price of racial jokes so high these days.)

When the Oklahoma City bombing occurred in 1995, who didn't automatically assume Middle East terrorists were responsible? Timothy McViegh exposed the tip of a subculture of white supremacist groups that has been steadily documented and evidenced in act after act of violence (the latest, at the time of this writing, was a twenty-one-year-old white student in the Chicago area who shot eleven blacks, Asians and Orthodox Jews in a two-day shooting rampage, killing two people).

Mixed with astonishingly good news about black America is alarmingly bad news. In the words of *Newsweek's* Ellis Cose, "Despite the lip service we pay to the concept of equality, we look with equanimity, even pride, upon a statistical profile of black Americans that, were it of whites, would be a source of horror and consternation."[6]

At the dawn of the twenty-first century, one out of every four blacks and over 40 percent of black children lived in poverty. Over 90 percent of those children had only Mom present at home, often barely an adult herself.

One of every three black men aged twenty to twenty-nine was in prison, jail, on parole or probation. A minuscule but highly dangerous 3 percent of African-Americans (nearly all males) were arrested for 45 percent of America's violent crime—almost all committed against other blacks.

Conditions within black families were perhaps most alarming of all. African-Americans had the lowest rate of marriage in the nation and the highest divorce rate of any major ethnic group. Teen black girls having children and irresponsible, absent fathers were national emergencies; 60 percent of black children have been abandoned by their fathers.

Making all this more complex is how much these are legacies of racial injustice versus *American* problems increasingly shared by all ethnic groups, as witnessed in a violent national subculture; a growing poor white underclass; rising white teen births and single-parent households; and an ever-widening, even immoral, national gap between "haves" and "have-nots." Many poor families work full time but cannot earn a livable wage.

Substantial resegregation of public schools has also risen since the early 1980s, even among suburban blacks. White students go to schools that are mostly white. More and more educated and middle-class African-Americans value equality over diversity, development of their communities over racial integration. In 1998 the NAACP hotly debated its historic commitment to integrated schools. The real issue behind school integration is persisting residential segregation.

Make no mistake, there is no end of racism. It lurks insidiously in literally tens of millions of souls. Some scholars estimate that as many as 25 percent of whites—*45 million*—are still hard-core racists. While far fewer than years ago, consider this alarming result: *for every two African Americans, there are three hard-core racist whites.*[7] Fueling outrage and injustice is the disproportionate presence of these racists in their lives. One persistent and public arena is hard-core racism among white law enforcement officers. Mark Fuhrman, a detective in the O. J. Simpson case, boasted on tape to a Hollywood screenwriter about planting evidence on black professionals, embodying a "Fuhrman factor" that repeatedly makes blacks (especially men) targets of police harassment and sometimes violence.

Millions of these hard-core white racists are in our nation's Christian churches. What is the church doing wrong that racists are comfortable in our pews, choirs and Sunday school classes—even in our pulpits? This brings us to the place of the Christian church in America within this paradox of progress.

Conviction 3: The Continuing Perversion

It is an institution, according to two analysts, "unmatched in its level of racial integration. . . [and] its broad record of African-American achievement. It is a world in which the African-American heritage is part and parcel of the institutional culture."[8] Would that they were speaking of the church. But no, this description is of America's leader in race relations—the military.

In stark contrast to national progress, a 1997 Gallup Poll concluded that the Christian church remains *the one "highly segregated" major institution of American public life*: 73 percent of whites and 71 percent of blacks still went to churches that were, respectively, all or nearly all white and black.[9] Adding insult to injury is sociologist Patterson's observation: *"The Christian church has failed miserably in the promotion of ethnic fellowship and is now the mainstay of segregation."*[10]

This is the real scandal of the Christian church. Citizens are not expected to act like family. Christians are—but we don't. In fact, the gospel's starting point for race relations is that black and white Christians are *more than family*. We are more brothers and sisters than with our own blood and kin. (Said Jesus: "My mother and brothers are those who hear God's word and put it into practice" [Lk 8:21].) Our accommodation to separation falls far short of God's intentions and robs the gospel of its power.

Social science may indeed show astounding progress in race relations. But these terms cannot describe the terrain as seen through the eyes of the gospel.

Through that lens, the white majority can "give ground" but be full of resentment, anger, guilt and shame. Millions of blacks can be "better off" but still hold bitterness and unforgiveness in their hearts. The races can know each other better and like each other less. National racial progress may be measured by statistics, but God measures by the content of the human heart. We can do the right thing, but if not for the right reason, if not inspired by sincere love, it doesn't even count (1 Cor 13:1-3)!

Every bit of racial progress in America has been fought for, inch by inch. The reign of God's kingdom, however, comes never by force but voluntarily—from the heart, not begrudged or demanded. The mark of reconciliation is not a truce but an embrace. And we have yet to experience that embrace within the body of Christ.

A church without embrace cannot break the entrenched cycle of ungrace between the races. It cannot cure descendants of hard-core racists of residual cancers of shame and superiority, nor empty the descendants of former slaves of poisonous reservoirs of dislike and disdain for former oppressors. Only those transformed by God's unfair, insane love—who then give it undeserved as willing victims back to each other—can break the cycle. There is no better—and no other—place to stage that embrace than within our churches.

The challenge is to come to see that embrace as a pearl of great price worth surrendering much. In the last months of his life, Spencer was reaching for a new language in describing that pearl to his black brothers and sisters—he called it "the culture of grace" (see chapter twenty).

Integration Versus Reconciliation
Sooner or later we are going to have to stop pretending that this antagonistic relationship can be healed by itself. It's going to take some work. The challenge of beginning to talk honestly and work intentionally toward living like family is the task of *racial reconciliation*.

Through our common struggle shaped over fifteen years of hard-won friendship, Spencer and I came to the same conclusion: *integration* and *reconciliation* are not the same. The two battles should be waged with different rules and on separate planes.

Integration is a political and social concept; the *beloved community* spoken of by biblical and contemporary prophets is a much higher calling. America may be more integrated, but it is far from being reconciled. Reconciliation is a deeply spiritual concept and must be approached spiritually. Trying to hold non-Christians to Christian principles is like trying to convince a cat that mice should not be eaten. The cat might see, and it might even understand, but it will not have the inner motivation or "vision" to stop chasing mice. When it gets hungry, it will interpret your request as going against its best interest. "Where there is no vision, the people perish" (Prov 29:18 KJV).

While this book may heighten your insight into our country's racial problems, it is a special challenge for those of us who have pledged allegiance to Jesus Christ to follow the tough but liberating teachings of our Lord. Analysis might be interesting, but what is most important is that we live out solutions that show the world another way.

While the Christian church has often failed miserably in demonstrating this alternative, this same church has a counterheritage. I believe the greatest stories of interracial partnership and progress in America—whether the underground railroad, the abolitionist movement, the civil rights movement, and even now in the growing, interracial, faith-based movements of churches taking on the inner city—are stories of courageous Christians. This is the heritage for us to reclaim.

Conviction 4: The Overlooked Partners

By now some are asking, "Is this just a black-white thing?" One of the critiques of *More Than Equals* has been its black-white focus. Well, some of my best friends are Latino and Asian and . . . no, I won't go there.

The fact is, Spencer and I didn't write as scholars but as practitioners. We focused on black and white because that is who we were and what we experienced. It's what we could address with authority.

Through further experiences and travels, however, we encountered a wider ethnic landscape. On many college campuses Asian Americans far outnumbered African-Americans. In Chicago I stayed with a friend who lived in a Latino neighborhood called "LaVillita." I went on my daily jog and got lost, and suddenly "little village" seemed vast and very foreign, especially when I asked three people for directions, and none of them replied in English. In Mississippi thousands of Latino employees have flooded into rural chicken-processing factories. Eventually Voice of Calvary Fellowship Church will be pushed beyond its comfort zone in a city that is no longer just black and white. One of the most defining symbols of black-white division in America is the 1992 Los Angeles riots. But more Latinos than blacks were arrested, and Korean-American stores suffered some of the worst devastation.

It is time to invest much more energy in extending the reconciliation challenge beyond black and white. Our partners have been in the room a long time. They've been overlooked, and I know they have felt it. Sometimes they can be pretty quiet too. It's time to welcome them—and challenge them—into the struggle.

There are three "significant others": Native Americans, Latinos and Asian Americans. Native Americans are an almost invisible presence, but the scar of unresolved original sin lies buried deep in the nation's soul. Latino and Asian Americans are changing the face of America and the church. By 2010, Latinos will be our largest minority group. Asian Americans are the fastest growing minority group, about one in ten Americans by 2050. Already outnumbering African-Americans in bellwether California, their influence is disproportionate because they are more educated and affluent than any ethnic group, including whites.

My closer familiarity is with Asian dynamics (having grown up in South Korea with a very positive experience and studied Chinese language in college). I will mention three issues added by their presence that probably touch similar dynamics in the Latino community.

First, where does reconciliation begin? For starters, "Asian American" is an ambiguous category. There are huge differences and tensions between Asian ethnic groups. It is more accurate to speak of cultures, neighborhoods and churches that are Vietnamese, Korean or Chinese than "Asian American." East Asian cultures (Korea, Japan and China—all based in Confucian culture) differ significantly from *Southeast* Asian. Korean immigrants, mostly educated and urban, have succeeded quickly in America. Cambodians, mostly poor and rural, have struggled. Japanese immigrants have been deeply assimilated into American life with an extremely high rate of interracial marriage with whites. By no means do Koreans first think of themselves as Asians. A Korean family friend always warns me not to go to Chinese restaurants. "Chinese dirty," she says. Like most Koreans, she also carried a fierce animosity for the Japanese, colonial oppressors of the Koreans. All these dynamics point to a deep need for intra-Asian ethnic healing.

At the same time, Asian cultures value the group over the individual, making the "birds of a feather" principle an even greater threat to unity with non-Asians. A cultural strength when it comes to mutual support, sticking together can keep Asian Americans isolated, self-satisfied and on the sidelines of the larger multiethnic arena. That must be resisted.

Second, are Asian Americans the "oppressed" or the "oppressors"? The legacy is decidedly mixed at both extremes. The long history of American Japanese and Chinese citizens is riddled with vicious discrimination, most familiarly when Japanese-American families were forced into internment camps during World War II. But throughout history, Japan committed notorious violence against other peoples, including colonizing Korea from 1910 to 1945. Thousands of Korean women were forced into brothels to service Japanese soldiers. Bullied by more powerful countries around it, Korea birthed a home-grown "theology of the downtrodden" called *minjung*. But they can't claim a clean slate either. Prejudice is intense against mixed-race children (mostly the progeny of American servicemen) and darker skin. In American inner cities, Korean storeowners are often detested. This is partly a cultural clash, but many of my black friends detect a dehumanizing superiority complex.

Ethnic chauvinism is an achilles heel for each of these East Asian cultures. There is much behind the fact that the Chinese dubbed their country the "Middle Kingdom." Japan has forced its culture upon others throughout history. Understandable Korean self-protection mechanisms and hard-won pride can erode into ethnocentrism. It would be easy for many Asian Americans to imagine they are superior, simply in comparing their economic performance to other ethnic groups. I have heard Asian-American students bemoan being labeled the "model minority." Well, there are worse things to be called. But perhaps they are voicing a deep insecurity that lies behind the image of success. Idolization of whiteness takes a sick form in the cut-and-paste surgery, common to Asian-American women, that "Westernizes" their eyelids.

Third, this complicated legacy of experiencing both pain and privilege, both discrimination and advantage, may point to a special role for Asian Ameri-

cans in racial reconciliation. Perhaps their experience on both sides of the fence has prepared Asian Americans to be bridge people in racial healing. They bring great cultural legacies to the challenge—perseverance, a willingness to delay immediate gratification for long-term success, and often fervent Christian faith. Back in Asia, the gospel was often accepted only at great personal cost. These are great assets for the reconciliation battle. Maybe Asians and Latinos even have a strategic role to play as bridges between the black-white divide that is undoubtedly our most insidious dilemma. The cultural strengths of our overlooked partners will be of great benefit to the whole church as we struggle for reconciliation in the twenty-first century.

While this book is not definitive, Spencer's and my ministry experiences across the nation proved that its biblical and practical principles can be readily applied to the entire body of Christ. I encourage you to add to its reading other ethnic-specific resources as listed in an endnote.[11]

A final word on a related subject: much debate has emerged over the use of the term *race* versus *ethnicity,* and *black* and *white* versus ethnic designations such as "African-American" and "European American." Some even prefer "Afro-American" to distinguish the ancestors of American slaves from the growing number of new African immigrants. An increasing and vocal number of mixed-race children, mostly of black and white parentage, no longer accept the "one drop" rule that persists in dubbing them only *black;* they prefer *biracial,* embracing the heritage of both parents. This debate raises important issues, including the fact that "race" is not explicitly mentioned in Scripture. New Testament divisions were between ethnic groups: Hebrews, Greeks, Samaritans and Romans. But to keep things simple, we will stick to the language of the first edition. In this book the terms *race* and *ethnicity* could be interchanged.

The Journey

Spencer's and my life stories are critical to this book's message. They illustrate both how differently the issue of race has affected different ethnic groups and how similarly we can be transformed as we become part of God's story. At times the anger from Spencer's bitter racial experiences sends sparks out from these pages, while my racial naiveté is embarrassingly evident.

But we all begin where we are. For the process of reconciliation to start, different responses are required from different ethnic groups. So each chapter in this book is written in one of our voices. As each of us sounds the particular notes of his own racial experiences and perspectives, I believe they blend into a clear and harmonious call to action.

We can't just snap our fingers and—presto!—suddenly be one in Christ. The task of bridging our racial divide and acting like a loving family is a journey, and three crucial steps are needed. They are the framework for this book.

First, *admit*. Christians must admit that a separation exists, that our ethnic and racial relationships are uneasy, and that this misrepresents what God intends for his people. Second, *submit*. We must hand ourselves over to God, fall on our faces before him for help, and recognize that we can't be healed apart from him. And we must submit to one another by embracing across racial and ethnic barriers and beginning to address the hurts and gaps between us. Finally, *commit*. Deep and lasting reconciliation will be realized only as we commit ourselves to a lifestyle of loving our racially different neighbors as ourselves.

Spencer's and my long friendship and ministry proved that it is still possible for the embodiment of reconciliation, this new family of God, to become visible on this earth. We wrote not as "experts"—not as sociologists, political scientists, economists or historians—but simply as brothers in Christ who walked a daily reality of unity. We stumbled much, forgave much and grew much. God always made a way when there seemed to be no way.

On January 27, 1998, Spencer's sudden death at age forty-four of a heart attack at his home in Jackson brought his witness on this earth and our long partnership to an end. For the sake of the gospel Spencer loved me " till death did us part." For the sake of the gospel, I loved him like a brother. Because of God neither of us was ever the same. Indeed, God made us family.

It is time that we, fellow citizens of God's kingdom, take our rightful place as the light—a city on a hill—in leading the way from separation and integration to the higher call of reconciliation. It is time that we, a holy race, no longer follow the world's lead but move beyond the quest for equality and mere tolerance to make visible the "one new person" that Jesus died on the cross to create. It is time that we, brothers and sisters, acted like family.

Part 1

Admit

1

Race Fatigue

As a black Christian I thought our freedom struggle in the *sixties would lead to reconciliation. I was wrong. Race seems to be one nut that even Christianity is having a hard time cracking. Chris and I believe that the first step in the reconciliation process is admitting that the race problem exists and that our inability to deal with race has weakened the credibility of our gospel.*

"I have a dream," roared the prophet, "that one day the sons and daughters of former slaves and the sons and daughters of former slave owners will be able to sit down at the table of brotherhood together."

If there was one word that captured the hearts and minds of black Americans during the sixties and seventies, it was *integration.* For many years we fought for it, and many even died for it. "We want our freedom," we insisted, and integration was one of the ways we were going to get it. "Register to vote." "We demand our civil rights." "We shall overcome." These were the battle cries of a generation of African

Americans who sought the life, liberty and pursuit of happiness articulated so beautifully in America's Declaration of Independence.

Now it is against the law to discriminate against someone because
of the color of his or her skin. We have a Fair Housing Act that outlaws
discrimination in housing. Black politicians control many of the major
cities in this country, and blacks have benefited enormously from the
well-intentioned attempt at restitution called affirmative action. But as
Boston Globe reporter Jonathan Kaufman has concluded, "A generation after the civil rights movement blacks and whites seem to know
each other better; but in many ways they seem to like each other less."[1]

We are all suffering from race fatigue. Someone forgot to tell us
along the way that you can't legislate people's attitudes. Changing laws
will not change hearts. The civil rights movement has run its course,
and we've gotten just about all you can expect to get from a political
movement. The dream of whites and blacks sitting down together at
the table of brotherhood is far from a reality.

Historically, American Christianity has failed to challenge racial
division. Sometimes we have even embraced separation—if not in theory, most definitely in practice. In 1974 our family and the tiny staff of
Voice of Calvary Ministries moved into a West Jackson neighborhood.
At that time the neighborhood was about 80 percent white. The meta-
morphosis that is now so familiar to American cities took place in just
six years; by 1980 our community was 80 percent black. It would make
me so proud to call myself a Christian if I could tell you that the white
20 percent who remained behind were the Christians. It would make
me proud if I could say that these white brothers and sisters decided to
befriend us and that their love for God was demonstrated to us by the
way they loved us. But only the whites who were too old and too poor
to escape stayed behind. Today our community is nearly 90 percent
black, like many other inner-city neighborhoods across the country.

I would love to be able to play the part of a Christian real estate
counselor (white, of course) who interviews Christians set on moving
out of their neighborhood when blacks begin to move in: "I suppose
you've prayed about this and concluded that it's God's will to get out.
Ever consider the statement you're making to black Christians by leav-

ing? I guess you figure you can do more for the cause of the gospel by moving to the suburbs, right? Ever consider what Jesus might do in this situation?"

Some frustrated blacks have described integration as "the period of time between the first black family's moving in and the last white family's moving out." For the most part, integration has been successful only when it could be forced on the white community. Given a choice, it rarely happens. White parents given the choice to send their children to a mostly black school would most likely choose not to. A white family with the resources to move out of a racially changing neighborhood will usually do so. A white church that can afford to leave the inner city will usually leave. These choices are second nature. I'm not sure if very many white Christians stop to think of the message they are sending to black Christians as they make these decisions.

Whites are not the only ones separating along racial lines. A new phenomenon is growing among blacks who are frustrated with the reality of integration: a call for black separation. Although the idea is not new (Elijah Muhammad and Malcolm X taught it during the fifties and sixties), more and more mainstream blacks are beginning to look at it as a feasible alternative. The train of thought runs the whole gamut, from all-black private schools, universities, churches and neighborhoods to a separate black state, federally funded as restitution for slavery. "If we can do it for Israel, why not for blacks?" is the rationale. Although this radical idea is not receiving much popular support, there is growing enthusiasm for the idea of blacks doing business with other blacks, living in black neighborhoods, worshiping with blacks and insisting that their children attend black universities.

The thinking goes something like this: the more we blacks can do for ourselves, the more we will respect ourselves and be respected by the American mainstream. The more we respect ourselves and are respected, the more control we will have over our own destiny.

Compounding this frustration with integration is what many black professionals have been calling a "glass ceiling." They are convinced that no matter how well they perform, their climb up the corporate ladder is eventually arrested solely on the basis of their skin color. A

growing number of black businessmen and women are leaving corporate America and striking out on their own, starting their own compa-
nies. They are refusing to be patronized by white corporations that
place blacks in high-profile but limited jobs like vice president of public affairs and personnel director.

On one hand, integration has helped to create a growing black
middle class. On the other hand, this middle-class group could and
did move up and out of black neighborhoods, taking with them economic, moral and spiritual stability and leaving behind only those
who were too poor to move out. It can be said, however ironically, that
integration has helped to create a new subculture that is now being
called the black underclass.

Separation is a natural path to take when you have bought the concept of integration hook, line and sinker. The problem is that blacks
tried integration with a mostly unwilling white partner. It was like
being the odd person out at a dance. The hosts and their other guests
would reluctantly dance with you, but you knew deep down that they
didn't want to. Then, as more of your kind showed up, the original
dancers slowly and inconspicuously moved their party to another
room. Before you knew it, you and your friends were the only ones left
in the room. "Hey! So who needs them? Let's throw our own party,
make it bigger and better and not invite them!"

I have to admit that my emotions run in this direction sometimes.
And speaking strictly from a human perspective, why not? What's the
alternative?

Credibility Gap

White Christians' decisions to choose the comfort of their own race
over the Christian ideals of brotherhood and oneness that our gospel
so boldly preaches have undoubtedly weakened their witness to the
African-American community. Because blacks have not been able to
distinguish between white Christians and white non-Christians when
it comes to racial issues and separation, major issues like abortion,
which should be cut and dried for us, become confused. When white
evangelical Christians stand against abortion, the first thought that

comes to the mind of many African Americans is, *What's in it for them? Whatever it is, it must be something bad for us.* Right or wrong, the fact that black Christians would even think like this demonstrates the ungodly mistrust that exists among the people who are supposed to represent a God of love.

The wounds of racism and oppression are still deep. Just how deep these historical scars are etched into our being was made plain to me by the comments of a black single mother as she watched white anti-abortion protesters on the evening news: "Do you think they would care one bit if only black babies were being aborted?" Many other blacks would echo her bitterness. I know her question sounds cruel and calloused, but it demonstrates the size of the gulf between us and illustrates our desperate need for racial reconciliation.

There is a huge credibility gap between us—a deep lack of trust. The historical gulf that lies between blacks and "right-wing" Christians is so deep that it's hard for some to imagine us being on the same side of any serious issue. Our lives have been so separate that we see issues like abortion from totally different perspectives. Abortion for many white Christians is an issue that can be discussed in a vacuum. Not for us. Even though an overwhelming majority of black Christians are against abortion, they are torn by the painful realities that surround them.

For blacks who have a huge stake in the survival of the black neighborhood, what does "zero abortions" mean? How many more female-headed households would be created? How many more young women would be trapped in the cycle of poverty, totally dependent on welfare? How many more gang members would these families produce? Wouldn't the ghettos be twice as large in just a few years? Wouldn't the crime rate soar? Wouldn't the prisons overflow? Who would take care of all of these children? Why should blacks not assume that as the ghettos become larger and more dangerous, the Christian antiabortionists will not move farther and farther into the suburbs, taking little or no responsibility for the social consequences of the lives they helped to save?

Let me tell you a true story—a story that illuminates the problems and illustrates black frustrations. Our congregation is rather unusual for a Southern church in that the black-to-white ratio is close to fifty-fifty. In 1989 some of our members were passionately involved in the antiabortion movement, so a Right to Life meeting was scheduled at our church. One local member of the organization, a white woman, obviously wasn't aware of our racial makeup or didn't prepare her two children for what they would encounter that evening. A black woman who had volunteered to tend the nursery happened to see this family as they walked into the building. When the white boys noticed the skin color of some of our children, one of them asked in disgust, "What kind of church is this?"

His brother's response summed up what these young white boys felt about their black brothers and sisters: "We'd better be careful what we touch while we're here," he said, drawing his hands back as if he feared contamination from some deadly disease.

Issues like abortion should not be too complicated for Christians. Who could imagine Jesus saying that because of social problems it is okay to terminate the lives of the unborn? But because Christians have not been consistent in fighting other social sins such as racism, the motives of antiabortionists are muddied for black believers.

All Bark and No Bite?

From a Christian perspective, integration has been weighed in the balance and found wanting. Even though it has produced a growing class of affluent blacks, it will never achieve the brotherly love Jesus calls us to. And black separation will produce much of the same frustration. Even though it might spark some much-needed self-respect, it falls far short of the Christian ideals preached by Jesus and the apostle Paul. White separation has compromised and weakened the power and witness of the gospel—so much so that it has confused us in responding to abortion and other social evils. And fear of the crime and violence of our inner cities is making opportunities for white and black interaction much more difficult.

Much water has gone under the bridge in the historical relationship between whites and blacks in this country, from the cruelty of slavery and the white racism that followed to the "Great Society" that tried to atone for past oppression through legislation like affirmative action. Now as we witness a white backlash and the confusion of a rapidly growing black "underclass," our mutual fear and distrust have only intensified.

Maybe it's time to consider some new leadership in this seemingly hopeless relationship. Maybe it's time for the people who should be the world's leaders in human relations to start living up to that high calling by seizing this great opportunity.

Every Sunday morning millions of us sit in church and sing that "Jesus is the answer for the world today." I often wonder whether the words "except for the race problem" should be added to that beautiful song.

My next-door neighbor used to have a little dog named Scottie. Every day when I would walk past Scottie's house, he would bark ferociously, leaping against the fence that separated us as if to say, "If I had the opportunity, I would rip you to shreds." One morning as Scottie and I went through our regular routine, he leaped against an unlatched fence. To his surprise and mine, the gate swung open, giving Scottie the opportunity of a lifetime. To my surprise and relief, though, Scottie would not come through that open gate. From that day on, I had no more respect for Scottie.

The tattered relationship between whites and blacks in this country offers Christians a historic opportunity. For centuries we have announced loudly and intensely that we alone had the answers to the world's problems. If that claim is true, it's time for us to move through this open gate of opportunity—or stop our barking.

2

Foot Soldier

THE WIDE-RANGING SOCIAL AND SPIRITUAL PROBLEM OF RACE HAS
*touched our individual lives in different ways. Chris and I dedicate much of
this book to sharing our personal stories. We do this to show that the process of
reconciliation must be made personal. For it is only when we feel a friend's
pain by making "his" problem "our" problem that we will harness the necessary passion to act.*

As a black child growing up during the sixties, I was shaped by two
powerful influences. First, I am the product of two strong Christian
parents who taught me and demonstrated their faith to me and everyone around them daily. Second, I am a child of race. Next to Christianity, issues of integration, voting, racism, segregation and "white folks"
were the things most talked about in my house and my neighborhood.

Sadly enough, this is the case for most black people of my generation. Race has shaped who we are and never seems to be too far
removed from any situation. Yet it was precisely because of our strong

Christian beliefs that my family took the point position in the battle for racial justice in our town.

As a child, I did not understand everything that was going on, even though I trusted my parents' judgment. But I was always sure of one thing. I knew down to the core of my being that what we were doing was right in the sight of God.

Until my school years, most of us didn't give much thought to hopes for racial justice. For years we had heard the grownups talking "hush talk" under their breath. We all cheered aloud with our parents as we listened to Martin Luther King Jr. make his famous "I Have a Dream" speech, but his marches seemed so far away.

Though most of the people in the country were shocked to see the Alabama police turn their dogs and water hoses loose on school-age children, we were not. We understood Southern justice. We had seen the evening news reports and could almost smell the smoke from Watts and Chicago. But we lived in Mississippi, "the Closed Society." Things would never change here. Still, something was in the air. All the teachers were talking about it, and I could see the fear and anger in their faces.

Harper Vocational High School ("Ha'pa High" to us) had an enrollment of about 750 students in grades one through twelve. It lay just across the railroad tracks in the "colored" section of the town of Mendenhall, Mississippi. The entire student body and all of the faculty were black. This was small-town Mississippi in 1966.

Some of the children in my seventh-grade homeroom cheered aloud and most nodded in agreement as Mr. Jackson, our teacher, voiced the sentiments of most of the teachers, who found the new talk of school desegregation frightening. After all, reorganization might threaten their job security. "Who do they think wants to go to school with them ol' peckerwoods anyway?" barked Mr. Jackson angrily, using one of our most derogatory terms for white folks. "I know I don't want to have anything to do with them." A couple of the more vocal kids added their "me neithers," summing up the attitude of most of the black people in Mississippi's school system.

For most of the kids, nodding in agreement with Mr. Jackson came easily. But not for me. I knew my father. He took his Christianity more seriously than most. He had left Mississippi in the late 1940s after his brother was killed by a white law-enforcement officer. But he'd returned with his family thirteen years later as a missionary, determined to make a difference in the lives of his people who, he said, "were trapped by sin, poverty and racism."

Instead of making him content, his Bible taught him (and he taught us) to be concerned not only about people's souls but also about justice for them. He had already been kicked out of a local church for trying to motivate the people to do something about their situation. Now he was the pastor of a small church he had founded, and he and my mother worked tirelessly with the youth in the area through Bible classes that were held three nights a week. They called it Voice of Calvary Bible Institute.

As I sat quietly in Mr. Jackson's classroom, I realized that if something radical was going to happen, my family would surely be squarely in the middle of it.

Up until that point the racial battle had mostly consisted of talk of what was going on in other parts of the country. It hadn't really affected my life in a personal way. But as I look back now and remember that day in Mr. Jackson's room, I'm aware that it was the beginning of my personal journey of trying to make sense out of the separation that existed between blacks and whites. For the next several years I would try to reconcile this separation with what my parents had taught me about Christianity.

In the spring of 1966 Mississippi began to yield to the pressure to comply with the nation's twelve-year-old school desegregation laws. But wholesale school integration wouldn't come for another four years. Instead, Mississippi opted for an ingenious plan called Freedom of Choice. This plan made it legal for any of Mississippi's school-age children to enroll in the school of their choice in their town or city.

As far back as anyone could remember, everybody in Mississippi had gone to either a black school or a white school. Now, in the fall of 1966, each family was "free" to make its own choice. Theoretically, any white parents could now send their children to a black school, while the black parents who were brave enough could send their children to a white school. But those of us who lived in Mississippi knew "freedom of choice" was an attempt not to integrate the schools but only to alleviate pressure from the outside world to do something about separate-and-unequal school systems.

As I said, I had given all this racial mess very little thought. I was content to live in the "colored quarters" (a term that harked back to slavery, when blacks lived in "slave quarters"). I was content, like most of my thirteen-year-old peers, to attend an all-black school. The white school uptown might as well have been on another planet as far as we were concerned. Sure, I was aware of the separation of the races, but I thought that was the way it was supposed to be.

But now, with the civil rights movement in full swing, I understood that we were actually second-class citizens and that God did not intend for it to be this way. And now—with my father's bold response to Mississippi's "freedom of choice"—I was willing to be one of the ones to do something about it. But why? Why did our family always have to be the ones to shoulder the responsibility? Why did we five school-age Perkinses have to take the brunt of white anger and black resentment? My father always summed it up in one word: *leadership.*

My father's response to "freedom of choice" was to send his children to Mendenhall's all-white school. This decision resulted in a nightmare of physical and emotional cruelty, a nightmare that scarred my whole family and left some of us cold and unforgiving. Only after ten years did I talk about the experience with my closest friends.

First Contact
I would love to say that all five of the school-age Perkinses—Joanie, Phillip, Derek, Deborah and me, the oldest—were unafraid on the first day of the new school year of 1966. I would love to say that we were poised and ready for battle. The makeshift Freedom School we attended that summer had tried to equip us for what we were about to experience, but there was no way it could totally prepare us.

Given that bravery is not the absence of fear but acting in the face of it, I'll have to settle for saying that we were very brave soldiers. It was the most fearful first day of school I've ever had. And this fear was not a one-time thing. It went on for most of the first year and even into the second. This would be my first up-close-and-personal look at white people, and you know what they say about first impressions—they're lasting.

Each day after school for months, I would compare the day's experiences with my brothers and sisters. We concluded that the severity of the cruelty varied according to our age groups, but overall our experiences were very similar. On one level we felt sorry for the white kids because we were pretty sure they were all going to hell for the way they treated us. But on the other hand we hated them and would probably have felt little remorse if the earth had opened up and swallowed them all.

I'm not saying that all the white kids participated in our constant harassment, but it might as well have been all of them. No one, not even the teachers, lifted a finger to make our existence at that school any easier.

One day while the teacher was out of the room, my desk became the target of innumerable wet paper bullets from rubber-band pistols. In my own opinion I had become a model of Martin Luther King's nonviolent restraint, never striking back even when the paper bullets found their mark and the entire class cheered with delight. I had learned to ignore or sometimes even make fun of such harassment: "Hope y'all are having fun," I'd say, or "Glad I can entertain y'all." Most of the time I would keep a straight face and my mouth shut.

This day was a little different—not because the children did anything different but because the teacher did not ignore their behavior. When he returned to the classroom, the evidence was irrefutable: dozens of paper bullets and rubber bands were strewn across the floor, all in the neighborhood of my desk. For some reason, this time it made the teacher angry. He had me point out all the boys who were involved. This I did with the naive notion that finally justice would be forthcoming. For me, this was to be a major victory; finally my existence in this hellhole would be a little more bearable. My fellow students could no longer torture me without consequences.

Before we reached the principal's office, I could see that I was taking this a little more seriously than my seven tormentors were. The principal, who was also a pastor, was one of the few people in the school I had considered somewhat sympathetic to me. I could tell he truly wanted to correct the situation. His first question to the boys was very short: "Why?"

I will never forget the puzzled look on the white boys' faces as they marveled that he, a white man, had asked such a stupid question. *What's the big deal, anyway?* One boy's response to the principal's question etched a wound in my soul that today, sometimes, still bleeds. His blue eyes twinkling with impatience, he pushed his blond hair out of his eyes and said in his immature Southern drawl, "He's just a nigger!"

The principal was stunned. He didn't know how to respond. I had lost another round.

Why did this cut me so deeply? I was used to being called "nigger" several dozen times every day. It was years before I understood what had happened to me that day. This was racism at its worst. For a thirteen-year-old black boy to realize that the highest authority in his daily world would not give him justice—even in the face of overwhelming evidence, including proud confessions from the perpetrators—was a devastating blow to his fragile self-worth. The principal's failure to convince the boys that they had committed any crime at all, along with his unwillingness to discipline them, painfully dashed my hopes of ever finding justice within a racist institution.

Paying the Price

Although the civil rights movement was underway in Mississippi, things were changing very slowly—at least from our perspective. A handful of blacks were now in the white schools and hating every minute of it, and blacks were being registered to vote all over the state. In our county, my father and his civil rights comrades decisively influenced the outcome of one of the powerful supervisors' elections. I will never forget how hard they worked to get their candidate elected and how proud they were when he won.

I never did understand why it was so important. The only white people we trusted were from the North, and this man was a Southerner. But my father insisted that the black community would reap some benefits and some jobs because if we put a man in office, we could take him out if he didn't keep his promises.

Still, things were pretty much the same. The whites hated us, and we hated them. The difference was that we knew it was wrong for us to hate them, even though most of the time we felt justified. Because we went to school with whites, the kids in our family probably felt a little more distaste for whites than most blacks did. The police were just as mean as ever—even more so to us because we were "stirring up trouble with all this civil rights mess." Medgar Evers, Martin Luther King Jr., Malcolm X and the Kennedy brothers were all killed. Every time one of them died, the white kids at school cheered. (Over the past few years I have had many honest conversations with whites, especially evangelicals, who are embarrassed to admit that they can remember their parents' negative attitudes about Martin Luther King Jr.—maybe they didn't cheer, but they were admittedly relieved at his murder.)

It always felt to me as if the white folks were winning. We never did figure out why when bad guys like Governor George Wallace and Senator John Stennis were shot, they didn't die, while our heroes did.

The movement in our town needed some momentum. The tiny spark needed to be fanned.

On a chilly December night in 1969, the wind seemed to change direction, and the tiny spark of Mendenhall's civil rights movement started billowing up into flame. Garland Wilks, a neighbor, had been arrested. He was pretty juiced, and my father was taking him home when the police stopped them, pulled Garland out of the car and took him to jail for public drunkenness.

Our reason for concern was that we knew what had happened in a store fifteen minutes earlier. It is said that often a person's real feelings come out after a few drinks. Maybe this was the case with Garland. Sober, he was definitely not one to step out of line. But this night, after having too much to drink, he had crossed the invisible line—he'd talked smart to a white woman, and we knew that would not be tolerated.

A group of about fifteen of us—children who had been practicing for a Christmas program along with three or four adults—made our way up to the jailhouse to protest Garland's arrest and to keep him from getting beaten. An hour later, all of us were peering out through those ice-cold steel bars.

This event captured the attention of the black community and tugged at its pride enough to catapult us into a battle of wills with the white community. They had now crossed our line. They had locked up children—girls as well as boys. And they would do that, of course, only to someone who could not or would not fight back.

That night my father gave his most unforgettable speech. "We ain't asking for some kind of special treatment," he said in a soft but determined voice. "We just want to be treated just like every other American citizen. We want a fair share of the decent jobs so that we can afford decent homes for our families. We want paved streets in our neighborhoods, just like they already have in the white neighborhoods. We want good education for our children. We want police protection instead of the police brutality that we always get. But most of all, we want to be treated with respect."

I'll never know if it was what he said, how he said it or the fact that he was saying it through the bars of a second-story window to a jail-yard full of people. But I know I'll never forget it. Even though I was shaking in my boots, I was proud to be standing there beside him in the jail. We had not bowed down but had stood up.

One of the statements my father made over and over during the course of this speech was, "If somebody's got to die, then I'm ready." This frightened me. I had heard how other people had been killed for standing up to white folks—one being my daddy's brother, Clyde—but I had never entertained the thought of my father dying. The notion that my dad might not be there to stand between us and this cruel system prompted new fears in me—fears that, in the months that followed, I would learn to live with.

If the true test of a good speech is whether it stirs the listeners into action, then this was a great speech. The next morning when the stores opened on Main Street, several unwelcome visitors were patrolling the sidewalks, carrying signs that had been fashioned during the long night. The store owners, police and authorities were caught totally by surprise. In response to my father's passionate plea a full-scale boycott, complete with demonstration marches and picketers, had begun in, of all places, Mendenhall, Mississippi.

During the previous night the police had realized it was a mistake to have children locked up in the city jail and had invited us to leave. But we had vowed not to leave unless everyone was released. Eventually the officers literally carried all the children out of the jail, beginning with the oldest male, me. They kept my father and his sidekick, a young white hippie named Doug Huemer, locked up for several days.

But that only fanned the fire. The Reverend Curry Brown, a friend of my father's from California, and Mr. Ruben, an elderly black man who had already had a cross burned in his yard, joined my mother in leading the daily marches and directed the picketers. Curry was our courage, and my mother was our symbol. She was a hometown girl who had gone to high school in Mendenhall. She knew everybody and everybody knew her, and she was well respected for her work with children. When the people saw her standing on the corner and heard her passionate appeal, most of them heeded. "They got my husband locked up in that jailhouse for no reason," she would yell. "Go spend your money somewhere else. We gon' hit them where it hurts!" Even some of the people who had put Christmas items on layaway sacrificed them in order to make the boycott work.

My father was released from jail on Christmas Eve. There weren't too many gifts that Christmas, but if Christmas is supposed to be the season of hope, there was plenty of that to go around. We'd discovered that there was something we could do about the situation we lived under. We had stood up to "them," and so far nobody had been hurt.

School resumed after Christmas vacation, and the daily marches became weekly but more intense. People were beginning to come from all over the state to help our cause. February 7 witnessed our biggest march ever, with more than five hundred people. To us, with our small-town mentality, it seemed like five thousand. We had grown used to the weekly rumors of white retaliation and the daily telephone threats. But so far nothing had happened.

The Saturday after our triumphant march, Doug Huemer and Louise Fox, a white Brethren Church volunteer, were driving two vans full of Tougaloo College students from Mendenhall to Jackson. Their caravan was pulled over by Mississippi state troopers for "reckless driving," and everyone in Doug's van was taken to the Rankin County Jail in Brandon. Suspiciously, the van driven by Louise was let go. Curry Brown, Joe Paul Buckley (my best friend's dad) and my father rushed the thirty miles to the jail to make bail. It was an ambush. That night Curry and my father were beaten to within an inch of their lives in the Brandon jail (Joe Paul, who was older and suffered from heart trouble, was only roughed up a little).

By morning our only clue to the events of the previous night had come over the phone in a rhetorical question posed anonymously to my mother in the wee hours of the morning: "Have they hung 'em yet?" All we knew was that Daddy and the other men were somewhere between Mendenhall and Brandon, and we had to find them. So early that Sunday morning we set out for Brandon, not knowing what we would find.

There must have been at least twenty people in the nervous group that approached the jailhouse that morning. Before we could even reach the front door, we could hear Joe Paul shouting as he waved frantically through his cell bars, "Y'all go back, y'all go back!"

"Don't let them boys come up here," he pleaded. "They'll kill all y'all. Go back. Go back." But my mother and I went in anyway. When we reached the front desk, the sheriff would allow only the immediate families into the jailhouse.

There was no visiting room, so we went up the stairs to the cell area. Every step of the way we were shadowed by a quiet police officer. He never spoke and neither did we. We could hear the young women before we reached the room. (My father later explained that those Tougaloo women had cared for him during the night, keeping him alive.) They were trying to tell us what had happened the night before. But when we saw my father—well, nothing more needed to be said.

I can still see vividly what my father looked like in that Brandon jailhouse; I suppose a sixteen-year-old boy would never be able to erase such a memory. His clothes were torn and bloody. His shirttail was half in, half out as if he had tried to tuck it in when he heard we were coming. His eyes bulged as if they were going to pop out of his head. They were as big as silver dollars. He had a lump on his head about the size of a fist (a few days later, a doctor drained a cup of blood out of it). His face was full of fear—but there was more there, much more. My sister Joanie figured it out as soon as she saw him. It was humiliation.

This is my toughest memory—the humiliation my father suffered. Although it was he, not the rest of us, who had been physically tortured, it might as well have been our whole family. We all felt the pain. An old biblical proverb sums up the situation well: "The fathers eat sour grapes, and the children's teeth are set on edge" (Ezek 18:2).

My mother tried to be brave. She held back her emotions until we were outside of the jail and out of sight of the policemen. Then she let it all out. "I didn't want them to see me cry," she sobbed. "I couldn't let them think they were beating us."

Sometimes I still resent what we had to go through just to get our "freedom." I would have done anything to keep my mother from having to cry like that.

Louise believed the whole thing was her fault. She kept apologizing to me. "I'm sorry, I'm so sorry," she said over and over. Even though I couldn't say anything to her, I understood what she meant. She was apologizing for two reasons.

It was now clear that she had been used in the trap to get Daddy to come to Brandon that night. She'd been allowed to drive her van away. Having watched the riders of the other van being hauled away to jail, she did what any of us would have done—she telephoned my father. And that happened to be exactly what the officers wanted her to do.

Second, she was apologizing for being white. All the pain and suffering we were experiencing was at the hands of white people, and she couldn't do anything to stop it, even though she was white. When she looked at me with tears in her eyes, I felt sorry for her. She seemed so helpless and so pitiful. In my heart I knew she was innocent, and I eventually told her so, but for the moment all I could see was her white skin.

In the months after, I watched with interest as my father struggled through a crisis in his faith. Frankly, I hoped he would conclude that the gospel and Christianity were for white folks. I hoped he would finally see the light and agree with Malcolm X that black people could not afford to be Christians because it cost them their dignity. I hoped he would decide that we should have nothing more to do with white people.

Accepting a Hard Truth

Over the next two years I struggled with these issues. I went off to college with many questions unsettled in my head. If Jesus says that the essence of Christianity is to love the Lord your God with all your heart, with all your soul and with all your mind and to love your neighbor as yourself, then is it possible to love God without loving your neighbor? As far as we could tell, no one in the white community loved us, but most claimed to be Christians. Was it fair to say that they were not followers of Jesus? Did they read the same Bible as we did?

These were not hollow questions to me. If these people who had made our lives so miserable were included in the body of Christ, I needed to know so I could get out of it.

When I was younger, sometimes disputes would break out among the children in my parents' Bible classes when they learned that we are to love everybody. "That don't mean white folks," one child would say. "Yes it do," another would rebut. Periodically I had asked my parents if loving my neighbor meant loving white people too. Their answer was always the same. Loving my neighbor meant especially loving white folks. But now that white people had nearly killed my father, would my parents answer differently?

I heard that my father was coming to California to speak at a black church pastored by a good friend, the Reverend George Moore. It was not too far from the private Christian college I was attending on a basketball scholarship. So I made it my business to go to hear Daddy. I had not heard him speak in over a year now, and I was anxious to hear if he had made any new discoveries or had any new revelations about his faith. I wanted to know whether he had settled any of the questions I knew he had struggled with after his jail experience.

As I sat in that church listening to him speak to an all-black audience, I felt disappointed. One side of me wanted some new insight that would justify my anger and bitterness. I got plenty of insight, but it was not what I wanted to hear. What I got was almost too simple. I listened as Daddy acknowledged that he had not been preaching the whole gospel, but that now he was determined more than ever to live the rest of his life preaching and living a gospel that would burn through all the racial, social and economic walls erected to keep people separated—some even in the name of God. He went on to say that a gospel that reconciles people only to God and not to each other cannot be the true gospel of Jesus Christ.

"Before my Brandon jail experience," he said, "I thought blacks were the only victims of racism. But when I saw the faces of those men in the jail, twisted by the hate of racism, I knew that they were victims too—I just couldn't hate back."

I can't possibly explain to you how much I hated to hear those words. After all we had suffered at the hands of white people, now we were supposed to forgive them? But I suppose it is what I knew I would hear. And deep down inside, I knew it was the truth.

It would be an understatement to say that the events of that night in Brandon had changed our lives. It was more than that. They had changed our Christianity. For my father there would no longer be a salvation gospel and a social gospel. There would be one gospel—a gospel that reconciled people to God but at the same time reconciled people to each other. To separate the two could allow the state troopers to beat Daddy almost to death and still be Christians. A gospel that taught no responsibility for your neighbor could not be accepted as the true gospel.

As I sat in that church with tears in my eyes, unhappy that I had come, I knew what I had to do. If I intended to follow Jesus, I could not allow my anger and bitterness to defeat me. If I was to be a follower of Christ, I would have to try to be like him—to keep on forgiving. This was hard for me to swallow, but I knew it was right.

But knowing is one thing, doing is another.

3

At the Crossroads

UNLIKE SPENCER, WHO WAS FORCED TO WRESTLE WITH QUESTIONS *of race from an early age, I was like most whites in that such issues were of little concern to me for most of my life. When I moved into a black neighborhood after college, this unfamiliar world began to touch me for the first time. Plunging across the dividing line was at first exhilarating. But there were painful surprises as I went below the surface and encountered the treacherous depths of the damage race has caused to both black and white. Admitting that there was a social problem was easy; acknowledging its stain on me, however, was another matter.*

Summer 1983. One more hot July night in Jackson, Mississippi. Only this night the sweltering heat outside was matched by the rising tempers inside our youth ministry center at 155 Wacaster Street. "Why are so many white people in charge around here?" one sharp, angry voice demanded. "Voice of Calvary isn't about developing white people, but us blacks. You whites need to step aside and we need to step forward!"

As I sat in the room full of white and black church members, the words pierced me like a knife. I was a twenty-three-year-old volunteer with two years' experience in VOC's black community. But I hadn't heard fighting words like these before. It was terrifying.

When the meeting was over, as I walked down the street alone to my house a few blocks away, my insides churned and my heart felt as if it were inside my throat. Desperate questions raced through my head: *Doesn't reconciliation mean not looking at color? Why are they so angry? Don't they know I came here to help?* For the first time since my decision to stay at VOC rather than return to college, a seductive thought rose to the surface of my consciousness: *Leave. Leave now. You're not wanted. You're not needed. Let these black people work out their damage and anger on somebody else. You have better things to do with your life.*

For me that difficult night has become a parable of America's race problem, a microcosm of where we blacks and whites stand with each other. Although most of us don't get that near the fire, there is certainly the fear that if we do, we will get burned by searing emotions.

Me—a Racist?

As I pondered my choices in the face of the accusing darts that seemed to be thrown my way, I found myself in uneasy camaraderie with the familiar voice of contemporary America: "I didn't cause it, and I shouldn't have to suffer for it."

After all, I was no racist. Racists burned crosses, told nigger jokes and threw black people out of their churches. I, on the contrary, was on the side of black people. By coming to VOC I had declared my allegiance to the cause. I had an upbringing free from prejudice, a track record of crosscultural sensitivity and a budding commitment to serving the poor to prove my progressiveness. No problem there.

It would be hard to uncover anything in my family heritage that could hold me responsible for the problems of black folks. Both Mom and Dad came from respected, well-established families in Niagara Falls, New York. Dad traced his roots to pure Vermont Yankee stock and further back to England, and Mom back to both Germany and

England. My great-grandparents on both sides were self-made entre-
preneurs who had started successful businesses in insurance and real
estate. My grandparents' world revolved around solid loyalties to family, the business, social life at the country club, the alma mater colleges
and participation in the local Presbyterian church.

As in many American urban areas, while whites and blacks lived
relatively near to one another in Niagara Falls, it might as well have
been two worlds. The white world's little contact with the "colored"—
as my grandfather always called black people in the common language of his era—consisted of cordial, comfortable relationships with
maids, custodians at downtown institutions and sometimes even cus-
tomers. There were few blacks in the city and none in the smaller
town down the Niagara River that my grandparents moved to and that
I grew up visiting regularly.

This was the world Mom and Dad, and I in turn, stood to inherit.
Dad was next in line to follow in his father's footsteps and head the
family business. But somehow, when he and Mom became adults, they
didn't fit very well into the predictable, secure life that was waiting for
them. Dad decided instead to become a minister in the Presbyterian
church. Thus began what eventually amounted to a big step away from
the security of my grandparents' culture and people.

Dad's first pastorate, in the white-populated coal-mining town of
Amsterdam, Ohio, was followed by an associate pastorate in Fairfield,
Connecticut. This second congregation had been started as a "First
Church" in nearby Bridgeport but was moved to the suburb of Fair-
field in response to a rise in the city's black population and the belief
that there was greater possibility for growth in the suburbs.

From this Middle America enclave Dad, swallowing his fear,
boarded a bus for Mississippi in the summer of 1964. He was joining
thousands of other young, idealistic, mostly white college students,
seminarians and ministers in responding to the call of Martin Luther
King Jr. and other civil rights leaders to descend upon the "Closed
Society" as Freedom Summer volunteers. Three weeks earlier in Philadelphia, Mississippi, three volunteers—James Chaney, Andrew
Goodman and Mickey Schwerner—had disappeared. Their bodies

were later discovered: they had been tortured, murdered and buried in a dam.

When I was six, my parents made a decision that destined me to be irreversibly crosscultural. They loaded Rick, me, Mark and Liz (the youngest at nine months) onto a plane and departed for Seoul, South Korea, as missionaries with the United Presbyterian Church. Korea's rapid development, as showcased in the 1988 Seoul Olympics, has been astounding and remarkable. It's hard to remember that the country was still recovering from the devastation of war when we landed there in August 1966.

Some missionaries in Korea affirmed and served the culture, while others didn't. I was always proud that Dad and Mom resisted living in a missionaries-only compound and insisted on Korean neighborhoods. They mastered the language and became close friends with their Korean coworkers. For twelve years I watched them serve Christ and the downtrodden. Mom worked to help two of the most discriminated-against groups in Korea: unwed mothers and mixed-race children (whose fathers were among the thirty thousand U.S. troops stationed in Korea during our years there).

Military-backed dictators dominated Korea in the sixties and seventies; tanks parked in front of campus gates and the tears in my eyes from tear-gas clouds in the midst of "demos" (as the Koreans called the street protests) are among my memories. Mom and Dad were active in helping Korean Christians work for democracy and justice. They hid fugitives in our home, lobbied the United States government and befriended political prisoners and their families. When eight Christians with no record of antigovernment activity were accused of being communists and hanged one night without a trial, Dad and four other missionaries donned black hoods, put nooses around their necks and demonstrated in front of the U.S. embassy. Their photograph later appeared in *Newsweek*. I remember our fear that night when men came to our house and picked Dad up for questioning by the Korean CIA.

Growing up in Korea shaped me in some significant ways. Attending a school of four hundred students representing thirty countries, I learned to be sensitive to and to appreciate cultural differences. I could easily adapt to the food, language and customs of other people. Being part of a racial minority, I didn't expect things to be done my way or assume that my way was better. I didn't accept people on the basis of their similarity to me.

I wouldn't trade my growing up in Korea for anything. It was the most important legacy my parents gave me. Their choices equipped me to cross cultural barriers readily.

When I left Korea to head off to college, the obvious choice was Middlebury College in rural Vermont, the small, private liberal-arts school that eight Rices had attended, starting with my great-grandfather. I decided to major in history and Chinese language, with aspirations of law school and a career in government.

I rarely crossed paths with or gave a second thought to Middlebury's few black students. I did occasionally wonder why all the black students sat together at meals and moved around the campus in a sort of hive, and about the mysterious Black Student Union I passed each day on the way to class. A few black students drifted in and out of our campus Christian fellowship.

I regard my two years at Middlebury as one of my missed opportunities for racial reconciliation. Many of us whites, like me during those years, rarely interact with black people. Yet nearly all of us can pinpoint times in our lives when there was such an opportunity. It might have been in high school or college. It might have been in the military or at a job. We've all had a chance for genuine contact, but if you're like most white Americans, you probably missed it. It would have meant going out of your way, just as I would have had to do at Middlebury—sitting at the lunch table where they gathered, visiting the Black Student Union, starting a conversation with a black classmate (maybe one was a Spencer).

Even on a small, isolated campus like Middlebury there was a tremendous social separation between white and black students. But it never occurred to me to do anything about it. All these "could 'a' beens" amount to a mountain of missed opportunities.

It's strange: while Korea had prepared me to be crosscultural, as easy relationships with Asians and even a Hispanic at Middlebury proved, somehow it was harder when it came to getting to know black people. Not until I went to Mississippi as a six-month volunteer would I begin to understand the reasons.

An Innocent Plunge

In September 1981 I sped along Interstate 20 through Mississippi's thickly forested hills, sprinkled white with patches of cotton blooms ready for harvest. When I pulled into the driveway at the VOC headquarters at 1655 St. Charles Street in black West Jackson, I was a green recruit to one of America's unique laboratories for racial reconciliation.

I was quickly won over by the biblical passion and action-oriented commitment of Voice of Calvary's staff. I settled in easily, found a niche among the many other short-term volunteers and got involved in the ministry.

Six months later, when the time came for me to leave, I faced a choice: Should I go back to school and continue my career plans or stay with VOC? Making the decision was an agonizing spiritual battle. It put me at an early crossroads of deciding what I would make of my Christian life. It was the first time since being in a black community that I considered the choice afforded to all white Americans: to go on with a life untouched by concerns of race. Finally I decided to stay, betting that if I left VOC I would probably never return. I know that God could still have used me if I had returned to Middlebury. But for me it was the right decision, consistent with where God was leading me in life.

At Voice of Calvary there are open doors for anyone willing to take the reins of a situation, and soon my responsibilities began to grow. I ran the warehouse of our Thriftco clothing store, working alongside another volunteer. Later I edited the ministry's newsletter. I was active in Bible studies and discipleship. It was exciting to use my talents to serve God's cause of justice.

With so much ministry activity going on I had little time for racial navel-gazing. We prided ourselves on how reconciled we were: black and white working, worshiping and living together. Where else in America was that happening? Visitors marveled at our interracial gospel choir and told us what pioneers we were.

Even as our witness for reconciliation was celebrated, I wrestled with questions about where I fit in as a white person. From time to time these racial tensions would rise to the surface. The first I remember was in a gripe session pulled together by a few of the younger single staff. My first unforgettable memory of Spencer dates from that meeting.

A number of people aired problems they saw: people not getting along, trouble in male-female relationships and other things. Then Spencer stood up and bluntly asked, "How come white people always come here and end up in charge? What are you white people doing here anyway?" Especially if you don't know him very well, Spencer has a way of making you feel uncomfortable with direct statements like that. His question cut right to my heart.

Looking back, I realize that I should have gone right to Spencer and asked him exactly what he meant. Instead I was left wondering what was behind his question, and I'm sure the lack of response from whites like me left *him* wondering what our motives were. One of the character traits of a reconciler is a willingness to confront conflict. I guess I wasn't mature enough to understand how vital it is to get everyone's honest thoughts on the table. If they aren't brought into the open and dealt with decisively, as our experience began to prove, they eventually boil over.

The Explosion

In the summer of 1983 my "progressive" assumptions were abruptly confronted by the hard realities of America's race problem. A series of gatherings that came to be known as "the reconciliation meetings" were initiated by several of our black members to challenge what they said was racism within our own church and ministry. Because VOC's development efforts were focused on a black community, there had always been a strong verbal commitment to black leadership. But some were beginning to point out that while the president of the ministry was black, the leaders of nearly all major ministry programs were white.

The easy answer voiced by several whites, "It's simply a matter of who is most qualified," was not quite good enough for this complex situation. The issue was much deeper. Clearly, whites had a head start in education and preparation for leadership. But was the "most-qualified" management style applicable at VOC, given that at the heart of the ministry's "prime directive" was the development of indigenous leaders? This was one of the key issues in that explosive summer of 1983.

I think I participated in the meetings mostly because I had a gut feeling that the experience would be decisive for my commitment to VOC, whether to stay or to leave. But I hated going to those meetings. I felt like a pig that was voluntarily walking into a slaughterhouse; the only question was who was going to be turned into bacon, ham or sausage tonight. It was just a matter of time before my turn would come.

At one meeting, discussion centered on how many ambitious whites had come to VOC and begun to take leadership positions. Some people argued vehemently that VOC's goal was not to develop whites but blacks. Whites could go anywhere and find no doors closed. Here they needed to step aside, while blacks needed to step forward.

This was when the thought of leaving entered my mind. I wondered whether I was really needed. I thought about an emotional scene from the movie *Gandhi,* when Gandhi has been arrested for leading a protest march and a white activist visits him in prison. Gandhi looks through the bars into the eyes of his comrade and says softly, "I've been thinking it might be best for you to go back to London, to your people there. We Indians have to see that we can do this for ourselves."

From what some blacks said, I concluded that what black people really needed was to separate and form their own institutions. Then they could see that they could do it on their own. Self-esteem would be raised in the process. Maybe white people could be involved after blacks achieved a higher level of self-confidence.

It was in the reconciliation meetings that I felt the heavy accusation of "racist" being leveled at me. And I didn't appreciate it. I looked back at my past and didn't see any oppression against blacks. What about my crosscultural badge of honor earned as a missionary kid? That ought to count for something. And I had given up so much to stay at VOC and help black people—not graduating from Middlebury, not pursuing law school or dreams of a career in government that could really count for something. Look, I sacrificed a lot to stay here!

As the smoke cleared after the end of the reconciliation meetings, a survey of the battlefield proved there was a clear victor. The basic conclusion was this: "Given the fact that white European culture is dominant in this country; given the legacy of racial discrimination that puts whites at an advantage in our society, even in the church; unless we make an intentional effort to affirm black leadership, culture and style, whiteness will always dominate." This painful realization put racial awareness decisively at the forefront of VOC's agenda. There was an intentional effort to identify black leaders and move them into more positions of influence throughout the ministry ranks and the church. Our life and direction became more visibly black in focus.

But a lot of casualties remained littered across the battlefield. Deep wounds of bitterness, unforgiveness, resentment, misunderstanding and guilt still remained unhealed. Some wounds were mortal. The conclusions reached at the reconciliation meetings were painful for both blacks and whites, and in the months following, many church members slowly began packing their bags and trickling away to greener pastures. Some whites saw the intentional emphasis on blackness as a threat to their potential leadership—not being allowed to use their gifts to the fullest. On the other hand, some blacks saw it as patronizing. It was hard to accept the fact that if we left things as they were, with no emphasis on color, whites would eventually end up in most leadership positions. Yet we had learned that this was indeed the case. For some blacks, the conclusions we reached were not only humiliating but unjust to the whites. But for some, like Dr. Ivory Phillips, who helped lead the meetings, and Spencer, the point was simply finding a better balance in what we valued in leadership. "We will not begin to deemphasize white," said Dr. Phillips; "we will just begin to value the qualities that blackness brings to the body."

As I surveyed the results of the battle for my own life, the greatest contribution of the meetings was that I had witnessed for the first time the depth of rage and bitterness that black people felt. I couldn't deny there was a gulf.

As the fires from our racial confrontation subsided, I realized that I had not won any deeper relationships with black people in the process. I came to the uncomfortable realization that for two years I had lived in a black neighborhood, worked in a black-led ministry and worshiped in a majority-black church, but had not gained a single close black friend. I realized that I really didn't know these black people with whom I had worked and worshiped for two years.

Each night after a grueling session was finished, I went home to an existence that didn't include any close black peers with whom I could talk through the issues. Looking back, I know now that I should have reached out more to the blacks who participated in the meetings. I could have asked someone to lunch or had one of the "angry blacks" over for dinner. A group setting is usually a highly charged atmosphere, whereas one on one there is more time to listen and understand and reason together. But the main thing is, I didn't have those personal relationships.

Whites often ask me, "How do I know when I'm really dealing with the race issue?" "When you begin to feel uncomfortable," I answer, "as I did in 1983." When blacks and whites start talking the truth to each other, it gets hot. During a racial reconciliation discussion that Spencer and I led in Wilmington, North Carolina, the blacks attending very honestly confessed their struggles with loving and forgiving whites. Afterward, a white woman approached me. Her eyes were sad and confused. She was a volunteer in a local black ministry, she said, and it hurt to hear the black people's honesty. "Don't they appreciate my help?" she asked. I understood.

In 1983 I was poised to become another casualty of America's race fatigue. The dynamic, hopeful vision of VOC had hooked my imagination and sustained my commitment to this point. But my awakening to what black people really felt made my stay increasingly uncomfortable. That "call of the wild" that had only been a faint whisper—put all this mess behind you and follow your natural survival instincts—now rang louder and clearer.

4

Who Is My Neighbor?

STRIPPED OF ALL THE THEOLOGICAL DEBATES AND BOILED DOWN TO *its raw essence, Christianity and Christians will be judged by two criteria: how much we love God and how well we demonstrate that by loving our neighbor. This is Christianity in a nutshell. But pushing these two great loves to the back pages of our practical theology has allowed Christians to join in with the world in separating along racial lines.*

A clearer understanding of the priority these two loves deserve should have us scrambling to figure out creative ways to demonstrate our love for one another. Understanding Jesus' definition of neighbor *should motivate us to show special love to those who don't love us. Growing up in Mississippi made the "neighbor" application very simple for me: I needed to accept the fact that God intended me to love even "white folks." Until Christians can admit to the importance Jesus put on loving our neighbor—until we can admit that not to do so weakens our gospel—it's unlikely that we will go out of our way to "prove neighbor." Instead, we will continue to pass by on the other side.*

One of the oldest strategies of warfare is to divide and conquer. Once you have isolated your enemy, you have robbed him of his strength. Then you can do just about whatever you please with him.

Christians have used a strategy similar to this in our attempts to deal with the hard teachings of Jesus. We have separated basic principles of Scripture that God never intended to be separated, consequently robbing them of their intended power.

The Bible can be divided into two broad categories: people and their relationship to God, and people and their relationships to other people. Everything in Scripture falls under one or the other of these broad categories. In the third chapter of Genesis man and woman broke their relationship with God by disobeying him and eating the fruit. In Genesis 4 we broke with each other when Cain killed his brother Abel. The rest of the Bible is a record of God's attempts to reconcile the human race back to himself and to reconcile us to each other.

If you had to sum up in one word the point God has been trying to communicate to the human race throughout history, that word could very easily be *reconciliation*: Paul says in 2 Corinthians 5:18-19, "All this is from God, who reconciled us to himself through Christ and gave us the ministry of reconciliation: that God was reconciling the world to himself in Christ, not counting men's sins against them."

Once Jesus was approached by a religious lawyer who wanted him to separate the two basic thrusts of the gospel (Mt 22:34-40). He challenged Jesus, "Which is the greatest commandment in the Law?" Notice that this lawyer was looking for one commandment. If the two could be separated, this would have been the time to do it. This was Jesus' opportunity to say once and for all what the point of Jewish religion was.

The first part of Jesus' response was expected. " 'Love the Lord your God with all your heart and with all your soul and with all your mind.' This is the first and greatest commandment." We have a tendency to want to stop here. We hear many sermons that concentrate on this one commandment. But Jesus did not stop here. Jesus says you can't reduce the gospel to just "me and God." There is a second commandment and it is like the first: "Love your neighbor as yourself."

Then Jesus goes on to make what must be one of the most over-looked statements in Scripture: "All the Law and the Prophets hang on these two commandments." Under these two categories falls every-thing that was taught by Moses and the prophets, and everything that Jesus taught, and everything that was taught by his disciples. Boiling it all down to its raw essence, what God wants is for us to love him and love our neighbor.

As I grew up, my parents tended to look at Jesus' teachings and try to live them—literally. By the time I was in elementary school, I could quote several dozen Bible verses, such as "Do to others as you would have them do to you" (Lk 6:31), "If anyone loves me, he will obey my teaching. . . . This is my command: Love each other" (Jn 14:23; 15:17), "If anyone says, 'I love God,' yet hates his brother, he is a liar. For any-one who does not love his brother, whom he has seen, cannot love God, whom he has not seen" (1 Jn 4:20). All these verses I could quote from memory, but our unsophisticated understanding of these Scrip-tures created a quandary for me.

I compared what I saw in the Bible to the reality we blacks lived under in small-town Mississippi. And at a very early age I concluded that it was impossible to be a white Southerner and a Christian, not because I understood all the different theologies and interpretations of Scripture and not because we had some special kind of black theol-ogy but because of what I read in the Bible. Since I saw in the Scrip-tures that if you loved God, you would love your neighbor, and since I knew the white folks didn't love us, it was easy to conclude that there were very few Christians south of the Mason-Dixon line—especially in Mississippi.

Separating loving God from loving your neighbor had cost white Christians a valuable witness to the power of God, at least to the black community.

A while back I was talking to an old man who lived in a Christian community in New York. This group of Christians takes the gospel as seriously as any group of believers I know. He asked me how they could get black folks to join their community.

"Why is that so important to you?" I asked.

He responded, "If we had whites and blacks living and worshiping together as brothers and sisters, we would make a much stronger witness to the gospel of Jesus Christ."

This old man understood how our lack of visible love for each other compromises our witness of the gospel to an unbelieving world.

Only five of every one hundred black Americans belong to a majority-white Protestant denomination. The number of whites who belong to majority-black denominations is even smaller. These numbers illustrate how hard it is for even the people of God to practice the Christian "prime directive"—love your neighbor as you love yourself. Maybe the problem is that we have misunderstood Jesus' definition of *neighbor*.

A Parable for Today

Let's say you live in a mostly white neighborhood. You hardly deal with people of other races. You work hard, and you teach your children to love God and other people.

Now suppose you hear about an unusual activist teacher who is going around preaching that same simple message you teach your kids: to love God and other people. But this teacher spends his time with poor people and members of the other race. You agree with what he teaches, but his lifestyle makes you uncomfortable.

Then one day you hear he's in town, so you go to hear him teach. Afterward, you approach him to ask a question. Your question is probing and goes straight to the heart of the matter. You believe that his answer will probably be theologically unsound, so that you will embarrass him, discount his lifestyle and in the process affirm your own. "How can I be sure that when I die I will go to heaven?" you ask, going straight for the bottom line.

Instead of answering, he asks you an elementary question. "What did they teach you in church?"

You reply from memory, from the first principles you learned way back in Sunday school: "Love the Lord your God with all your heart and with all your soul and with all your strength and with all your mind; and love your neighbor as yourself."

He smiles and says, "You have answered correctly. Do this and when you die you will go to heaven."

But you feel a little slighted. His answer was too simple. You think, "If we agree, why then does his lifestyle still make me feel so uncomfortable?" And you realize that the difference must have something to do with the "neighbor" part.

Needing to justify your own existence, you decide to probe a little deeper. So you ask the question—the one whose answer was as ignored in Jesus' day as it is today: "And who is my neighbor?"

His reply comes in the form of a story.

"One evening a man was driving from his suburban home to his downtown office. Because he was pressed for time he decided to drive the most direct route, which led right through the roughest part of the inner city. It just so happened that while driving through this mostly black part of town he had a flat tire. Because his white face stuck out like a sore thumb in this part of town, he was tempted to continue driving on the flattened tire but decided it would only take a minute to change it. While he was changing the tire, though, a gang of black youths attacked him, stripped and beat him and left him half dead.

"Now it happened that a preacher on his way to evening service also had to drive through this dangerous part of town. When he saw the car up on a jack he slowed down, and then he saw the man slumped over the steering wheel. But the preacher hurried on his way, deciding that it would be too dangerous to stop.

"A little while later another man, who had been a Christian all his life and was well respected in his community, also saw the injured man, but he too decided not to get involved.

"Finally, an old black man driving a beat-up pickup truck drove up and stopped, pulled the injured white man out of the car, laid him in the back of his truck and drove him to the hospital. He paid the hospital bill and then continued on his way, never seeing the injured man again."

His story finished, the teacher then asks you, "Which of these three do you think proved neighbor to the man who was attacked by the gang?"

You answer, "The one who had mercy on him."

And he says to you, "Go and do likewise." (See Lk 10:25-37 for the original version of this story.)

When Jesus was asked, "Who is the neighbor I'm supposed to love like myself?" he didn't say "Your family," or "The people of your neighborhood—people who are like you." For all practical purposes Jesus turned the question into a racial issue. It was no coincidence that Jesus picked a Samaritan to demonstrate the meaning of *neighbor* to a Jewish expert in the law. Jews didn't see the Samaritans as their neighbors. Samaritans were half-breeds, the scum of the earth, outcasts. The Jews believed that if a Jewish person's shadow happened to touch a Samaritan's shadow, it would contaminate the Jew. If a Samaritan woman entered a Jewish village, the entire village became unclean.

But in this story Jesus says that our neighbors are especially those people who ignore us, those people who separate themselves from us, those people who are afraid of us, those people we have the most difficulty loving and those people we feel don't love us. These are our neighbors. In Matthew 5:46 Jesus says, "If you love those who love you, what reward will you get?" Anybody can do that.

Christianity doesn't require any power when its only challenge is to do something that already comes naturally. But it will take a powerful gospel—a gospel with guts—to enable us to love across all the barriers we erect to edify our own kind and protect us from our insecurities.

Sometimes in my weak moments I wish the lawyer who asked that question two thousand years ago had never opened his big mouth. But now, because he did, I am without excuse. I cannot plead ignorance to the question of race. Now, because of Jesus' answer, I have to go beyond my comfort zone and embrace neighbors I would rather do without.

The answer to the question "And who is my neighbor?" has much to say about the priority we place on loving people who are different from ourselves, especially as it relates to our eternal future. Hidden behind Jesus' simple lesson on helping others is an intense spotlight aimed right at one of our most serious blind spots—race.

Do You Recognize Your Neighbor?

It doesn't take much imagination for each of us to figure out who Jesus would use as an example of "neighbor" in our own towns and cities.

For an Israeli, how about a Palestinian?

For an Arab, how about a Jew?

For a rich white, how about a black welfare mother?

For a poor white, how about a middle-class black who got where he is through affirmative action?

For a black male, how about a white male—better yet, a pickup-driving, gunrack-toting, tobacco-chewing, baseball-cap-wearing white man who still refers to a black man as "boy"?

For a feminist, how about an insensitive, domineering male chauvinist?

For a suburban white family, how about the new black or Hispanic family that moved in down the street?

For all of us, how about the unmotivated, undisciplined, uneducated poor? Or an AIDS victim who contracted HIV not through a transfusion but through homosexual activity or intravenous drug use?

Who would Jesus use as the neighbor if he were speaking to you?

As I mentioned earlier, when I was growing up, I used to ask my parents if loving your neighbor as yourself meant we had to love white people too. I'm sure you can imagine the answer I wanted to hear. But they would always say loving your neighbor meant *especially* loving white folks. Even though sometimes I could see them struggling with the answer, especially after my father was almost beaten to death by white men, they still managed to say and demonstrate to me that loving my neighbor did mean loving white folks.

How are you answering this question to your children—and to the world?

Maybe the question is not being asked in words, but believe me, it's being asked. Maybe you are not answering in words, but you are answering—if not in words, then surely in deeds. As the old saying goes, "Our lives speak so loudly that the world can't hear what we are saying."

Jesus said our witness, our credibility to the world, is demonstrated by our love for each other. There is no greater witness to the genuineness of our gospel.

Think about it. If, because of Christ, blacks and whites could bridge our country's greatest schism and live out a model of reconciliation that has not been attained by any other force, the world would have to ask, "Why?"

To many blacks the idea of racial reconciliation, given all our problems, is low on the priority list. But here's a sobering thought for blacks who are still dealing with unresolved anger at white America. Our forgiveness from God hinges on our ability to forgive others (Mt 6:14-15).

On the other hand, for many whites the idea of intentional racial reconciliation may sound extrabiblical. But remember that the "And who is my neighbor?" question clarified the answer to the question "What must I do to have eternal life?" Living out the answer could have eternal significance.

The Fruit of Worship

At the Lausanne II Conference on World Evangelism, Indian church leader Vinay Samuel voiced this concern:

> The most serious thing is the image around the world that evangelicals are soft on racial injustice. . . . One sign and wonder, biblically speaking, that alone can prove the power of the gospel is that of reconciliation. . . . Hindus can produce as many miracles as any Christian miracle worker. Islamic saints in India can produce and duplicate every miracle that has been produced by Christians. But they cannot duplicate the miracle of black and white together, of racial injustice being swept away by the power of the gospel. . . . Our credibility is at stake. . . . If we are not able to establish our credibility in this area we have not got the whole gospel. In fact we have not got a proper gospel at all.[1]

I experienced the truth of Vinay Samuel's plea in 1989 when I had the opportunity to take part in a remarkable worship service. There were about six thousand Christians present, of whom about 5,990 were white. People spoke in tongues and danced and prayed in the Spirit. They sang beautiful songs about how wonderful Jesus is and how Jesus is the answer to all the problems of their country.

But it was difficult for me to take part in this worship, because the service was held in a "whites-only" area just outside Johannesburg, South Africa. I had just come back from visiting one of the all-black townships only a few miles away. I had seen with my own eyes the extreme poverty in the black townships and the abundant wealth of the white minority. I had seen naked black children rummaging through garbage piles in search of food, while only a few miles away white children were being served by their black servants. I had seen very clearly how wealth was divided according to the color of one's skin. I had seen how the laws were designed to support this concept, and how South African Christianity had no effect on it.

Though the majority of the white Christians we talked with in South Africa could demonstrate outward "gifts" of the Holy Spirit, these signs did not translate into concern for the desperate situation of their thirty million black brothers and sisters. Six thousand white Christians, with hands raised, all calling on the name of God, and yet they were not demonstrating the fruit of the Spirit toward their black brothers and sisters. How could this be? If the God they were worshiping gave all this his approval, then there was no way I could bow down to that God.

It is estimated that 80 percent of white South Africans claim to be born-again Christians. As a black man, I have to thank God that we don't have more of such "Christians" in the United States. What I experienced on my 1989 trip revived an old question of my youth: *What is a Christian, anyway?*

The Bible is full of sayings like the ones I learned when I was a child: "If anyone says, 'I love God,' yet hates his brother, he is a liar" (1 Jn 4:20). "If anyone has material possessions and sees his brother in need but has no pity on him, how can the love of God be in him? Dear children, let us not love with words or tongue but with actions and in truth" (1 Jn 3:17-18).

Is it possible to have beautiful, authentic worship experiences yet not lift a finger to oppose the injustice that systematically oppresses a whole group of people? It would stand to reason that if our worship of a just and holy God does not lead us to confront the evils in our communities, our cities and our nations, then we are deceiving ourselves when we think we are spending time with the God revealed on the pages of the Bible. If we were spending long periods of time praying, singing and worshiping in the presence of this God, then some of his qualities of love, justice, forgiveness and self-sacrifice would certainly rub off on us.

A world confused about race needs to see a gospel with guts enough to break the idols of race, not only through our words but also through our deeds.

5

White Blinders

*Take sides. Neutrality helps the oppressor,
never the victim. Silence encourages the tormentor,
never the tormented.*

ELIE WIESEL, NOBEL PEACE PRIZE WINNER
AND SURVIVOR OF A NAZI CONCENTRATION CAMP

ALTHOUGH I GREW UP IN THE CHURCH, THE POWERFUL RACIAL *implications of the gospel that Spencer laid out in chapter four were unknown to me until I ventured onto the soil of a black community. Recognizing that we whites have racial blinders on is crucial to understanding and admitting that there is a problem of racial separation. Blacks and whites don't have the same options when it comes to race. It's vital for us whites to take an honest look at the world around us and begin to see how our blinders have affected us in ways we've hardly realized.*

As Spencer has said, for two painful years he was one of only two black students in his high school. Whenever he sat down, the seats around him immediately emptied. He was the brunt of cruel jokes, he was spat on, and countless times a day he was called "nigger." Yet only a small minority of the white students actually participated in these acts of hatefulness. The vast majority just stood by and watched.

Today very few Christians would consider outright bigotry acceptable. *Nigger* is a bad word. The Ku Klux Klan is a hateful organization
that blasphemes the name of Christ by calling itself Christian. The rise
of racial hate groups is abominable. Acts of hate are surely against the
very nature of Christianity. On these points most Christians are in
agreement.

We have also learned that even more subtle acts of discrimination
are wrong. Black people should be allowed to live wherever they
want—next door to me if they so choose. It would even be fine if a
black person joined my church.

It's harder now to identify the "good guys" and the "bad guys."
Questions of race are more ambiguous. Like the majority of the kids at
Spencer's high school, while most of us don't intentionally, actively
choose to hate, neither do we take a positive stand to show another
way. Some of us close our eyes and pretend there's no problem. Others stand by and watch as people are treated unjustly. But most of us
lack the peripheral vision to see what's going on around us.

Blinders were an ingenious invention designed to keep a horse single-minded, focused on one thing—moving forward in the direction
the master desired. They are put around the horse's eyes, limiting its
peripheral vision so that the horse can see only a part of reality. So it
forges forward in that one direction. Meanwhile, all around are dan-
gers, difficulties and even opportunities of which the horse is totally
unaware. Even if the horse cannot see them, they still exist.

Four hundred years of slavery, forced segregation and discrimination have left a stubborn residue within us all. For blacks, the residue
is anger, bitterness and blame. For whites, the residue is racial blinders.

If you drink polluted water, you'll probably catch hepatitis; if you
were born white in America, as I was, chances are you're wearing
those blinders.

A Whites-Only Option

After a volunteer group from the Midwest had worked hard one week
to renovate a house for a low-income family in Jackson, some VOC

staff members spent a lot of time in our kitchen preparing a generous "soul food" dinner for the volunteers. During dinner we overheard several offhand critical comments from them about the food. After the meal we retired to the living room, where several of us shared brief testimonies, and Spencer gave a message about God's concern for racial reconciliation.

When he finished, there was a long pause before one adult leader spoke up: "Thanks for the food, but I'm tired, and I came here to serve Christ, not to talk about black and white. So I'm going to leave." Other group members joined him in making it clear that they weren't interested in learning about racial reconciliation. Soon after that, they left the house. We felt devastated and rejected.

Blinders keep us from understanding how differently whites and blacks are affected by race. It was all too easy for this group of whites to avoid the whole problem. They thought helping renovate one house was enough. They could return home and go on with their lives, not giving a second thought to the hurts and struggles of people different from themselves.

This lesson was driven home to me again a few years ago when Lisa, a college friend who lived with a white Southern farming family in the summer, invited my wife, Donna, and me to join her for a weekend. It was a peaceful, relaxing two days. We were treated with warm hospitality: we swam in the family's pool, ate wonderful home-cooked food and were invited across the way for Sunday dinner with the farmer's mother. Donna and I also attended church with the family and were treated kindly.

But when we were alone with Lisa, I listened with sadness as she confided that when she had asked if we could visit for the weekend, one of her hosts had looked at her for a moment, then asked, "Are Chris and Donna black?" The woman wouldn't have allowed us to come if we hadn't been white. Since we are white, Donna and I received the finest treatment. But our black friends would not have been welcome in the house, the church or the neighborhood.

Although attitudes like this family's are slowly disappearing, the experience taught me a valuable lesson: race is an issue for me only when I choose to think about it. I can walk away from black West Jackson any time I like and be welcomed readily anywhere I go. But my black friends don't have that option.

On the turf of race, because we who are white do not experience the stigma of being black, we have the option to walk away. So given that the very nature of the solution—reconciliation—calls for us to share the burden, we whites face a special challenge to step out of our normal existence and understand the hurt of our black brothers and sisters.

Where Was Your Starting Line?

Another effect of white blinders is the deeply ingrained belief that everyone in America starts out the same. Many people remark, "My family pulled itself up by its own bootstraps. Why can't black people do the same?"

One of the United States' great strengths is that we are largely a nation of immigrants. Most Americans, including me, can trace their family history back to the point of hope for a better life that brought our ancestors here. Whether our people first stepped bravely onto the shore of virgin land or wept with joy as they steamed past Lady Liberty into New York Harbor, they all became part of a great "pot" of ethnicity. Stories abound of how folks of different nationalities and races came from all corners of the world, many penniless, and through hard work and determination managed to carve out a piece of the American dream for their children.

Each ethnic group capitalized on the American creed that all people are created equal, endowed by their Creator with certain inalienable rights, among which are life, liberty, and the pursuit of happiness. They gradually worked their way into the mainstream of American life, doing what was necessary to become solid citizens of their new country. That's the American way. It's one of the things about our country that deservedly make our hearts swell with pride.

Yet this is not the family story of all Americans. Casting a dark shadow against the glow of the melting pot are the lives of those who were already here when Europeans came and those who were brought here against their will, chained in the holds of slave vessels, to help tame this resource-rich land. We didn't really all begin on the same starting line.

Black people are the only American immigrants who did not choose to come. Slavery deprived black people of three crucial rights available to every other group that came to America—rights that enabled each group to establish an economic foothold.

First, blacks had no right to *leadership*. Enslaved Africans had no right to determine the nature of their families, their customs or their futures. They were stripped of their native languages. Husband was often ripped apart from wife, parents from children. They had no right to celebrate their native traditions.

While I can trace my family history via Jamestown Colony all the way back to England, Spencer can go back only one generation past his great-grandmother, who died in 1983. Her father had been a slave. There's no way for Spencer to know for certain where his ancestors came from, what their native tongue was or what customs his family practiced.

Second, African slaves had no right to *ownership*. Without the right to own property, slaves could not learn how to capitalize on the economic system. While my great-grandparents were establishing businesses in the mid-1800s, Spencer's great-grandparents tilled the soil and picked cotton to benefit the next generation of white children. Despite all their labor, blacks had nothing to pass on to the next generation.

Spencer and Joanie have told me about rising early as a family on Saturdays to pick cotton to help make ends meet; they labored together till sundown. That was harder work than I ever had to do. I had access to the system and a stable environment in which to learn marketable skills. Clearly my family didn't attain its standard of living just by working hard and being good American citizens. Social benefits were passed on from generation to generation, each building on the foundation inherited from the previous one.

Finally, black Africans had no right to *worship*. They could worship God only as the slavemaster allowed them. The black church thrived during slavery *in spite of* the system's attempts to make religion a tool to induce submissiveness.

Tom Skinner used the analogy of a baseball game to illustrate what's happened to black people in America. The game begins and team A quickly takes the lead. Soon they are leading team B 10-0. Although team B has been continually yelling foul, it's not till the sixth inning that the members of team A suddenly realize that team B members have been playing with one hand tied behind their back. "Okay, we'll let you untie your hands," team A tells team B. "Now let's continue the game." Well, by now the score is 20-0, with two innings to play. Team A has been free to develop the skills necessary to master the game. Team B, though now able to play with both hands, has not acquired the same level of skills. Can there be any doubt as to the outcome of the game?

George Jackson, a teacher at Messiah College in Grantham, Pennsylvania, brought a group of students to Voice of Calvary one January for a three-week crosscultural course. After a week of inner-city life and numerous lectures, the students' major concern was still "Is this going to be on the test, George?" So George devised a new teaching method.

One morning he divided the students into two groups—a brown-eyed group and a blue-eyed group. For one day, he declared, the Brown Eyes were designated the superior group. Blue Eyes had to do whatever Brown Eyes told them. Brown Eyes ate first, gave all their housecleaning and menial work to Blue Eyes, and insulted them with all kinds of putdowns.

What started as lighthearted role-playing turned serious. After two hours of name-calling, exclusion and putdowns from Brown Eyes and "General George," several of the blue-eyed "inferiors" were visibly upset. Some withdrew. One girl ran outside in tears. For a few hours these students had experienced what it was like to be treated as inferior, and it was almost too much dehumanization for them to tolerate. Mercifully, George soon brought the experiment to an end. He had made his point.

A One-Way Street

The dominant culture of America is white European. People from northern Europe shaped our nation's institutions: the legislative system of democracy, our free-market economy, separation of church and state, our language.

Whether you were originally European, Asian, African or Hispanic, blending into the melting pot means giving up a piece of your individual cultural identity. Italians become Italian-Americans; Jews become Jewish-Americans; Hispanics become Hispanic-Americans. As citizens we rightly expect every ethnic group to participate and cooperate in what we call the American way. The name of the game is *assimilation*. It's the way things work in America. It may not always be fair, but it is reality.

Black people are no exception. If they expect to gain the political and economic respect other ethnic groups have gained, they must also learn to take advantage of the free enterprise and political freedoms of this great American experiment.

But the fact that this is the way things work for the country does not mean that the church should function the same way. One of the problems in trying to achieve racial reconciliation is that we apply political and economic principles to what should be a spiritual realm. Reconciliation isn't a commodity to be competed for in the marketplace; it is a state of being that needs to be nurtured in the protective womb of the body of Christ.

In the world of the marketplace white European is the dominant standard for success. But in the fellowship of the church—the body of Christ—God is no respecter of culture or race. Although assimilation has worked somewhat well for the nation, it cannot and should not be used as the basis for racial reconciliation.

No, we don't "see color" when people of other races are entering our world on our terms, but suddenly color becomes very important if we have to enter the process on equal terms. Unthinkingly, whites often approach reconciliation with the expectation that black people will assimilate and "become white." It's okay for blacks to join our church or move into our neighborhood, but we don't consider joining their church or moving into their neighborhood.

Blacks and whites rarely have close, confiding friendships. As a result, whites don't know what black people really experience and think. Because blacks have to operate in a white world, though, blacks generally know whites much better than whites know blacks.

The movie *Driving Miss Daisy*, which won the Academy Award for Best Picture in 1990, depicts the touching relationship that develops over many years between Miss Daisy, an Alabama white woman, and her black chauffeur, Hoke. At the end of the movie Miss Daisy, now a lonely old woman, is visited by Hoke in the nursing home where she will spend her last years. She tells Hoke that he is her best friend. The movie ends as Hoke feeds her with a spoon, for Miss Daisy's arthritic hands are unable to reach her own mouth.

I heard many comments from whites about how much they enjoyed the movie. Many blacks I spoke with, on the other hand, couldn't figure out why *Driving Miss Daisy* received so much attention. Why was this movie received so differently by whites and blacks?

Hoke and Miss Daisy's relationship is a one-way street; it develops on the terms of her culture and her needs. The closest Miss Daisy ever comes to seeing Hoke's world is a time when, as he is driving her on a long trip, he can't find a place to stop to use the bathroom because he is black. Hoke knows everything about Miss Daisy's world. But Miss Daisy knows very little about Hoke's. Miss Daisy and Hoke have a "safe" relationship, and Hoke is a "safe" black person. Hoke makes us feel okay about ourselves as white people. He doesn't bring up tough racial issues. Whites can relate to a black person like Hoke and think, *See, I'm progressive. I have black friends.*

A relationship of mutual respect can't happen unless each party learns to appreciate what's important to the other. We all know what kind of bread goes with spaghetti, but do you know what kind of bread goes with greens? Everyone can sing "My Country 'Tis of Thee," but what about "Lift Every Voice and Sing"? We all can tell you who Thomas Edison is, but what about Garrett Morgan?

Take heart. Not many whites have learned to eat cornbread with greens (I'll take mine with hot sauce), sing the black national anthem or recite the many accomplishments of the black inventor of the stop-light. We need to start learning, though. In fact, we can and must turn a cultural street that's currently marked "one way" into a crosscultural thoroughfare of mutual respect, understanding and appreciation.

Because whites rarely cross into the foreign territory of black culture, often we don't get to hear what black people really think. Whites are often surprised when black people they thought they knew well begin to reveal some of their deepest feelings.

During a reconciliation workshop for the staff of an inner-city ministry in Alabama, it became clear that the whites and the blacks on the staff had completely different impressions of the state of the ministry. The whites believed that the ministry was basically in good shape. As the workshop got under way, however, the blacks began gradually to reveal feelings of being undermined and mistrusted. This is a scenario that is often repeated in our interactions with interracial groups. We are too rarely honest with each other.

Missed Opportunities

How separated is your life from the other race? One of the results of our blinders is that we underestimate the extent of our separation and make little effort to bridge the gap. The following questions make up a "reconciliation inventory." The purpose of these questions is not to provoke guilt, but to help you examine your everyday life and determine what level of contact you actually do have with people from the other race. While the questions are addressed to whites, readers from any background can ask themselves the questions in terms of their contact with members of another race.

Neighborhood

☐ If you had to borrow a tool, is there a black family on your street you would ask for it?

☐ Who is the black family that lives closest to you?

Children
☐ If you needed a baby sitter for your children, is there a black person you would trust to do it?

☐ Do your children have black friends they might invite to spend the night?

☐ Look at your children's bookshelf. Do they have any books about or by black people?

☐ If you wanted a black Christian to have an impact on your children, is there someone you would invite to participate in their lives?

Work
☐ If you were to choose one coworker to do a vitally important project with, is there a black person you could choose?

Church/Spiritual
☐ If you were to choose a black prayer partner, is there someone you know well enough to ask?

☐ Is there a living black Christian who has had an influence on your spiritual development?

Social
☐ If you decided to ask a black person out to dinner, is there someone you could invite?

☐ If you're married, is there a black couple you and your spouse would invite to dinner?

☐ If you were to invite someone to join you in your favorite recreational activity, is there a black person you would invite?

Mentors
☐ Is there a living black person who has made a significant impact on your life?

☐ Look through your bookshelves. Do you have any books by black authors? What about black Christian authors?

If nearly all of your answers were no, ask yourself why. Is it because you simply don't cross paths with people from the other race? Or are there people who could become the "yes" to these questions—people in your neighborhood, at work or in your area who could become more influential in your social and spiritual life if you were willing to invest some energy?

Let's assume that God desires for us as whites and blacks to make a real mark on each other's lives. Now go through the questions again. This time strip off your blinders and ask yourself: What opportunities am I missing to develop relationships in this area? In my neighborhood? At work? In my spiritual life? Maybe you don't know any black (or white) Christian well enough right now to start a prayer partnership, but perhaps there's someone you could begin developing a friendship with. What about your children? Are they being equipped to be crosscultural? If your children don't invite kids from the other race to your home, maybe they don't know any. Talk to them about it. Maybe you live in an all-white world, and it's time to take some risky steps into unfamiliar places. Or maybe you're black and have retreated to close relationships with blacks only; it's time to gird yourself up and take a chance again.

It feels awkward to bend over backward to make genuine contact. And it's sad that something so close to God's heart should seem so strange. But maybe after we've put real energy into developing deep, mutually beneficial relationships across racial lines, such friendships will come to feel normal.

Whites outnumber blacks in many American towns and cities. But even in areas where there are large numbers of both blacks and whites, we have too few environments in which to interact, whether as friends, coworkers, fellow Christians or parents. Why is this so?

One reason is that we have inherited choices that were originally made specifically in the interest of racial separation. In fact, many suburbs in America were founded to accommodate "white flight" from places where blacks were moving in. The only reason many whites were born in the suburbs instead of in places where races mixed was that their parents decided to move out of the city when blacks moved in.

If you were born there, you didn't make the choice. But you did inherit the negative consequence—separation from the other race. A great many other choices grow out of where we live: who our children's schoolmates are, what Christians we interact with, what people influence our life's direction.

Taking Off the Blinders: The First Step

Because most whites' lives don't intersect with black people's lives, we must begin to go out of our way to become educated. We need to put ourselves in situations that will enable us to peel off our blinders and see how our actions and unconscious attitudes affect our brothers and sisters who are not a part of the dominant culture.

One of the qualities that made basketball legend Magic Johnson such a great floor general was his peripheral vision. Magic knew the position of all his teammates at any given time. Although this talent was a great gift, it alone did not make him basketball's greatest playmaker. There are many players who have the same ability. The difference was Magic's willingness to give up the ball. He took delight in helping a teammate score a basket. As a result everyone loved him, and he will undoubtedly go down in history as one of the greatest basketball players of all time.

In a narrow sense, wearing racial blinders serves our self-interest. The less we see of other people's lives, the more we can concentrate on taking care of ourselves. So taking our blinders off is an act of unselfishness. It means willingness to go out of our way to help others score—and, like Magic Johnson, taking delight in their successes.

Instead of plodding ahead seeing only the things that are useful to our own interests, we will become aware of the needs and interests of others. Jesus put it this way: "Whoever wants to become great among you must be your servant" (Mt 20:26). Of course, it will take extra energy and extra effort, but the reward—being considered great in the kingdom of God—is worth it.

Because race awareness is optional for the vast majority of whites, and because our economic or social interests are not at stake, our willingness to deal or not deal with it becomes purely a spiritual issue. Unfortunately, because it's "only" that intangible part of our integrity

before God that's at stake, and not our survival, we feel little motivation to bridge the gap between our normal existence and the everyday
reality of our black brothers and sisters.

That weekend Donna and I spent in rural Mississippi would be a
wonderful memory now if not for a simple fact. My friends Spencer,
Melvin and Arthur would have been treated like yard boys at that
home. If I hadn't had friendships with black people, I probably
wouldn't have even noticed the racial attitudes in that family and that
town.

It is no accident that Republican Jack Kemp and Democrat Bill
Bradley were for years two of their parties' most passionate voices for
racial healing. They both had backgrounds in professional sports—
Kemp played with the Buffalo Bills, while Bradley spent ten years in
the NBA's black world—where racial discrimination became a personal issue in friendships with black teammates. "I could not face my
friends Ernie Ladd, Cookie Gilchrist or Tippy Day or all the black football players I know and lived with and lost and won with, if I were not
their voice in the cabinet," said Kemp when he was HUD secretary. "It
is my way of redeeming my existence on this earth."[1]

Kemp and Bradley found common ground with blacks on the playing fields of professional sports. Finding common interests is a good
starting point for building interracial friendships.

One day a white church leader who had just heard Spencer and me
speak grabbed me in the hallway and outlined his quandary: "Our
church is Presbyterian Reformed. We have a burden for the black
community, but we don't want to lose our theology. We don't know of
any black Christians who share our doctrine. What should we do?"

Make the task too great, and you can lose the race even before you
put one foot forward. Rather than start relationships where we disagree, we need to start where we agree and see where it leads. Focus
on building personal trust rather than on reaching agreement on
every point of theory and theology. Get into the trenches in a common
ministry rather than debating the pros and cons of affirmative action.

Racial reconciliation should not begin with a debate over affirmative action and quotas. It is about personal relationships, getting to

know names and faces. Let race take on a name and a face. Build relationships and share in your new friends' concerns for their families and communities. Go into their neighborhood. Visit their church. Get involved in their community. Let their experience speak to your life.

An Environment for Learning
Putting yourself into an environment where you are the minority is one of the most effective ways you can begin to understand the hurts that didn't concern you before.

During the course of a political discussion with a group of college students several years ago, the name Nelson Mandela was mentioned. One student innocently asked, "Is he one of the civil rights workers that was killed in Mississippi?" This student was a senior at a Christian college. He was dedicated to his political party and had talked about all his reasons for voting for his candidate in the upcoming election. But he wasn't educated at all on issues that didn't affect his life.

Before the summer of 1991 Richard Parks might have shared that need for awareness. He certainly wouldn't have had a clue how to relate to a black person like Yolanda Green, who is from the tough streets of Detroit. Richard comes from an affluent California suburb; the few blacks he'd seen took care of his neighbors' gardens and cleaned their houses. He took his faith seriously but wasn't confident around people who were different from him. While a college student at the University of Southern California, Richard decided to spend a summer doing inner-city ministry with Voice of Calvary. The relationships he developed with VOC's black staff and children opened Richard's eyes to a reality he had never experienced before.

But as he returned to campus in the fall, he still wondered if his unusual summer would change anything back at school. Then he met Yolanda. "I wouldn't have been comfortable reaching out to a black person like Yolanda before my summer in Jackson, especially since she wasn't a Christian," Richard admits "But I gained a lot of confidence from living in a black community. It helped me to understand black people, to be sensitive to their culture and to be more confident in relating to them."

As a result of her friendship with Richard, Yolanda eagerly began seeking God, even attending Bible studies led by Richard and others. A few months later she came to Richard and said, "I'm ready to give it all to Jesus."

Our need to admit that we wear racial blinders is similar to an alcoholic's need to admit that he has the disease of alcoholism. Alcoholics have a natural tendency to abuse alcohol. Initially confronted, an alcoholic will swear up and down that he doesn't drink too much and that he can control himself. The first and most critical step on the road to recovery is for the alcoholic to admit that he has a problem (some say that admitting is 70 percent of the solution) and that he can't manage his problem without God's help. He knows that if he lets down his guard and forgets what his inherent weakness is, he'll slide into abuse again. The introduction that Alcoholics Anonymous members use in their meetings, "My name is Joe, and I'm an alcoholic," recognizes that inherent tendency to abuse alcohol.

We whites need to come to the point where we can say, "My name is Chris, and I've been wearing racial blinders." Admitting helps me remember that left to my own devices, I will look out for me and mine first. Only by admitting our blinders can we begin the process of stripping them away, piece by piece.

6

School Daze

LOOKING BACK AT MY RACIAL EXPERIENCE, I SOMETIMES BELIEVE *that it was in God's design all along for me to be involved in a specific ministry of racial reconciliation. If I can be reconciled with whites, anybody can.*

Most blacks can tell you story after story of what it feels like to be on the negative side of America's race issue. The severity of our personal experience is in direct proportion to how much and how often we ventured outside the safety of our black-controlled environments. For those of us who were among the first black "settlers" to venture into the unknown lands of integration, the stories are especially intense. I share some of these stories now not to cause shame or guilt but in the hope of creating understanding.

It was late summer 1970 in Mendenhall, Mississippi. In a few weeks I would be starting my senior year in high school. Although it had been six months since my father was beaten in the Brandon jail and the racial tension had cooled, there was a different nervous anticipation and excitement around town, at least in the "quarters." This was the year that the schools were to be totally desegregated.

On the black side of the tracks no one was quite sure if things would go smoothly. The adults were angry because so many of the black schoolteachers lost their jobs. The black high schoolers were resentful because the whites had taken down all the pictures of blacks from the walls of Harper High and because the school (which had been named for a beloved black professor) had been renamed Mendenhall Junior High. But all these inconveniences and many more were chalked up to integration. We'd known it would carry a price tag.

The white community was restless as well. There was anger and resentment for being forced into something against their will. Those with enough money would escape by creating a private academy. But for the majority the unthinkable had happened. The North had imposed its will on the South once again. I suppose next to going to church with blacks, this was about as bad as it could get.

There were rhetorical bets around the black community as to whether the white folks would finish building their private school in time for the new school year. Although we all knew they would, the bets were our way of poking fun at their intense disdain for us. We looked at it like this: for some of the most dyed-in-the-wool Confederates, just the thought of having to send their children to school with us would fuel enough negative energy to complete any task. We were right—they had it ready for the new school year.

Football practice traditionally began three weeks before the school year, so those of us on the football team were the first to test the new reality. For my black friends, this would be the first visit "up on the hill" (what we called the white school), but not for me. Many of the white boys who were now on the football team had been my classmates only two years before. Most of them politely pretended they didn't remember me, and I did the same. After all, it had been two years since I had seen any of them. I'd completed tenth and eleventh grades back in the security of the all-black environment. The constant stress of our experiences in the white school had finally gotten to my mother, so she had decided to put us back in the all-black school and wait for the total desegregation of the schools. Now that time had come.

But this time it was different. I was not alone. I was back with a whole army of black comrades. Because I knew most of the white kids, I could give intelligence reports to my black friends as to the particular whites—students and teachers—who had made known their negative feelings about blacks.

As it turned out, most of those who had given me the most trouble were no longer there. They had either dropped out or had left for the security and racial purity of the private school. In a perverted kind of way I was disappointed that these guys were not there. I had so much looked forward to seeing how they would respond when they no longer had the security of numbers.

It turned out that the football team was indeed a good indication of how our school desegregation would go. For the most part things went more smoothly than anyone had expected at the newly integrated Mendenhall High School. There were only a few racial incidents that year. During one game, our football team almost unraveled when some of the black players, who were unaccustomed to losing (Harper High had lost only two games in the previous three years), walked off the field before the game was over, not understanding why they were sitting on the bench.

All in all, my senior year of high school was one of my best. I was glad for the experience of integration before I went off to college. Not only did it help round out my experience (I'd now attended an all-black school, a white school before total desegregation, an integrated school in southern California for a couple of months during tenth grade, and then total desegregation in the South), but it helped me see that integration was possible. I hoped the whites realized by now that being with us was not the end of the world.

Then I took off to a small Christian college in southern California. The difference between my new campus and Mississippi was like night and day. While in the South being black determined my identity, in California it didn't seem to matter. Many people say that college is the best four years of your life—and you won't get much of an argument about that from me. My first semester was exhilarating. The freedom of being on my own in an atmosphere with very little racial tension, combined with the opportunity to play basketball—life had never been better.

Best Friends

During that first semester, I became very good friends with a white guy I'll call Dick. For some reason we were drawn to each other. We spent most of our free time together and would often stay up late at night talking. Dick had grown up in the Northwest and could not understand how Southern whites could harbor such ill will toward blacks.

Because we spent so much time together, some of the older black guys would sometimes rib me about it, accusing me of wanting to be with Dick over them. One of the black seniors issued a brotherly warning. "Dick is no different from the rest of them," he cautioned. "When push comes to shove, you'll still be black to him." He spoke with great conviction.

His warning nagged at me because it reminded me of another caution I had gotten from a senior back in high school. "There is a little snake in all white folks," Reggie would sometimes say with confidence, as though he were an old man whose experience was irrefutable. Reggie, who endured that first year of "Freedom of Choice" with me in 1967, would often remind me of this "truth" when we were discussing which of the white kids were "good" and which were rotten to the core.

Of course, I defended Dick because he was my friend. "Dick doesn't see color," I insisted. And as far as I could see, my black skin made no difference to him. Since my senior mentor could not convince me of Dick's guilt, his final words were a calm "You'll see."

My friendship with Dick continued to grow. We were together so much that a picture of the two of us appeared on the cover of one of the school's PR pieces. Dick and I were shown seated on a lounge sofa shaking hands as if we were heads of state who had just signed a peace treaty. The purpose was to demonstrate the harmony that existed at our school.

It happened that Dick's roommate decided to leave school after the first semester. Dick and I had often talked about being roommates.

Since we were such good friends, we both thought that it would be ideal for us to room together and had excitedly talked about it on many occasions.

After Dick's roommate left, we planned that I would move in after I returned from a basketball trip. Upon my return to campus, I was eager to tell Dick all about the trip and how I had played, and then to set up my move. But when I entered Dick's room, I was confused. Someone else's belongings were already there. My first thought was that Dick's roommate had returned, but I could tell by the expression on Dick's face that it was something else.

I will never forget the conversation that followed. It probably governed the way I related to white men for the rest of my college years. "After thinking about it more," he began, "I've decided that it will be best for us not to room together." Aware of my bewilderment, he continued, "It has nothing to do with you. I like you and would love having you here, but I don't think I could handle your black friends hanging out in here."

My first thought was instinctive: *Defend your black friends.* But I didn't have the energy. I was devastated. What was he saying? What was wrong with my black friends? Did being accepted by whites mean that I would have to give up my black friends—my blackness? Had I assimilated so much that now Dick could think of me as white? But I wasn't white, and like many blacks in that era, I had grown to be proud of my blackness.

I don't remember what I said to Dick, but I can remember what I thought. It is almost embarrassing now, but during that painful conversation I was concerned about his feelings. I can picture very clearly the embarrassed look on his face as he tried to explain his decisions. I actually felt sorry for him for the inconvenience of having to explain something that clearly embarrassed him so much. I left his room as soon as I could, showing very little emotion.

I am not by nature a quick-tempered person. Attending an all-white school in Mississippi for two years had taught me to restrain my thoughts, my anger and my actions. But I'll never forget how I felt as I walked back down the hall to the security of my own room and my black roommate. My first emotion was sorrow. I felt sorry for myself. But the more I thought about it, the angrier I became. I dreaded hearing all the I-told-you-sos from my black friends. I had made such a fool of myself. *I guess they are all alike,* I admitted to myself. *Maybe there is a little snake in all white folks.*

Retreat into Safety

"No matter what you do or become, to them you're still just a nigger" was the conclusion my angry black friends and I reached a few nights later, as we discussed not only this situation but the state of America's race problem. It amazed me that my older black friends had predicted the outcome of my friendship with Dick. I kept thinking, *How did they know?* But they had been around for three or four years, and as the saying goes, "Experience is the best teacher."

The one thing that didn't add up was that we were all Christians, but being Christian didn't seem to mean anything when it came to this issue. During my early years in Mississippi I had always had trouble reconciling the behavior of white Southerners with the Christianity I saw in the Bible. But this was not the South.

I have always been a person of ideals, even as a young boy, so in my head there were only two options. If white and black Christians could not be reconciled, then either the gospel was a lie or we really weren't indwelt by the Christ we said had taken up residence in our lives.

This was only the second semester of my freshman year, and the damage had been done. And as I look back, I can see how this incident affected my later behavior.

When I was a boy of six or seven, one day my uncle brought home a huge turtle and announced that it would be our supper. The trick was to kill the turtle. Being aware of his precarious situation the turtle, for some time, refused to stick his head out of his protective shell. So my uncle instructed all of us to stand perfectly still and be quiet. Eventually the turtle assumed the danger was over and poked his head out. I'm sure he never saw the ax coming. We had turtle soup that night.

I was like a turtle that had stuck his head out of his shell but only got the tip of his nose cut off. After Dick reneged on our plans to room together, I stuck more closely to my black friends. I sat with them at mealtimes, and we spent our free time together. The sad truth is that I never had another white male friend during the remainder of my college years.

In 1974 most of the black guys, including me, were asked not to come back for our senior year. We had been pretty disrespectful of some of the school rules. We all went quietly; we knew we were guilty. So I moved back home and attempted to transfer to Jackson State University, an all-black school only a few blocks from where we lived. But this school would not accept many of my credits from the Christian college. Therefore I reluctantly enrolled in a local Presbyterian college that had just begun accepting blacks. I was one of only six or eight blacks enrolled.

My first three years of college in California had basically been fun. Even though racism lurked beneath the surface, life there had been a breeze compared to life in the South. Coming back to Mississippi and attending a white school was like going back in time. No one at the Presbyterian school was ever mean to me, but no one talked to me either. It was as if I didn't exist. At the time I considered this an improvement from what my junior-high years were like—and believe me, it was.

Although I've learned that others perceive me differently, I see myself as a competitive but shy person. I lived off campus when I attended the Presbyterian college, and I suppose that had something to do with my lack of friendships. Maybe an extroverted black person would have had a different experience from mine; perhaps my isolation and loneliness were partly my own doing. But I suppose abused women and children sometimes think this way too.

I often wonder what those two years would have been like if a few white kids had reached out to me. And I wonder whether some black kids on majority-white college campuses today are feeling out of place and bewildered, needing someone to acknowledge their existence and offer friendship.

Two years after my return to Mississippi, I graduated with a degree in business administration. The thought of participating in the com-

mencement exercises never even crossed my mind. I picked up my
diploma from the dean's office and drove away relieved that I'd never
need to return. Years later I realized that I had attended classes there
for two years and had never held a single conversation with a white
student.

7

Black Residue

U NFORTUNATELY, THE RACIAL PROGRESS AMERICA HAS MADE *cannot simply wash away the effects of our negative history. We blacks will undoubtedly continue dealing with the residue of our history for many years to come. For us, the first step toward removing the residue involves coming to terms with some very painful truths that we don't like to face. I hope that this discussion will help us begin that process, and that it will also help whites understand the extent of the psychological barriers that must be bridged if we are to build and maintain healthy crosscultural relationships.*

The oppression of the black race is a matter of historical fact. This part of our history is painful for blacks to recall and shameful for whites. Thanks to the civil rights movement, the oppressive laws that physically bound blacks and gave whites a false sense of superiority have been wiped away. But to the bewilderment of blacks and whites alike, an elusive residue remains.

One TV commercial demonstrates how a certain soap is the only one that doesn't leave a film behind after rinsing. It claims to leave no residue. How wonderful it would be if history were like that—if just wiping away the old oppressive laws could make us all squeaky clean! But the residue of a racist legacy is slippery and resilient. Both whites and blacks struggle with the residue left by years of living in a divided society. For black people who are still struggling to join the mainstream of American society, this residue is excess baggage that slows down the soul train.

Residual Anger and Blame

One of the more obvious relics of the historical oppression of black folks is black anger. I'm not talking about anger in general. I'm talking about an anger that is specific to being black in America.

Most black people are angry—angry about our violent history, angry for the hassle that it is to grow up black in America, angry that we can never assume that we won't be prejudged by our color, angry that we will carry this stigma everywhere we go (it is hardly ever a positive asset), angry that "black" always seems to get the short end of the stick. And most of all, angry that white America doesn't understand the reasons for our anger.

Even blacks who are embarrassed by the black "underclass," who insist that race is no longer an issue, will sometimes let that residual black anger slip out in moments of weakness.

This anger can be a very destructive force, as proved by the rioting in South Central Los Angeles after the police who beat Rodney King were acquitted. Backed up against the wall, most blacks will concede that the violence and looting were wrong. But deep in the recesses of most black minds was a tiny voice whispering, *If this is the only way we can make them understand how we feel, then so be it.*

As I sat in church the Sunday after the riots, a black friend passed me a note that read, "I'm kinda glad they are rioting in L.A." My friend would never have made this statement in public.

Anger is not always hurtful. When channeled positively, it can be a valuable ally. Sometimes it surfaces as passion or, as some prefer to call it, "righteous indignation." Christians who believe anger is always wrong say that Jesus' emotion when he drove the moneychangers out of the temple was nothing more than "intense passion." Those who believe there is such a thing as righteous anger, though, insist that anger in the name of justice is godly.

Regardless of what you think about anger, it is present in nearly all American blacks—even in Christians like me—and must be reckoned with. If blacks and whites are to achieve long-term intimate relationships, blacks must learn to channel their anger and reserve it to fight injustice rather than directing it at whites who are sincerely trying to reach out. Whites, on the other hand, need not make it their mission to convince blacks that there is no justifiable reason for their anger. Instead, whites must seek to understand the reasons behind this anger and learn not to fear it.

Though I've said our anger can be channeled for good, it does have a dark side. To say that it is deadly would not be an overstatement. Left to simmer, unharnessed anger has very little redeeming value and will eventually twist and distort the personality trying to accommodate it. Mental wards, prisons and morgues are full of people paying the price for unresolved anger. Many of our best and brightest blacks, because of their anger, cannot redirect their energies toward reaching their God-given potential. The end result of this anger is paralysis.

One of my long-time friends is a walking casualty of unresolved anger. I'll call him Jack. Jack has a brilliant mind. In fact, his brilliance is what attracted me to him. But he is angry at his lot in life and the lot of black people in general, and he blames the bulk of it on the white folks. Years ago, I would just sit and listen to him exegete the problems for hours—what's wrong with white folks, and how they will never change, and how sad the plight of "our folk" is.

But I believe that sooner or later the time for talking is over. I began asking, "Okay, what are we going to do about all these problems?" Jack found no pleasure in expending his mental energy on entertaining possible solutions. He would get visibly irritated when I steered the conversation in that direction. He wanted to keep talking about what's wrong between whites and blacks.

Eventually we drifted apart, and Jack became more self-destructive. Although brilliant, he has no future. I believe it's his unresolved anger that keeps him from getting along with anyone long-term. So he bounces around from job to job. Being around him for any length of time drains my energy. But I still hurt for him.

I suppose I am sympathetic with Jack's untiring analysis of America's racial problems and the unmistakable role white America has played in creating the black "underclass." But as my father says, "It is a foolish waste of time to think that the people who got you into this mess will get you out of it." Jack will eventually have to be responsible for himself. As the old folks used to say, "E'ry tub's got to sit on its own bot'um."

What alarms me is the lack of Christlike compassion in a breezily announce that blacks must now be left on their own. It took three hundred years to create our racial problems, and already white America is beginning to feel that it has done its part. Even professional civil rights activists like Eleanor Holmes Norton lamented, "We don't have a clue on how to proceed. I would have never said that in 1978 or 1968."[1]

Ms. Norton, you are not the only one. It frustrates me to try to address problems like this outside the body of Christ. To be honest, if I were a white non-Christian, I don't know if I'd have any motivation to care. But I am a Christian, and claiming that distinction carries responsibilities. I don't have the option to be unconcerned about the poor, or about a brother or sister who is hurting. If I want to enjoy the benefits of following Christ, this responsibility goes with the territory. This is why it excites me to talk about our race problem in the context of the body of Christ. Here we are equipped with guidelines, precedents and commands. It is the absence of these absolutes that has everybody else, from white liberals to black activists to conservative Republicans, scratching their heads and moving farther into the suburbs.

Black anger must be defused with sincere love, not negotiated like a minefield. And since the intended target of black anger is white arrogance and apathy, one of the best first steps toward its healing is to build meaningful, nonpatronizing peer relationships with the targets of our anger—white brothers or sisters. It is easy to remain angry with a faceless white race. It is much harder to direct that anger at a particular white brother or sister who has a name and a face.

Some blacks attending our church for the first time are struck by the black and white friendships that extend beyond the worship service. We need more environments where such relationships can develop. The church offers the best hope of filling that void. We should be able to draw on the common denominator for both black and white Christians—Christ himself.

Residual Self-Doubt
Another negative phenomenon, hatched and fattened during the years of our racial oppression, is black self-doubt. It has slithered through the nets of the civil rights years and even to this day reaches up and threatens, and sometimes strangles, the efforts of some of our most secure black Americans.

As I try to explain this reality, I'm often challenged by white students who are aware of their own insecurities. "What's so different about black self-doubt?" they ask. "Everyone has self-doubt to one degree or another." This is true. Even the healthiest white people suffer sporadic bouts of self-doubt. But whites who have experienced the devastating effects of a normal dosage of self-doubt should be all the more understanding of the struggles of blacks. Our normal insecurity is compounded by additional doubts related to our skin color.

Blacks in the fields of sports and entertainment may benefit from the accomplishments of their black predecessors enough that they suffer from only a normal degree of self-doubt. The rest of us, though, carry a nagging demon that routinely whispers discouraging words peculiar only to blacks: *You must remember, you're black. You don't come from as stable a background as these white people. No black person has ever held this position before. If you don't succeed in this task, you will let down the whole black race.* Then, finally, the ace: *Don't the years of oppression of my people make me less capable—don't they make me, in fact, inferior?*

In his book *The Content of Our Character* Shelby Steele does a much better job than I ever could in probing black vulnerability to self-doubt. He writes, "This vulnerability begins for blacks with the recognition that we belong, quite simply, to the most despised race in the human community of races. To be a member of such a group in a society where all others gain an impunity by merely standing in relation to us is to live with a relentless openness to diminishment and shame."[2]

If it is true that we are at least partly products of our environment, it stands to reason that all of the negatives that we face in being black help shape who we are. I come from a stable Christian family. We were always taught, not just by our parents but also by the culture, that we were just as good as anyone. The sad implication is that if we had to be taught this, then there must be some doubt in someone's mind about the truth of the matter.

Being as good as anyone ("anyone" usually meant white folks) and then gaining opportunities to demonstrate it was a major part of my identity as I grew up. In junior high, when I found myself surrounded by whites for the first time, I felt it my responsibility to prove to them and to myself that I was not inferior. As I look back now, I have to thank God for those experiences. For I believe that somehow they add fuel to my quest for racial reconciliation.

One of the barriers that had to be broken down if blacks were to join mainstream America was segregation in Southern schools. Being one of only two blacks in an all-white high school was not a prospect I anticipated with delight. But I knew it had to be done.

Up to that year the first day of school had always been filled with eager anticipation. Exaggerating summer experiences, sizing up the competition for recess football and trying to make a good impression on the new teachers were the only concerns of the day. But on my first day in the white high school, before I could make it to my first class, I had been called "nigger" or referred to as "the nigger" several times.

My homeroom teacher, who was about as good as white Mississippians could be in 1967, spent the first fifteen minutes trying in vain to answer the questions of thirty white eighth-grade boys. "Do you mean we really have to go to school with a nigger? We have to be in the same class with him? If God wanted us to mix, why did he make us white and him black? They can make me go to school with a nigger, but they can't make me like him. They can make me go to school with him, but they can't make me sit by him." From that day, for the next two school years, there was always an empty seat on either side of me.

Every time someone accidentally jostled me in the hall, he would brush himself off as if to remove the germs. No one ever talked to me, unless it was to insult me or to make fun of me. For two years I was the repulsive creature the girls would refer to when attempting to insult a classmate. "You like Jimmy," one would say, but the other had a chilling retort: "Well, you like Spencer." Then they would both shudder and make faces indicating the ultimate "gross-out." Nothing that passed through my hands—money or homework papers—was ever touched directly by any of my classmates. I was considered unclean. The teachers, though more mature and sophisticated, felt much the same as the kids and were reluctant to object to the relentless harassment.

Although the notion of my inferiority was absurd to me in my head (and most of the time my actions did back up that reality), sometimes my psyche was not so progressive. There were always unanswered questions in the back of my mind—questions that if answered might legitimate white people's attitudes toward us: Why did we all live in a little ghetto on the other side of the tracks? Why did the white folks not want us to be in the same school with their children? Was there something wrong with us? Such questions always hovered somewhere in my mind, though most of the time they were unconscious.

Even to this day I have a tiny fear that one day I will open a newspaper and find, printed for all the world to see, the story of some nerdy scientist who has uncovered undeniable proof that black people are innately inferior to every other race. I can see the headlines now: "German Scientist Wins Nobel Prize for Genetic Discoveries Proving the Inferior Status of the Black Race." And the lead paragraph will explain that his findings have been confirmed by a team of scientists hand-picked by the NAACP.

Granted, I am exaggerating. No black person is haunted by all these thoughts at one time. But in our most insecure moments many of us do entertain them.

James Brown's song "I'm Black and I'm Proud" probably helped to decrease the number of fistfights in many all-black elementary and high schools around the country. The word *black* from the mouth of another black student followed by a string of unflattering obscenities—as in "He called me a black so-and-so"—had been commonly cited by ruffled combatants whose teachers asked why they were fighting. It is a painful and embarrassing memory for adult blacks and probably a total surprise to most whites that black children put each other down with the word *black*.

It still happens today, although not nearly as much as it did before the sixties. Much of the sting has diminished with the gradual acceptance of our blackness that began, for many of us, with James Brown's song.

Although this song did as much as anything for our self-esteem by helping us embrace our blackness, it also troubled me from the first time I heard it. I knew there must be a problem with believing that we were black and proud if we had to, as James Brown put it, "say it loud, I'm black and I'm proud."

As a teenager in the early seventies, sitting in an audience whipped to fever pitch by the charisma of Jesse Jackson, I felt an unmatched pride when we repeated his famous "I am somebody" chant. But even then my euphoria was tainted by a twinge of shame at having to repeat this to ourselves.

The truth is that our racial legacy has damaged us. Our unwillingness to confront our fears, I believe, is one of the reasons we are beginning to insist on black separation. I can think of several leadership-quality black men who left our biracial church for the security of an all-black congregation, but only after the baton of leadership had begun pointing in their direction.

I know in writing this I run the risk of being attacked by some of my black brothers and sisters, who will stiffen their necks and move their heads from front to back and side to side at the same time (as only black women can do), insisting quite passionately that being black has had no adverse effect on their self-image. This is a taboo subject. We hardly talk about this, even in all-black company. My laying the problem out to white readers may seem like airing our dirty laundry—an act of treason.

My only reason for this "treachery" is to help whites understand and recognize where we are coming from, and to help blacks begin a dialogue that will lead us to face our fears head-on.

The Urban "Underclass"

The Pasadena, California, community where my parents used to live is one of the highest crime and drug neighborhoods in southern California. This and many other inner cities were once described in a popular rap song, appropriately titled "The Wild Wild West."

Not five minutes after my wife and I got into bed on the first night of our visit, we heard two gunshots right outside our bedroom window. Gunshots in this neighborhood are not uncommon, so there was no mad rush to look outside. But when we got up and looked out, our jet-lagged eyes saw a young Hispanic man standing across the street and quietly calling for help. Seconds later, I watched in disbelief as he fell to the ground. My father got outside about the same time I did. By the time we got to the wounded man, two young men were flagging down an ambulance that was on its way to another call.

Red and white lights flashed and a crowd gathered. As I watched the paramedics, they reminded me of a team of busy beavers doing their job systematically, almost without thinking—applying oxygen to the man's face, vigorously pumping his chest and inserting an IV. The sad truth is that their expertise has come at the expense of hundreds of young black men. As they worked to save this man's life, even I in my inexperience could tell they were fighting a losing battle.

In a desperate move to free up another pair of trained hands, they asked me to hold the IV bag. Then I saw why even with all their training and sophisticated technology they would lose this battle: two bullet holes, one through the chest and another in the head.

Two minutes later, the frenzy was over. He stopped breathing. Two days later we read in the newspaper the reason for this senseless killing and so many others: two boys had just wanted to experience the thrill of a kill. These two happened to be only twelve and fourteen years old.

Ever since the days of the early church there have always been a few Christians who were willing to take the gospel message to places

that were neglected and dangerous. Years ago the mention of dangerous places would have conjured up visions of "deepest darkest Africa"
in the minds of many Western Christians. Today if you asked an American Christian where she or he would least like to live, serve God and
raise a family, the answer would likely be different. Our most dreaded
mission field might be no more than a few miles away—the inner city.

Much has been written about the evolution of the urban ghetto and
its ability to survive despite efforts to locate its "Achilles' heel." In the
1950s and 1960s the racism that separated black from white was said to
be the culprit. In the 1970s, 1980s and 1990s the very opportunities
gained from the civil rights struggle worsened the plight of the inner
cities, as upwardly mobile blacks moved to the suburbs. The inner city
finds itself suffering from a lack of moral, spiritual, economic and
political leadership. Everybody who is somebody, black or white, views
the inner city as a place to be avoided.

I suppose it's important to understand the reasons for the development of this modern phenomenon, if for no other reason than to
keep from participating in its perpetuation. I'm often asked by both
blacks and whites, "What do you see as the reasons for the rise in law-
lessness, drugs, crime, single-parent families and the black prison population?" I know it shouldn't, but my answer sometimes depends on
who's asking and for what reason.

When I address blacks, it seems self-defeating to recount all the
injustices done to blacks in the past—from slavery and sharecropping
to the damage of the welfare system—and to say that these are the reasons for inner-city problems. Learning history and understanding
how you got into a particular situation is one thing. But whining and
wallowing in the self-pity and hopelessness that can result from this
emphasis has undoubtedly burned up energy that should have been
used in the hunt for solutions. I believe time and energy could be better spent discussing how members of the new black middle class can
take more leadership and responsibility.

On the other hand, when I'm asked such questions by whites who
seem to be seeking an excuse for washing their hands of the problem,
my emphasis is altogether different. Yes, it is imperative that blacks

take primary responsibility for the problem. But the cruel and devastating history of white America's treatment of black Americans demands that white America feel equal responsibility for finding solutions. In short, when it comes to the residue from our racial history, ain't nobody clean.

I listen to, read and marvel at the discussions concerning the "underclass." I listen for any ideas that will help us in our efforts to address this problem. I listen to the liberals and I listen to the conservatives. I listen to the black activists, and even to the white supremacists who gloat over the problem. But for now I want to concentrate my energies with the people of God—not with blacks only or whites only but with Christians. Because our motivation is not guilt or selfish gain, I believe that ultimately the power to unravel the mystery of the "underclass" rests in us.

As Christians governed by common convictions we should be able to relate to each other and work toward solutions together. We study the same Bible, we worship the same God, and we seek out ways to obey his commandments. So the question of who is at fault for the problems of the inner cities is not our most pressing issue. Since we are all Christians, and since following Jesus will usually lead us among the poor, the problems of the inner cities fall under our domain.

The underclass is neither proof of black inferiority nor a living legacy of white racism alone. Seen through my Christian spectacles, it is a living testament to our disdain for the poor and our disobedience to a Christ who commands us to love our neighbor as we love ourselves. Given the lessons of the past decades—the failure of the government, the dependency fostered by well-intentioned liberal programs and the conservatives' lack of compassion, I believe it's time for Christians to step forward and add the personal touch of Jesus to a desperate situation.

In this case, loving our neighbor will probably mean more than social programs; it will entail making new friends. Surely we will not muster up enough arrogance to even entertain the thought of asking the two-thousand-year-old question "And who is my neighbor?"

8

Silence Gives Consent

T HE LEGACY OF OUR RACIAL HISTORY THAT SPENCER DESCRIBED AS *a scummy residue left on blacks has stained white Americans also. I described it in chapter five as racial blinders. Seeking the source of these blinders begins with the understanding that people are more than individuals. The positive and negative values of society rub their imprint upon our attitudes, understanding and choices. Everyday social institutions—popular videos, history textbooks, even Bible dictionaries and Christian children's books—are powerful influencers that inform, educate and shape us, and unfortunately often keep our racial blinders intact. How can we see beneath the surface of these "normal" social institutions to understand the often unconscious ways we, and even our children, are tainted? You may not be aware of it, but even our Christian institutions can perpetuate separation and distrust.*

Even though I grew up as a missionary kid in Korea, many of the institutions that shaped me were typically American. My favorite TV shows were *Good Times* and *Star Trek*. The foreign church I attended was Protestant, founded by Americans. At our small missionary-founded school we were taught by American teachers with American textbooks. I attended a small, highly regarded liberal arts college in Vermont. In our campus Christian fellowship we benefited from the fine staff and Bible-study materials of a parachurch organization. I graduated from a Christian college in Jackson. Churches ranging from mainline to charismatic provided me with solid Bible teaching all along the way.

But after I arrived at Voice of Calvary, my already well-worn Bible began to get highlighting on new Scriptures. I heard my first sermon ever on racial separation. I knew John 3:16 but not Luke 4:18-19, the words that kicked off Jesus' public ministry: "The Spirit of the Lord is on me, because he has anointed me to preach good news to the poor." In history classes I had learned about slavery but not about the African civilizations that preceded it. I counted Americans, Swedes, Germans, Koreans, Brits and Argentineans among my friends—but not a single black person.

I had been educated and discipled by some of the best, but my eyes were still surrounded by blinders. And I'm not at all an exception; the same institutions of which I am a product teach, disciple, inform and entertain the Christians of America. What's caused the gap in our understanding?

When Hurt Begins to Look Normal

Seoul, Korea, where I grew up, is a congested city of ten million. The air is gray and smelly from pollution. Every day for twelve years I breathed it in. Gradually I accepted the pollution as normal and didn't give it a second thought. Even now when I'm walking down a street and a passing bus throws a wave of exhaust in my face, I get a little homesick.

Sometimes we Christians get so acclimated to the environment around us that we don't know what's dirty and what's clean anymore. We can be hurting ourselves, and overlooking the hurt of others, because it just seems normal. It takes God-vision to discern the difference between clean and dirty, especially when it comes to social institutions.

In one sense, all individuals are powerful. Every human being carries the sin-powered weapons to damage and destroy themselves and their relationships with others. Often our careless words hurt others even when we don't intend to. But some individuals have much more power than others. And when powerful groups and institutions are thoughtless and careless, the possibility for hurt is much more frightening. A blind elephant is more dangerous than an angry mouse. A herd of blind elephants can really do some damage.

It's easy to take our institutions for granted. Institutions shape us in ways we hardly question—textbooks we are taught from, news shows and newspapers that inform us, television programs that entertain us, and Bible translations, dictionaries, study guides and Sunday school materials that disciple us. As we listen to our pastors preach, we indirectly put our trust in the seminaries that train them.

Throughout history, however, we Christians have often failed to have enough collective God-vision to discern the sin—both obvious and subtle, deliberate and unintended—carried out through social institutions.

"How is one to explain," asks Holocaust survivor Elie Wiesel, "that among the [Nazi] S.S. a large proportion were believers who remained faithful to their Christian ties to the end? That there were killers who went to confession between massacres? And that they all came from Christian families and had received a Christian education? How to explain that the Christian in them did not make their arms tremble as they shot at children or their conscience bridle as they shoved their naked, beaten victims into the factories of death?"[1]

Wiesel's haunting questions, prompted by one of Christianity's greatest failures, should help us learn from our mistakes. If our Christian forebears did not have enough collective God-vision to discern what we recognize now as the obvious evils of slavery or Nazism, how much easier must it be to overlook the more subtle damage our social institutions are doing today. Once we put our most extreme failures under the microscope, we can begin to see what pollution consists of and how it creeps into the air, and then maybe we can determine how to not breathe that hurtful air again.

The result of our social blinders is that subtle and careless patterns, traditions and systems that encourage racial separation and inequality remain unnoticed, intact and unchallenged. They even seem normal. We need to take a closer look at the institutions that shape us, and begin recognizing some of the separations and hurtful choices caused by our collective blinders.

Holes in Our History Books

Dr. Ivory Phillips of Jackson State University gives a powerful talk on black history. Many people who attend his presentations are in positions of influence and are extremely well educated—pastors, educators, business executives and community developers. It is telling that so few of these people, including blacks, have heard the story of African-Americans. Ivory's relentless communication of the facts confronts the stereotypes and unspoken assumptions of his "educated" audience. I was alarmed to see how it happened to me, a college history major.

Ivory starts with the early African civilizations, pointing out that discoveries by archaeologists, including L. S. B. Leakey, have located the earliest known human being in East Africa. As the accomplishments of the great world civilizations of Ghana, Mali and Songhay in western Sudan are recounted, Ivory's listeners begin to see a people of intelligence and dignity rather than field hands and house servants. Many world leaders were of African heritage, including arguably the greatest theologian (Augustine), the greatest general (Hannibal) and the greatest composer (Beethoven).

In case you accept the commonly held myth that the Africans passively accepted slavery, Ivory will tell you about the slave revolts, the difficulty of escaping through unfamiliar territory with black skin (and how many risked that journey in spite of the odds) and the everyday covert things slaves did to undermine the slavemaster. There is no way to argue that slavery was part of God's plan to give Africans the gospel after you learn how millions of Africans died in Africa after their capture, during the savage "middle passage" and on plantations after arriving in America. To trot out the old at-least-they-got-Christianity line is to make God an accomplice to the torture and murder of millions of Africans.

As you learn this history, you begin to see the resilience of the black family and the black church. You come to grips with the fact that Africans were the only ethnic group that didn't come to America by choice, that were stripped of their native languages, cultures and families.

Finally, in response to the unspoken assumption many of us have that blacks contributed very little to American civilization, there is the record of black accomplishments in spite of overwhelming odds.

Black Americans pioneered as missionaries to Native Americans, the Caribbean and Africa. They included John Marrant to the Cherokee Indians in 1775, George Leile to Jamaica in 1782 and Lott Carey in the 1820s (sent from the missions society of his Richmond, Virginia, church) to Sierra Leone.

Crispus Attucks was the first of five persons killed in the Boston Massacre. Black and white minutemen fought British soldiers at Lexington, Concord and Bunker Hill. There were black soldiers in the Revolutionary Army from all thirteen original colonies. Blacks fought in the land and sea battles of the War of 1812. Some 185,000 black soldiers served in the Union Army during the Civil War—37,638 lost their lives.

After escaping slavery Harriet Tubman returned to the danger of the Deep South nineteen times to bring out more than three hundred slaves. During the Civil War she organized slave intelligence networks to spy behind enemy lines. After the war Ida B. Wells showed similar courage as an investigative journalist documenting the widespread practice of lynching—ten thousand deaths between 1878 and 1898 alone. And Mary McLeod Bethune, once a field hand, studied at Moody Bible Institute and later started a school for poor black laborers in Florida; today that school is Bethune-Cookman College.

Jean-Baptiste Pointe DuSable, a black trader and trapper, established the settlement that eventually became the city of Chicago. When Commander Robert Peary reached the North Pole, the only American with him was a black man, Matthew Henson.

Dr. Charles Drew set up and ran the pioneer blood plasma bank in a hospital in New York. Dr. Percy Julian's pioneering research led to contributions including a treatment for glaucoma, development of a synthetic male sex hormone and a fundamental product for aerofoam fire extinguishers. Dr. William Hinton developed the famous Hinton test for detection of syphilis.

Over a span of nearly fifty years, Elijah McCoy of Detroit received more than fifty-seven patents for inventions on automatic lubricating appliances and other devices pertaining to telegraphy and electricity. His prolific ingenuity sparked the phrase "the real McCoy."

George Washington Carver made nearly 250 products from the sweet potato, pecan and peanut—including peanut butter. Jan E. Matzeliger created the first machine for attaching soles to shoes. Garrett Morgan invented the gas inhalator—the prototype of the gas mask—and the automatic stop sign.

Philadelphian Augustus Jackson was known in the nineteenth century as "the man who invented ice cream." Hyram S. Thomas of Saratoga, New York, reportedly created the potato chip, and George F. Grant invented the golf tee in 1899.[2]

By the end of Ivory's two-hour lecture, at least one puzzled hearer usually exclaims, "I can't believe I never learned this before!"

Can You Imagine Wanting to Switch Colors?

Sadly, many of our children are infected with a highly developed racial value system at an early age.

An African couple from our church enrolled their five-year-old in a day-care center at a white church. When the leader of a local soup kitchen was shot and killed (an incident that devastated our entire city), the day care's head teacher, who was white, talked to the children about what had happened. For some reason she emphasized that the murderer was black. At home that night, our church members' daughter asked her parents, "Why are black people bad?"

From that point on, this little African girl began to take note of who was black and who was white. At school, as a result of the teacher's emphasis on the murderer's blackness, the children began to turn on the little girl and make comments about her black skin. It was too much for her parents to see her suffer. "I feel like getting out of this country before my children get too damaged," said this Kenyan mother.

A search for the influences that reinforce superior attitudes could begin in your nearest Christian bookstore. On a visit to one of the largest ones in my city, a book caught my eye. It was titled *Jesus Was a Child like You.* I paged through it and looked at the pictures of boy Jesus, his family and his friends. All were white.

Well, surely this is an isolated example, I thought. So I began looking through other children's books, including titles like *My First Bible* and *Baby Jesus.* The more I looked, the more my disappointment grew. Illustrated Bibles, Bible storybooks, Sunday school materials and children's videos lined the aisles. Not only was Jesus white in every single one, but all the other major Bible characters were also white—Adam and Eve, Abraham, Moses, David, Peter, Paul, and so on. Angels had blond hair and blue eyes. There was not even a brown person.

As I left the store (which, by the way, was in a neighborhood that is 85 percent black), I understood the frustration of black parents who face a daily battle with society's messages—even, unfortunately, the messages of Christian society. Those publishers surely didn't intend to hurt anyone. But it seems that not one of them had stopped to ask, What does it do to a black child's self-esteem to open a book called *Jesus Was a Child like You* and discover that, really, Jesus *wasn't* a child like her at all?

And I'm not troubled only for my black friends' children. As my son's little hands clumsily turn the pages in his Bible storybook, are its images already beginning to shape a racial hierarchy in his head? Do we want our white children to grow up thinking that they're the center of the universe? Don't we have a responsibility to show them that they can learn from and be led by those who are different from them?

If you're white, imagine that practically every character in the books your children read, practically every actor they see on TV, is black. Can you imagine your children wanting to be black? Imagine explaining to them that it's okay to be white: "Hold your head up and be proud of your whiteness! Don't let anybody tell you that something's wrong with being white!" White people don't have to spend time thinking about this, because society automatically and unconsciously affirms being white. But that need for constant affirmation is what black parents have to accept and live with. Very little in the world of black children affirms their blackness.

Consider the protagonists of the most popular children's books, cartoons and videos: Cinderella, Sleeping Beauty, Dorothy (from *The Wizard of Oz*), Alice in Wonderland, Peter Pan, Ariel the Little Mermaid, Superman, Batman, Tarzan, Mickey Mouse and Willie Wonka. Oh, and don't forget Snow White.

Spencer and his wife, Nancy, were considering ordering a set of videotapes on the life of Christ that had been advertised on a Christian TV show. They believed this well-produced animated series would help their children learn more about Jesus. But when they saw excerpts from the series, they quickly changed their minds. It wasn't the fact that all the characters looked like white Europeans—they're used to that. What was most troubling was that Jesus was a shade whiter than everyone else. And to top it off, Jesus was the only one who had big blue eyes.

The producers of this beautiful series didn't consider what this kind of imagery does to little children who already have to fight the notion that they are inferior because of their skin. We see the negative effects of this example around us every day. During the course of a Bible discussion with a group of black teenage boys in our neighborhood, I asked them what color Jesus was. "Of course he was white," they all answered.

If you are trying to represent a Jesus full of compassion, why not use the awesome power of the media to affirm everyone, instead of instilling a false sense of superiority in white children and reinforcing inferiority in children with darker complexions? Why not make some characters brown with dark hair some curly, some straight? Surely no one actually believes that the people of the Middle East at the time of Christ were white Anglo-Saxon.

Some will insist that Jesus' skin color is not important. Yes, it shouldn't be. But how would white parents feel if every picture of Jesus were black? Think about it. If skin color were unimportant, it wouldn't matter, would it?

If you're white, imagine for a moment that it was discovered that Jesus really was black. Imagine that all the pictures of Jesus in your books, in the movies and in your wall paintings were suddenly black. Imagine the faces in Leonardo da Vinci's famous painting *The Last Supper* suddenly being black. Imagine being approached by black Christians trying to persuade you to accept Christianity. All the people in their literature are black, all their depictions of Jesus are black, even the angels are black. How much consideration would you give to this Christianity?

Think about it. Would you feel that you needed to come up with an alternative religion, as Black Muslims have done? Would you feel that black must be better than white? How would this affect your self-image?

Sound extreme? Maybe to whites, but I'm sure black folks are enjoying every minute of this game.

The Church Wears Blinders Too

These reflections should lead us to examine our theology. Theologians have studied every nuance of Scripture, giving us eschatology, Christology, ecclesiology and many other "ologies" that I can't even pronounce. Some theologians are involved in a heated argument about the molecular makeup of Jesus' resurrected body: was it his actual body, or had it been somehow reconstituted? Bestselling Christian books predict the exact date and location of Jesus' second coming.

But when was the last time you heard a sermon on racial reconciliation? When did you last take part in a Sunday school class discussion on the topic, or a workshop at a Christian conference? Are other theological concerns so much more important that no one has had time to do in-depth research on racial reconciliation?

Precious little Christian energy has been put into considering what God thinks about racial separation. Try to find an entry for *race* or *rac-*

ism in a Bible dictionary, or entries about ethnicity and crosscultural subjects; you won't find any. One dictionary offers the following reference: "Race: See Games." Yes, they carry an entry on biblical sports events but none on how Gentiles and Jews got together!

The evidence for a biblical call to reconciliation and unity across barriers of race and culture is overwhelming. The first two sentences of one Bible dictionary's listing for *unity* sum up the neglect of the topic: "The theme of Christian unity fascinates many. Yet there is little agreement about the nature of that unity or about the way unity is best expressed." Thanks, I needed that strong advice! Would we dare to summarize what God says about adultery, or gossip, or even abortion in such an ambiguous way?

But the evidence for our theological and cultural blinders does not appear only in Bible dictionaries. Christian organizations are deeply affected by these blinders as well.

Mark Dyer, a former missionary to the Philippines, is the president of International Teams, an evangelical missionary organization that sends teams to Europe, Asia and North America. Several years ago God began stripping away Mark's racial blinders. For the first time Mark began to ask why there were no blacks on his staff of over two hundred people. A message by Elward Ellis (president of Destiny, a black organization that promotes missions) brought Mark to a startling realization: "We excluded blacks not by design, but by not going out of our way to build relationships. We were going out and seeking whites to join our organization, but not blacks."

At an annual conference of black Plymouth Brethren pastors and church leaders, Mark publicly asked forgiveness for International Teams's exclusion of blacks. "It was a powerful experience in my life," remembers Mark, "and the beginning of many friendships." He began learning how foreign missions agencies, supposed experts in crosscultural communication, actually lag behind corporate America in inclusion of American minorities. He realized that in his suburban Chicago-based ministry and scores of other Christian organizations, "our financial structures, literature, locations, networks and even style of worship often create barriers to non-Anglo involvement with us in ministry."

Attitudes and choices that used to seem normal took on a new light. Mark heard white leaders contend that blacks shouldn't be sent as missionaries to certain European countries where there was deep prejudice against them. "But we never asked that same question about whites," maintains Mark. In some Middle Eastern countries, for example, whites are not readily accepted, and in many parts of the world a person of color who is seen as part of an oppressed group would, in fact be trusted more readily than a white person. Other barriers in Christian institutions, Mark found, have to do not with right or wrong but with the fact that whites and blacks sometimes value different things; organizational choices in these areas, however, generally favor white preferences.

Mark began to see how his ministry's music and worship style were comfortable for whites but often not for black Christians. Another consideration was the tradition of asking missionaries to raise their support. While this practice is familiar and acceptable to white churches, many black churches assume that if missionaries' services are valuable, they should be getting a salary.

Coming to these realizations was often painful. "Over the past couple of years, I have had many tears run down my cheeks with African-Americans," Mark admits. But his racial "conversion" is leading to deep changes. One of two new key objectives International Teams adopted was to become multiethnic in its ministries. The ministry brought on its first black board member. Staff members have been exposed to black and Hispanic culture in Chicago. Black leaders have been brought in for staff education. Several International Teams members have begun attending black churches in the city.

International Teams is not the only group that is benefiting from these changes. The organization is now serving two churches in Chicago, one black and one Hispanic. These churches are being strengthened in local outreach, and International Teams's foreign expertise is also leading those churches to look overseas. The black church, for example, is sending a mission team to Guatemala.

Traveling to build new relationships, attending unfamiliar conferences and bringing in speakers to help raise awareness have taken new chunks of time and money. But Mark is convinced that the atmosphere in his organization is changing for the better: "When an African-American young person comes to us now, there will be a lot fewer hurdles than there were a couple of years ago." It's not clear where all this is leading for International Teams, but Mark is confident that God will honor these steps of faith: "As we develop friends in African-American churches, we'll see where God wants it to go from there."

Many Christian institutions wear racial blinders. Thank God that some like International Teams are courageously beginning to recognize and remove them.

Not only have the blinders on evangelical institutions failed to instill a passion for reconciliation in our young Christian leaders, but our silence in this area has actually been an obstacle. Evangelicals have often dismissed Martin Luther King's contributions to the church because of his liberal theology. But if King had attended an evangelical seminary (which in the early fifties didn't exactly welcome blacks with open arms) or worked in an evangelical ministry, would he have become the prophet for reconciliation that he was? Given our institutions' silence on race, would Dr. King have been able to stand tall and embrace a theology that included a passion for racial justice and reconciliation? How many young pastors and future Christian leaders today are failing to fill his shoes because they aren't being filled with that same biblical passion?

Getting Our Souls Back

Many of us are tempted to say, "Racial inequities just happened. I'm not responsible." But consider Kay Muller of Evanston, Illinois. The day Beverly Jordan matter-of-factly shared a piece of local church history with Kay, the two friends had no inkling where their conversation would lead. Beverly had learned that until 1873 First Baptist Church, which is white, and Second Baptist Church, which is black, had been one church. But because blacks had been relegated to the balcony during worship services and were not accepted into full membership, in 1873 the blacks had left and formed their own church, Second Baptist.

Intrigued, Kay began to do some research. No one at First Baptist knew about the history Kay called "a stain on our church." Many asked her, "Why bring up the past?" But Kay couldn't put the disturbing events out of her mind. Eventually she pieced together a clear picture of First Baptist's history from the local library and old newspapers.

Kay didn't stop there. She immediately went to right the wrong. As a result of her efforts, eventually First Baptist unanimously adopted a resolution to take responsibility for the wrong the church had committed 120 years earlier. On June 2, 1991, in the packed sanctuary of Second Baptist, both congregations watched as Kay presented the resolution on behalf of her church, asking forgiveness and acknowledging the continuing sin of racism. First Baptist's white pastor preached in a joyful celebration. Afterward over one thousand members from the two churches, led by their singing choirs, marched four blocks down the street to First Baptist, where Second Baptist's black pastor preached. For the first time in 120 years the church building that was once home to both congregations was common ground again, but this time black and white worshiped side by side.

"Scars like that need to be opened to the air and acknowledged," says Kay, who has developed close friends at Second Baptist and is now attending services at both churches. "The church is an ongoing body. It's not just who is there now, but who was there and who will be there. We needed to get our soul back." Because one person believed that even things that "just happen" affect all of us, two churches were touched, and an example was set for all of us.

Yes, you're just one person. But reconciliation can begin with you.

If you are a white person, the point is not to fall at the feet of every black person you meet and ask forgiveness. You could spend the rest of your life doing that without accomplishing anything. It may be good for your soul to ask forgiveness of a particular black friend, or for your church to acknowledge its sin before another church. But what's most important is how we turn our recognition of wrong into a lifestyle of reconciliation.

Let us learn from Nehemiah, who was miles away from Jerusalem but took personal responsibility for the fall of the nation of Israel. "I confess the sins we Israelites, including myself and my father's house, have committed against you," he prayed. "We have acted very wickedly toward you. We have not obeyed the commands, decrees and laws you gave your servant Moses." (See Neh 1:4-11.) Nehemiah understood that no one is an island. He saw himself as part of a people whose corporate sin had left a stain on each individual.

It's easy to shift the blame—to the hard-core racists, to the textbook industry, to the doll manufacturers, to the video makers, to earlier generations. But our identity as part of God's people should prompt us to focus responsibility on "us" instead of "them."

The task before us is to take off our collective racial blinders, take on the vision of God and act as the "we" that Nehemiah and Mark Dyer and Kay Muller acknowledged. Otherwise our silence gives consent.

9

A Little Respect

M OST OF US AFRICAN AMERICANS KNOW PLENTY ABOUT WHITES. *And this knowledge allows us the freedom to respect or disrespect them. We have had to learn all about white folks in school, and how to get along with white folks in work and in play. Our survival depends on it. But most whites don't know much about us. Their survival did not require knowledge of us in the past, and it still doesn't.*

Being reconciled is an intentional step, and it will require intentional learning. A failure to know and understand others' history and culture can lead to a low opinion of them and an overly high opinion of our own selves and our culture. That is called ethnocentrism. In crosscultural relationships we need to understand ethnocentrism and keep it in check.

Going out of our way to learn about others' ways and customs not only teaches a healthy respect for them but also shows them that we respect who they are and value what they can bring to the relationship between us. It's next to impossible to be reconciled to someone you don't respect. Admitting that we sometimes don't value each other's history and culture and that we don't take time to find out what is important to each other is an important step in the reconciliation process.

In the late sixties, during the height of the civil rights movement, Aretha Franklin captured the emotions of the black community by belting out some well-timed lyrics. Although she sang of the unequal relationship between a man and a woman, many of us used her words to voice the way we felt as a people: "R-E-S-P-E-C-T . . . All I'm asking is for a little respect."

My father drilled into us from childhood that "we [black and white] are all created in the image of God, and because of this fact we all have dignity. You cannot bestow dignity on people; they already have it. Dignity must be affirmed; it cannot be given." Sometimes it is hard for us to see God's image in those that Jesus called "the least of these." But regardless of what you see, regardless of what a person looks like, regardless of how that person has suffered or prospered, because of being created in the image of God, he or she has dignity. In this sense we are all equals.

A Question of Cultural Values

Unlike integration, reconciliation requires mutual respect and always assumes *equality*. It's next to impossible to be reconciled to someone you do not respect, or who seems not to respect you. And attempts at racial reconciliation between two unequal partners will be superficial and result in further damage. The negative consequences for the "inferior" partner are more obvious, but the other person's false sense of superiority is just as negative. Such a relationship will inevitably produce future conflict. Until both parties accept and internalize their need for equality, they will only spin their wheels.

The negative effects of an unequal relationship on the "inferior" partner have, over the years, been the subject of much study and debate. We all feel that the "inferior" partner receives the short end of the stick. That assumption makes sense by worldly standards. But kingdom principles must guide any discussion of racial reconciliation. And in most cases, kingdom principles are just the opposite of the world's principles.

If we assume that our values, intellect and style (including our worship style) are superior to another's, we will approach the relationship paternalistically. Paternalism in areas of race and culture is called ethnocentrism. It is a very close cousin to racism. As we will see later in the book, Jesus' disciples were full of ethnocentrism. And for the most part, so is Western society.

In the fall of 1988 I traveled to New Zealand with my father; we had been invited to encourage reconciliation between the Maori (native to the island) and the whites. The history of the two groups is very similar to the history of whites and Native Americans in the United States. The similarities between the social condition of Maori in New Zealand and blacks in America are astounding. Both groups suffer from disproportionate unemployment, teenage pregnancy and single-parent families, welfare, rising gang activity and a high prison population. Maori, like African-Americans, make up about 10-13 percent of their country's population. The Maori tend to mistrust white New Zealanders, while many whites are anxious about the new Maori nationalism (which is calling for the return of all Maori land taken illegally). All that is needed to ignite this powder keg is a lighted match.

Among many reasons for the conflict between the two groups is the fact that the two simply value different things. The Maori are unquestionably the most giving people I have ever met. But the Europeans have another word for the Maori's generosity: *irresponsible.* "They never seem to have any money," complained one frustrated white man. "They will give their entire dole [welfare check] to a friend or relative. They just don't handle money properly."

The Europeans value nice things like houses, cars and sailboats, and spend much time keeping them clean. Many Maori don't understand why a white will spend so much time washing a car, given that it will get dirty the next day. They say it seems like idol worship.

The Maori value their relationships. Money has value only inasmuch as it contributes to a relationship. "If another Maori has need of the money, we give it," explained a confused Maori, not understanding why the whites were complaining. "I know if I'm in need, he will do the same for me. Isn't that what the Bible teaches?" For the Maori the quality of one's life is in direct proportion to the quality of one's relationships with friends and family. For them, good financial stewardship is not saving more for yourself but spending it freely on behalf of everybody.

New Zealand's whites, on the other hand, seem to value the money itself or what it will buy. They see it as security and as a means to a better life. And because they are "better stewards" of money, they have more material possessions.

Now, which of these value systems is more biblical, given the upside-down nature of the kingdom of God?

> Do not store up for yourselves treasures on earth, where moth and rust destroy, and where thieves break in and steal. But store up for yourselves treasures in heaven, where moth and rust do not destroy, and where thieves do not break in and steal. For where your treasure is, there your heart will be also. (Mt 6:19-21)

In 1980 I had made another international trip—this one to Kenya. Then too I traveled with my father, who was frequently sponsored by World Vision to teach community development in underdeveloped countries. One of the first cultural differences that caught our group's attention was the Kenyans' easygoing, laid-back style. Although they were always busy, whether working the fields or conducting business, they were never too busy to enjoy each other's company.

I remember one time we were nearly four hours late in leaving for a meeting. We Americans had become quite frustrated; but on the way, much to our surprise, our host stopped at a coffee shop to have tea. Of course it was difficult for us to enjoy our tea, realizing how late we would arrive at the church. But when we finally arrived, much more than four hours late, all the people were still there. No one was upset. These people had lost nearly a full day's work because we were late, but it didn't seem to matter.

One of the American businessmen in our group commented several times during our stay about the thousands of "man-hours" that were "wasted" in Kenyan culture. The difference, again, is what is valued. The Kenyans valued being with each other and spending time with their guests. In fact, several of the Kenyan businessmen who had invited us took most of the three weeks of our stay off from work. Surely they lost a lot of money, but that didn't seem to matter as much as being with us and each other.

It is very difficult for Americans not to make value judgments on other cultures. If a society is less productive, we assume it must be inferior. Never mind that its people love and care for each other better than we do.

The Eye of the Beholder

America was built on the ideal of equality. The signers of the Declaration of Independence announced, "We hold these truths to be self-evident, that all men are created equal." But even when these inspirational words were written, some of the men who wrote and signed the document owned slaves. It was easy to proclaim equality when in their minds the document referred only to men like them. America's struggle for liberty and justice for women, blacks, Native Americans and other minorities began the day this great document was signed.

From the beginning of this great experiment of "liberty and justice for all" there has been a gap between the theory and the reality of equality. Is it possible to be equal with someone who is your slave or who used to be your slave? If your father was a plantation owner, how can you be equal with someone whose father was a sharecropper? If your father is an upper manager for a major corporation, how can you be equal with someone whose father, if he knows him, is in prison and whose mother is on welfare?

Take a mental look around the world. Whites fare better than blacks. Europe is more prosperous than Africa. Whites are readily tempted to think, *We pulled ourselves up by our own bootstraps. Why can't they do the same? They must be inferior.*

But again, the question is what is superior: a culture that values technological advancement or one that values relationships? A people who because of their aggressive nature and military might were able to conquer and colonize, or a people who because of their simplicity and trusting nature were able to be conquered and colonized? Who is superior—the people who accumulate wealth and power or the Maori who give it away? Who is the greatest—the servant or the master? Jesus, laying a cornerstone of kingdom principles for his disciples, put it this way: "For who is greater, the one who is at the table or the one who serves? Is it not the one who is at the table? But I am among you as one who serves" (Lk 22:27).

The question of superior and inferior is much like the question of beauty. It is in the eye of the beholder. So from a historical perspective it is understandable that some blacks, Muslims in particular, have concluded that white people are innately an inferior race. They say that it is innate in the white race to oppress, kill, conquer and enslave. Many whites look at history and conclude their superiority, but many of those looking at history from the bottom up have come to the opposite conclusion.

Learn Why They Do It That Way

It is psychologically difficult to oppress someone whom you consider your equal. Therefore, in order to justify oppression you must devalue the oppressed group's way of being.

Supporters of slavery insisted that the Africans were savage head-hunters who ate their young and had no rhyme or reason for what they did. Their black skin was a curse, they did not have souls, and therefore it was okay to take and keep them as slaves. Similarly, characterizing American Indians as savages who would kill innocent people for no reason—instead of a heroic people trying to defend their land and their way of life—made it easy to kill them, break treaties and steal their land.

It's much more difficult to oppress people when you learn their ways and customs, begin to understand why they are the way they are and learn to respect that. A scene in the movie *The Mission* illustrates this principle.

The movie centers on the relationship between two Jesuit priests and a reclusive, misunderstood tribe of South American Indians. One conversation finds the priest trying to convince other church leaders that the Indians were not like monkeys but were human. "Don't they kill their young?" asked one concerned layman.

"Yes," replied the priest. "They do kill their third child. Each parent can only carry a single child when they are running. A third child could endanger the whole family."

"Why must they run?" asked the layman.

The priest replied, "They must be able to move quickly in order to escape the white slave-catchers."

Learning to respect others' way of being will mean finding out why they do what they do—and assuming from the beginning that they are just as intelligent in their own way as you are. Sometimes what looks like stupidity to us is actually habits and customs that have developed over the years in order to ensure survival.

Some of the habits and customs among today's African-Americans were developed under years of extreme oppression and will take years of not only freedom but also creative development to overcome. Says Shelby Steele, "Oppression conditions people away from all the values and attitudes one needs in freedom—individual initiative, self-interested hard work, individual responsibility, delayed gratification, and so on. In oppression these things don't pay off and are therefore negatively reinforced. It is not that these values have never had a presence in black life, only that they were muted and destabilized by the negative conditioning of oppression."[1]

Slavery, sharecropping, perpetual welfare and general oppression have left behind a survival mentality among American blacks. "I'm just trying to make it" and "Just trying to survive" are common greetings among black men. Even though these greetings are spoken mostly in jest, they hint at a mentality of thinking only short-term. Success is just making it to the next day. Planning for the future is a luxury beyond our means. This mindset has its roots deep in the history of the oppression and humiliation of the black man.

America's brand of slavery was one of the most cruel systems ever devised among humankind—not so much for its brutality, though it was very brutal, but for its basis in skin color. Once the color black became synonymous with slavery, blacks and whites alike received the message that black was inferior to white. Nothing you could do could change the color of your skin. Therefore, no amount of hard work, saving or planning would ever change your condition. Your labor, your efficiency, your creativity all went to benefit someone else. The concept of working and saving now so that your life would later be better made little sense to people just trying to survive. These virtues that so many people take for granted were not encouraged but were discouraged.

If the quality of your life is determined by something as permanent and visible as the color of your skin, then a situation that allows others to "pull themselves up by their bootstraps" might look hopeless to you. Success will be making it through another day with food to eat and a roof over your head. Up until the mid-1960s, many blacks felt it didn't matter what they did or how hard they worked. Their skin was still black, and that was the determining factor in their future. They could progress only as far as white people would let them.

The great northward black migration in the 1920s, 1930s and 1940s was largely an attempt to escape the dehumanizing control whites had over blacks. But in my childhood we had a saying, "You can take a person out of the country, but you can't take the country out of the person." Even though many blacks migrated to the North to escape the harsh racism that controlled their lives, a physical move could not undo the negative conditioning they had received under the years of oppression. The sharecropping cabins of the South simply evolved into the notorious ghettos of the North.

Today, though there is still plenty of racial discrimination, skin color is no longer the single most important factor in determining success or failure. Sure, it's still harder for some of us blacks to achieve because of the color of our skin. But the obstacles can be overcome. Future generations of blacks need to learn this and—more important—believe it deep down in their being. That won't happen without a kind of intensive, hands-on development that our government and most Christians have not yet understood.

The real miracle is how so many black children do learn and practice the work ethic and deferred gratification, even with very limited exposure to such values. Value messages are internalized primarily through one's immediate environment—by watching how one's parents live and their parents before them. Each generation learns and benefits from the one that preceded it.

Many of my white friends come from families that handed down valuable traditions from one generation to the next. Grandparents and other relatives of some have died and left them financial inheritances as well. My great-grandmother died in 1986; her father had been a slave. That's as far back as our family history goes. Because the African-American family has been in existence only since the Civil War, most of us have only recently begun to benefit from family traditions.

But being on the short end of the equality equation does have one advantage. Blacks, for the most part, do not have a problem accepting the American ideal of equality. Being in the dominant culture has put whites at a disadvantage in this part of the reconciliation process. Accepting the reality of equality and attempting to learn from people of whom you've had only a negative impression can be a difficult obstacle to overcome.

One white pastor in New England got excited about doing outreach through his church to the poor community in their city. In order to begin training his congregation for this ministry, he showed them a video of John Perkins explaining indigenous leadership development. After the video, instead of taking up the content of the presentation, most of the comments centered on why the pastor used a black man to try to teach his parishioners. They were hardly able to learn, because they couldn't get past the color of the speaker's skin. In this case, the people who believed themselves superior were actually proving themselves too simple to learn from and be enriched by the life experiences of someone who happened to have a different skin color.

Minority people seldom have this problem to overcome; we more easily take on the values and customs of the dominant majority. For a white person to come into a black church and be heard is much more common than for a black person to come into a white church and do the same. In most cases, blacks readily accept white people into their functions (especially church services) and go out of their way to make them feel comfortable.

Still, there are times, places and events where white presence and participation are discouraged. Such exclusion has nothing to do with superiority or inferiority, but with trust.

Many blacks feel that the only setting in which they can be fully respected is among other blacks. Usually this is not based on a sense of superiority to white people. The rise of black student unions, black dorms and separate black functions on college campuses suggests that young blacks are not sure they will find acceptance and respect among whites. For blacks, this intentional separation is saying, *We always have to expend energy to conform to your environment and your way of doing things. We don't feel that you respect us as equals, so when we're with you we are forever trying to prove our worth. This drains us and makes us weary. So we need to set aside havens in which we can escape the ever-present issue of race. If and when we can feel that more real trust has developed between us, we will feel less need for this type of sanctuary.*

Since the lack of trust that blacks feel is unintended by most whites, blacks-only settings look and feel to whites like reverse segregation, which only agitates the fragile relationship. It is these types of no-win situations that leave me feeling hopeless for our country's race situation and have driven me to place my hope of reconciliation in Christians who are sincerely seeking Jesus.

Once Nancy and I were invited to share dinner with a white family who are close friends. I am especially fond of this couple's daughter (then fifteen), who is very intelligent and lively. As she served dessert, vanilla ice cream, she made what was to her an innocent joke. "Maybe if you eat lots of ice cream you'll turn white."

Naturally, this innocent comment tripped sirens and flashing red lights in the heads of the adults. Nancy, who likes to use situations like these to educate, jumped in quickly. "All black people don't want to be white," she explained.

"They don't?" gulped the youngster with a confused look on her face that easily read, *I thought everybody wanted to be white.*

This young girl had never been verbally taught that everyone wanted to be white, but somehow she'd made this assumption, based on careful observation of her environment. But she had also not been explicitly taught to value people who are different from her as much as people who are like her.

I'm sure it's obvious to most Christians that there are no such things as inferior or superior races. But we have to go a step further. If we intend to change the unconscious cultural mindset, we will have to be intentional. Telling our children the truth will not suffice. We will have to show by our deeds the truth of our words.

It's unfortunate that to some whites the phrase *racial reconciliation* conjures up images of angry, sign-toting blacks demanding to be included in the mainstream of society. This is inaccurate. Reconciliation is a spiritual concept. It is not a right that can be demanded by any group. And it is not a commodity that one group can give. Reconciliation is white Christians and black Christians recognizing their need for each other. It is seeking from each other ways to demonstrate this love to each other, to our children and to the unbelieving world.

Reconciliation will not be achieved until both parties learn a healthy respect for each other. But more important, reconciliation will be achieved only when Christians come to understand the importance of sincerely seeking it.

Part 2

Submit

10

From Anger & Guilt
to Passion & Conviction

U NDERSTANDING SOME OF THE PAIN CAUSED BY OUR STORMY RACIAL *history is only the first step in the reconciliation process. This second section of the book is devoted to the step of submitting, which involves two things. First, as with all the difficult problems that face us individually and corporately, we need to turn racial separation over to God. Second, we need to submit to one another, white to black and black to white.*

There will be little hope for genuine healing and trust unless we seek contact with our racially different neighbor. Voice of Calvary's racial reconciliation meetings in 1983 were a turning point in our efforts to submit to one another. In chapter three Chris began the story of that crucial time, and here we pick it up again. The meetings affected us differently. So each of us will give his perspective on the aftermath of that tumultuous summer, which was when we really began to get to know each other.

Spencer: The Showdown

The racial reconciliation meetings marked yet another showdown in a long personal history of dealing with race. Up until 1983, although I understood what following Jesus meant, I took it seriously only once in a while. Now I was twenty-eight years old and had begun to give serious thought to how much I really believed in the teachings of Jesus that had been drilled into me as a child. That summer the reality of all those ideals was put to the test in a series of meetings that shook our church and ministry to the core.

The racial reconciliation meetings were the stuff that church and denominational splits are made of. Hardly ever do black and white Christians discuss their true feelings about race. It was explosive. Even today many VOC old-timers, when recalling an event or a person in our history, speak of "before the meetings" or "after the meetings." The meetings were a test of the strength of our Christian commitment—much as teenagers test the soundness of their parents' beliefs to determine if they warrant personal sacrifice.

I saw these encounters as a showdown between two of the most powerful forces in the universe: God and Race. Thirteen years earlier I had watched intently as my father struggled between these two foes after his beating in the Brandon jail. But up to this point I had never seen Jesus win over Race on a large scale. Was Jesus Christ the one superhero who had the power to defeat the shrewd, powerful villain called Race? A racial split that had occurred at Circle Church in Chicago a few years earlier was a haunting reminder that others had fought and lost.

Relationships between blacks and whites in America have been so strained that the trust needed to begin and sustain a relationship does not always come easily. Some blacks, whether consciously or unconsciously, will throw up a defensive obstacle course for whites to overcome before they will open up and begin to trust. A white woman attending one of our Christian community development workshops commented, "There is no way I could tolerate this type of game-playing. I would just give up, assuming that the black person didn't want a relationship." It's unfortunate that sometimes blacks carry such excess baggage when whites attempt to reach out. But as we've already shown, as we try to sit down at the "table of brotherhood" together, we all bring racial residue. Many blacks and whites, like this woman, are not willing to tolerate the inconveniences that come with trying to break through the ice of suspicion and mistrust in crosscultural relationships.

In the months following the racial reconciliation meetings, there was a slow exodus of people, both black and white, from our church. Though it saddened me to see people go, I was encouraged by the strong contingent of people who emerged from the battle with the look of determination that said, *We will stay and fight.* Before the meetings I hadn't been secure enough to climb into the same foxhole with the people of the church—especially my white sisters and brothers. After the meetings, I saw many of these people through different eyes. Not only my faith in them but also my faith in Christianity had been strengthened because of their commitment.

In some ways the shrinking of our fellowship reminded me of the process Gideon had to go through before God would let Israel go into battle. Gideon had gathered an army of thirty-two thousand soldiers. But the Lord said to Gideon, "You have too many men for me to deliver Midian into their hands" (Judg 7:2). God didn't want Israel to assume that its own strength had been its salvation. So by the time the Israelites went into battle, God had dwindled their number to just three hundred—the most determined few. At VOC, maybe God was saying that the only witness to racial reconciliation that he would allow us to make would be a small one; otherwise we might think we'd done it ourselves.

I've always been a team player and have never been able to understand how you could follow Jesus alone. The people who emerged from this battle had, I felt, been tried by fire. For me, these were the brothers and sisters who had "the right stuff." I had finally found the people I could trust enough to fight with—who would not turn tail and run in the heat of a conflict. Together we would take up our cross and follow Jesus, even against a villain as formidable as Race. These were the people who could help me deal with my hurt and anger—and who finally helped me turn my anger into a passion for reconciliation.

Voice of Calvary Fellowship is broken into small groups that meet in homes one night a week to pray, study the Bible and support one another. That winter my wife, Nancy, and I started a new small group that solidified the direction I would take in following Jesus. It was in this small group that I got to know Chris and to see that he and I, like most blacks and whites in our church at the time, had experienced the reconciliation meetings totally differently: in the aftermath of the meetings he faced the decision of joining the exodus or staying.

Chris: Holding Up the Mirror

As I shared in chapter three, the atmosphere of blunt truth in Voice of Calvary's reconciliation meetings in the summer of 1983 confronted me with uncomfortable challenges. Even if I denied that racism had tainted me, there was something deep here that I couldn't quite grasp. I contemplated packing up and joining the slow trickle of church members who were leaving for greener pastures.

As I wavered that winter, I was asked to join Spencer and Nancy's new small group. I had some reservations. I didn't know either Spencer or Nancy very well. When I thought back to Spencer's question from a couple of years earlier—"Why are all you white people here?"—I feared that the new group might bring more of the same old truth-sharing, and I was reluctant to try again.

But if there was any possibility for hope, this was it. The new group was solidly biracial, many of its members were veterans of the battle for reconciliation at VOC, and all had committed themselves to be in Jackson for the long haul. I wasn't sure why Spencer's brother Derek and a white friend, Donna Wheeler (whom I married four years later), had taken a chance and invited me to join, but just the fact that I was asked was affirming and gave me hope. I decided to give it another try.

Every week we gathered in Spencer and Nancy's living room. We started by sharing our life stories. Each person took about an hour to tell us about his or her family, growing up and formative experiences. This took several weeks, but the testimonies began to draw us closer together. While I had not developed a single close black friend in my previous two years at Voice of Calvary, now I was getting closer to black brothers and sisters like Spencer, Gloria, Joanie, Lue, Derek, Karyn, Perry and Billy Ray. I began to see that Spencer was not the black terrorist I'd thought. In fact, I saw that he had a gentle spirit, hard on truth but soft on people. People I found difficult, he seemed to relate to easily, yet without sacrificing his honesty.

Through these friendships, God slowly knit a safe place of acceptance where I could assess my racial baggage more objectively. These secure relationships provided the context in which I could face the truth of the reconciliation meetings. It was one thing to be told that my skin color was not a stigma. It was quite another to become friends with a black sister like Gloria and hear her tell how her five-year-old son, Kortney, had come home from his Christian school telling her he didn't want to be black because his teacher said that when God washed away your sin it made you "white as snow." I wanted to wipe away the destructiveness of a society that confused children about race, because I wanted to wipe it away for Kortney and his mother.

The relationships in our Bible-study group also gave me the courage to examine my deepest motives. I began to ask myself, *Why am I here?* Some of my reasons were good and pure. After all, I had stepped out of my world and come to Mississippi because I wanted to follow God and help lift poor people up. I was motivated by compassion, to meet a need, to accomplish a task that would glorify God. My skills and resources were needed. God had blessed me so that I could give something back to him. I felt the satisfaction of giving and helping.

But there was another side to my "do-good" motives. My life was all mapped out: I would offer my skills to the black community for a while and then leave and get on with my real life. Maybe I would even use what I'd learned in a political career. Subconsciously, I had struck a deal with God: I'll do some good for the poor, but don't mess with my mind, my lifestyle or my life plans.

I realized that I was a kind of caseworker. People in need could, so to speak, come into my office, sit down in front of my desk and outline their problems and needs, and I would do whatever I could to help them. I would be the giver; they would be recipients. But when the recipients started saying that maybe the desk needed to be turned around and I needed to learn from them, I had begun packing up. I became aware that my real, deep-down motivation to leave during the reconciliation meetings was that I didn't want to go through the pain of looking into a clearer mirror, especially if it meant my potential for leadership and exercising my gifts might be limited.

God began showing me that he wanted me to move from giving to receiving, from leading to being led. God reminded me that when I made a commitment to Jesus, I put all of my life under his lordship. But there was still lots of unconquered territory, and one of the major terrains was marked "racial." God controlled some of it, but he wanted it all.

My motive for racial reconciliation needed to be for my own sake. Do-goodism wasn't good enough. It put the focus on what I was doing for others rather than on what God wanted to do in me. As God purified my motives, I found myself becoming not only a more effective soldier of reconciliation but also a more mature disciple of Christ.

Side by Side

My racial conversion process had been birthed with my arrival into the black community at Voice of Calvary in 1981. The racial reconciliation meetings of 1983 had brought the issue into turbulent adolescence. I had been tempted to rebel and go my own way. Now I decided to stay, and new friendships with blacks offered an opportunity for my commitment to mature another step.

The fact that the black people of our small group were reaching out to me created a tension. Hadn't blacks made it clear that we whites were getting in the way of their development? Despite their anger, despite the focus on "black," they were opening up their lives to me. *Why?*

An event in the fall of 1985 solidified my move toward racial conversion. A group of us from VOC Ministries staff had been meeting regularly on Thursday mornings. We had decided to spend more time together outside of work hours struggling with the muddy issues that were so much a part of our daily ministry.

One morning Lem Tucker, VOCM's president at the time, reminded the group that when he had asked me to step in a year earlier as acting fundraising director, it had been with the understanding that a search for a black replacement would begin immediately. But now, said Lem, he and I had met, and he had asked me to accept the full responsibility of being the ministry's development director. "This morning," continued Lem, "I want to discuss the role of white people at VOC—and Chris is our guinea pig!"

I was taken off-guard. I fidgeted in my seat. Sweat began to drip under my arms. I enjoyed friendly relationships with everybody in the room. But I knew that the members of the group—which was mostly black—would speak their feelings honestly. All of them put a high priority on developing black leadership.

Nearly everyone in the room responded. And through it all, the message was clear: "Chris, we accept you as part of us. We appreciate the gifts you bring to this ministry. We've seen you up close over the last four years, we've seen your struggle with your racial prejudice. We affirm your being in a leadership position." Melvin Anderson's words encouraged me the most: "You know, I don't think of Chris as being white. He just seems like one of us."

It was as if God had reached out through my black friends, put his hands on my shoulders and said, "This is where I want you." I flashed back to one of my mental arguments for leaving VOC: I'm not wanted here. I'm not needed here. Now I understood: The blacks hadn't rejected me. I'd been the one to think I should leave. When they said, "You need to be willing to step to the side," I had heard "Step back." When they said "mutual submission," I'd heard "black domination." When they mentioned the importance of black leadership, I'd heard "No room for white leadership."

What the black brothers and sisters were saying throughout the reconciliation process was "Stay here with us. Stay and serve. Let's show the world that when black and white Christians come together, we can work as equals." Finally I understood that the reconciliation meetings had not been a purge, or a coup that would elevate black over white.

We were *partners*, moving ahead side by side.

Just exactly how the newfound ideal of partnership should be expressed in the practical life of our church still had to be worked out. One important question was how our church should be led. Spencer was deeply involved in facing that challenge, so I'll let him tell you how we began to work it out.

Spencer: Our Tiny Witness

One of the results of the racial reconciliation meetings was a renewed resolve to develop black leadership. Although our church was about 50-50 black to white and our surrounding community was nearly 90 percent black, the church leadership was made up of five whites and two blacks, and the pastor was white. There had never been any overt plan for whites to have a majority in leadership; it just happened that way. In an all-black church setting blacks have no problem taking leadership. But we realized that when blacks and whites come together for a common cause, the whites tend to feel more secure taking on the leadership roles—whether it's volunteering to lead in a church project or being willing to be considered for eldership. So we decided to make an intentional effort to affirm black culture and encourage black leadership. This was an attempt not to put blacks over whites but only to balance the scales—especially since we lived and worshiped in a black neighborhood.

In the fall of 1983 four people—three blacks and one white—were confirmed as elders in our church, and I was one of them. As a result of the racial reconciliation meetings, we decided to return to interracial pastoral leadership. When our church was born in 1977, we had appointed biracial copastors, Phil Reed and Romas McLain. But Romas served only a few months before leaving for seminary. Because we all loved and trusted Phil, we allowed him to continue as pastor even though we didn't think it ideal for an interracial church in a black neighborhood to have a white pastor. (Sometimes, though your ideal seems so clear to you, God will not give it to you. Struggling to reconcile ideals with reality has been a way of life for VOC ever since I can remember.)

After the racial reconciliation meetings, the elders and congregation felt the best form of leadership would be a three-person pastoral team. Only a few weeks before this decision was reached, Phil had offered to step down in favor of a black pastor. But the black members of the body had affirmed him, insisting that he stay.

Over the next couple of years the church's leadership stumbled around, trying to find the right combination of pastors. Then in 1985 the Reverend Donald Govan (known as Mr. G) and I joined Phil to form the pastoral team for Voice of Calvary Fellowship.

Even though Phil is white, he chaired the team. He was the one paid by the church and who did the day-to-day administration and most of the preaching. He served in this fashion even though the authority is shared by the pastoral team. Not many people would be willing to work in such a structure. I praise the Lord for Phil. In my opinion, he is an unsung hero—one of the few pastors in this country to be a part of a truly interracial body of believers with interracial pastoral leadership.

Any plural leadership, and especially when it is interracial, has special risks. As the unity of the pastors goes, so goes the unity of the church. Since we became a team, Phil, Mr. G and I have had to fight for our unity. My relationship with Phil has been the toughest. We are both more opinionated than Mr. G, and therefore we have had to struggle harder to maintain our unity. Several people have commented that our relationship reminds them of a marriage. If we don't spend time together, our relationship deteriorates, and when it deteriorates, it's much harder to attain unity in decision-making. Marcia, Phil's wife, marvels at how we are able to remain committed to each other. It has been said that the first and most important rule in a marriage is "Never mention divorce as an option." In the same way, in order to maintain unity among ourselves as copastors, each of us must be confident that the other two will not decide on their own to walk away. This confidence is essential for survival.

Voice of Calvary Fellowship still struggles with how to live out our witness of racial reconciliation. Even though our church has many people coming and going, our membership still runs about 60 percent black and 40 percent white. I often wish that every member had to experience something like the racial reconciliation meetings. Many new members are attracted by our witness and lifestyle but were not part of the fellowship during this trying time. Sometimes newcomers take our interracial character for granted without understanding the blood, sweat and tears it took to reach this point.

God told Israel that he would bless them so that they could in turn bless the other peoples of the world. Over the years God blessed us greatly at Voice of Calvary, and the evidence to me is that the faith of many people around the country and world has been strengthened because of our tiny witness here in Mississippi—a witness to the power of a God who can bring together and reconcile those who have been most divided.

Chris: Autopsy Versus Recovery

Beneath the surface of the racial harmony that was a marvel to VOC visitors before 1983, a volcano was sizzling. When it erupted, explosive emotions spewed forth. Blacks and whites who had worked and worshiped and lived side by side were suddenly at odds. We realized how little we really knew each other. Past incidents had ignited sparks that should have been immediately extinguished. Instead, later problems had fanned the flames of mistrust and misunderstanding. It seemed that a raging fire was out of control.

Yet if you visit Voice of Calvary today, you will see many of the same people who endured the fires of 1983 now sharing genuine, deep friendships. You'll see us worshiping together, living on the same streets, reaching out to our neighbors in ministry. You'll see our children enjoying friendships together. You'll see us continuing to talk about and work through racial struggles.

What happened? Why didn't we blacks and whites go our separate ways?

The story of another group that attempted to reconcile the races might illuminate the issues. The Student Nonviolent Coordinating Committee, called SNCC (or Snick, for short), was arguably the most creative and idealistic civil rights organization of the 1960s. SNCC's student leaders adopted radical grassroots methods and constantly butted heads with their more traditional counterparts at the NAACP and Martin Luther King's Southern Christian Leadership Conference (SCLC). SNCC's staff lived in the poor communities where they worked. Their vision was not only to fight injustice but also to show how black and white could live and work in harmony. This caused great disturbances in Southern towns. Their dangerous ventures—voter registration, community organizing, sit-ins and marches—paved the way for some of the more well-known political gains of the civil rights movement. SNCC's bold goal? To rid America of racial segregation and discrimination in every arena of life.

SNCC's efforts helped to break down tremendous legal and political obstacles. In town after town, enemies like Alabama sheriff Bull Connor were defeated. On the national level Congress passed the Civil Rights Bill of 1965.

But in the aftermath of these victories SNCC found that its dream for racial harmony was dying. The conflict hit boiling point at a staff retreat in May 1966 when SNCC debated asking whites to leave the staff. Mary King, a white SNCC worker, recalls the divisive mood of the debate: "[Some blacks argued that] white people . . . were inherently incapable of comprehending the black experience. For SNCC to become the type of organization they desired, it would have to rid itself of white staff members and become 'black-staffed, black-controlled, and black-financed.'"[1]

In the months afterward white SNCC staff and blacks who were supportive of interracial cooperation trickled away. By the following year only one white staff worker remained.

Bob Zellner hung on until a meeting in Atlanta in 1967, where he was planning to propose a new organizing campaign. "I was in one room, and the executive committee was in another," he says. "They offered me a compromise: you can do the project, but you can't come to meetings. I wouldn't accept that because SNCC never required second-class citizenship of anyone. Then they said, Okay, you can come to meetings, but you can't vote. I said no. They finally said, Okay, good luck."[2]

Only two years after the landmark civil rights bill, SNCC was a blacks-only organization. The racial unity that SNCC had dared to proclaim, and had pursued at great risk, ended in divorce—"separated due to irreconcilable differences." SNCC's political victories had been considerable, but the relationships between individual blacks and whites had not been strong enough to hold the organization together.

The same challenges that split SNCC in 1967 were faced by VOC in 1983: mistrust between the races, whites' tendency to dominate the leadership of an interracial group, unresolved residue from growing up in an unequal society. Yet VOC's confrontation did not result in a racial split. Why?

In the difference between SNCC and VOC lies our only hope: *Reconciliation is ultimately a spiritual issue.*

SNCC had the weapons to win a political war but not a spiritual one. Like SNCC, VOC reached a point of painful conflict that looked impossible to transcend. But a deeper motivation enabled us to persevere and make the sacrifices necessary to stay together. Even after 1983's racial confrontation, blacks at VOC didn't ask whites to be second-class citizens. None of the white church leaders or ministry staff were asked to leave. In fact, when the church picked new elders, a white was added along with three blacks. During that same time Derek, a black brother, asked me to join the new small group. Then Lem, another black brother, asked me to take a key leadership position, directing the ministry's fundraising efforts. Black friends as well as white encouraged me to accept the position. The actions of VOC's blacks proved that they desired not to separate from whites, or to be our superiors, but to be partners in a shared mission.

The powerful lesson in these two stories is that the gulf between black and white can be crossed only on a bridge built by the hands of God. This is what SNCC lacked and—by the grace of God—what VOC grasped. This is what sustained us through the racial reconciliation meetings. Without God at the center, there is no basis for reconciliation.

11

Weapons for the Battle

O<small>NCE I ADMITTED THAT YES, I HAD FALLEN SHORT OF GOD'S WILL FOR</small> *reconciliation between black and white, I felt indicted and frustrated. This is a common response, especially for whites. At best, we want to wipe away the pain that race causes; at the least, it's tempting to look for a quick fix to rid ourselves of our pangs of guilt. But God is taking us through a process, and it's important not to try to find shortcuts.*

Without God as architect, our plans for building reconciled relationships will eventually collapse under the weight of our old racial residue. When we put our racial struggle at God's feet, though, he doesn't just grab us under the armpits, jerk us up and push us back into the battle. Instead, he gives us effective spiritual weapons to use in the struggle. These weapons have proved indispensable to those who seek to submit themselves to the deepest purposes of God in the area of race.

> All to Jesus I surrender,
> Humbly at His feet I bow;
> Worldly pleasures all forsaken,
> Take me Jesus, take me now.

I surrender all, I surrender all,
All to Thee, my blessed Savior,
I surrender all.

Whenever our church sings that beautiful song, I find my voice getting softer when the chorus comes: "I surrender all." It would be closer to the truth for me to sing "I surrender some." I know I fall short of where God wants me to be.

But I suppose it's okay for Christians to be shy about that song. Feeling that tension reminds us to be dependent on God. It reminds us that we've forsaken "worldly pleasures" not because we're anything special, but because Jesus Christ has taken up residence in us. We can't be good citizens of God's kingdom without a great deal of help from our King. Solving our racial problems must begin at the foot of the cross.

The wide gulf separating blacks and whites can easily leave you feeling helpless and hopeless. When you reach this point, it's tempting to rationalize your way out of taking responsibility. Blacks often wash their hands of the need for reconciliation by reasoning, "All white folks got a little snake in them. Every one of 'em will eventually turn their back on you." Many whites who are confronted with the racial gulf feel guilty, but then, not seeing any way beyond the guilt, we also find ways to rationalize our retreat from responsibility. "Blacks will never be satisfied. So why keep feeling guilty?" Yes, both races conclude, *the gulf is great. But it's not up to me to cross it.*

This hopelessness is why we must begin the journey at the feet of Jesus. For it is only through his power that we will be able to take the next step and allow God to turn white guilt and black anger into positive forces of conviction and passion.

At a crucial moment in Israel's history the people cried out to God. They were exiled in captivity, banished by God because of their sins against him. Once feared and respected, they now cowered in defeat, demoralized and without hope. Jerusalem, the once-esteemed city of their holy nation, lay in ruins. The stones of the city wall lay in a pile of rubble, and the city gates were burned to the ground. "Ha! How small is your God that we should defeat you!" their enemies sneered.

But one Israelite had not forgotten who he was or the God he served. Captive in faraway Persia, consigned to duty as cupbearer to King Artaxerxes, a man named Nehemiah faithfully made his way back to Jerusalem to rally the people and rebuild its walls. As he did, three spiritual weapons enabled him to persevere. You will find these same weapons to be indispensable in waging spiritual battle for reconciliation: *purity, passionate purpose* and *perseverance*.

At Voice of Calvary, these three weapons have been dented and dulled in battle over and over but have always proven sufficient for victory.

Our Weapon of Purity: Forgiveness

When Nehemiah first heard the awful news from Jerusalem, he fell on his knees and wept (Neh 1:4-11): "For some days I mourned and fasted and prayed before the God of heaven." He grieved for four months. The Israelites' exile, Nehemiah understood, was the result of their disobeying God. And because God took the sin seriously, Nehemiah prayed passionately: "We have acted very wickedly toward you. We have not obeyed the commands, decrees and laws you gave your servant Moses." Nehemiah didn't justify himself. Though he was far away from the land of his ancestors, Nehemiah accepted personal responsibility. He saw that the sin of Israel had left a stain on him that he needed to confess. The beginning point for national healing was his personal healing.

When the world sneers at our God because we cannot conquer the racial giant, we ought to fall on our knees as Nehemiah did. Unfortunately, instead we usually accept racial separation as much as the world does. *Guilt* has become a dirty word, something we go to therapy to get rid of.

We need to learn how to mourn and grieve because the name of God stands disgraced by our racial problem. It is only as each individual starts with himself or herself, confessing and receiving forgiveness from God, that there will be a basis for racial reconciliation.

Seeking forgiveness is risky. As Ben Carson says, taking healthy risks means "doing what [you] know is right even when [you] have no assurance of the results."[1] And we are called to the risk of seeking forgiveness and offering it.

Forgiveness is choosing not to base your actions on how others have hurt you. No, you can't always forget those hurts. But you can choose to return another's angry word with an act of love. Even if you got beaten up at the last meeting, you can choose to go to the next one. You can base your actions on the trust that God is at work in you and in everyone else, and that it's just going to take time for his way to win out. You can go to God and choose to pray for the best for a person who hurt you. You can suck up your pride and apologize for the angry word that you said. You can admit that you were wrong or that your attitude was wrong.

Voice of Calvary's racial reconciliation meetings of 1983 were extremely painful, and as we began to recover, we felt like spouses whose marriage had been saved on the very brink of divorce. Yes, we were making a fresh start. But there were no false hopes that we wouldn't disappoint each other again. We knew that one day we would say something hurtful and insensitive. We might have sharp disagreements. Some would still have advantages over others. But our hope was not in our human ability to be more committed to each other. It was the power of God that allowed us to continually forgive.

Without this spiritual weapon of forgiveness, every disappointment will tempt us to give up and retreat. With it, we can move forward, allowing God to turn each disappointment into an opportunity to become the pure, refined gold he desires us to be.

Our Sword of Purpose

Nehemiah's prayer began with a confession of his guilt, but it ended in an earnest commitment to correct the wrong. His passionate prayers were not a substitute for action but preparation to do battle. He prayed that the king would grant his request to go to Jerusalem and rebuild the wall. He asked God to open a door for action, and for the boldness to move through it.

Even as we humbly confess our shortcomings at God's feet, God's desire is to move us from guilt to conviction and then to action. Paul expresses this concern for purposeful action in his second letter to the church at Corinth:

> Even if I caused you sorrow by my letter, I do not regret it. Though I did regret it—I see that my letter hurt you, but only for a little while—yet now I am happy, not because you were made sorry, but because your sorrow led you to repentance. For you became sorrowful as God intended and so were not harmed in any way by us. Godly sorrow brings repentance that leads to salvation and leaves no regret, but worldly sorrow brings death. See what this godly sorrow has produced in you: what earnestness, what eagerness to clear yourselves, what indignation, what alarm, what longing, what concern, what readiness to see justice done. At every point you have proved yourselves to be innocent in this matter. (2 Cor 7:8-11)

Nehemiah's earnestness to act, and thus "prove himself innocent," grew out of a deep sense of purpose based upon understanding who God is. His prayers reveal his familiarity with the Scriptures. When Nehemiah prayed he cried out, "O LORD, God of heaven, the great and awesome God." He knew that he was limited and weak, but his God was mighty and powerful. One of God's past promises gave Nehemiah a basis and hope for moving forward, and he reminded God of his own words: "if you return to me and obey my commands, then even if your exiled people are at the farthest horizon, I will gather them from there and bring them to the place I have chosen as a dwelling for my Name" (Neh 1:9).

Only God-inspired daring will let us see beyond our impossibilities to God's ability to overcome them. While we are part of a people that have fallen short, we are also part of a people to whom God has promised blessing.

A sure lifeboat that has seen us through our racial storms at VOC has been an unswerving commitment to keeping God's Word at the center of our church life. Without the conviction that what the Bible says is true and right, we would have long abandoned any passion for racial reconciliation. Our belief that reconciliation is close to God's heart has kept us from giving up.

Because John Perkins was committed to obeying Matthew 5:44,

"Love your enemies," he returned love for the kicks and blows of those Mississippi patrolmen in the Brandon jail, and afterward he reached out to whites with even greater passion. Because they believed Ephesians 2:14, which says God has torn down "the dividing wall of hostility," the Perkins family, who are black, and the Spees family, who are white, moved into a racially changing West Jackson neighborhood to show that whites and blacks didn't have to run from each other. Because the Antioch church's interracial witness opened the whole church's eyes to the possibilities of the gospel, as explained in the book of Acts, we at Voice of Calvary have struggled for a witness of black and white that would inspire the many people who visit and work with us today.

Being close to the purpose of God enables us to be clear about our mission, to move forward even in the face of difficulty and risk and to be faithful in spite of the odds.

Our Weapon of Perseverance

Racial reconciliation is surgery, and surgery is never painless. Fear of this pain prompts many Christians to ignore their racial blinders. But the point where we feel pain is the beginning of the surgical process. The pain of the Racial Reconciliation Meetings was the beginning of my dealing with the racial residue in my own life. When we feel the first cut of the knife, the pain of confronting our true attitudes, we want to cry out, "Stop! I can't handle it!" But how we respond to pain determines whether we grow. As Ben Franklin said, "What causes pain, instructs." Or as my high school basketball coach used to say before running us through wind sprints, "No pain, no gain."

After Nehemiah's four months of prayer, the rest of his story is one of persevering through struggle after struggle to rebuild the wall of Jerusalem. The spiritual weapon of prayer gives us direct access to the power of God. It is how our will becomes God's will. We can cry out to him for help and gain the strength and perspective we need to continue the fight.

Because Phil Reed carries the heaviest load in leading our church, he is often the lightning rod for the frustrations and conflicts that arise as people of different cultures and races learn to be family to each other. As a white pastor in a majority-black church, he finds that sometimes it's still hard to win the respect he deserves after more than twenty years of commitment to reconciliation at VOC. Add to this Phil's quick temper, and things can really get heated. Over and over again I have seen Phil take the heat. At the racial reconciliation meetings especially, the actions of white leaders were often pointedly challenged.

An outsider might say Phil Reed was addicted to punishment. But the secret to Phil's resilience is, I believe, that his knees are familiar with the floor of his study. In the times of pain, he goes to prayer. There he wrestles with God. When he walks out and takes the pulpit, we have learned to expect that even after the most heated times of conflict, Phil will give a word born out of prayer. Phil's honesty in the pulpit has enabled all of us to look into ourselves to see where we have given the forces of darkness a foothold. Phil would be the first to say he's made many mistakes. But he always bounces back.

Building on Solid Rock

"Eleven o'clock Sunday morning is America's most segregated hour." Thirty years after Martin Luther King Jr. first preached those words, they are still all too true. It is often said that the church is dead last in bringing black and white together. But ironically, while the church falls far short of God's highest purpose for black and white, it is the followers of Christ who are the greatest hope for reconciliation.

Businesses, recognizing what's good for the bottom line, now invest in improving understanding between black and white employees. The military has moved in the same direction with similar motives. Since the Vietnam War, the U.S. Army has instituted some of the most progressive racial-awareness programs in the country. Army leaders have recognized that black and white need to be better teammates if they are to win in battle.

Paid employees and soldiers are captive audiences for racial-awareness seminars and exercises. We in the church, however, follow Christ by choice. It is precisely because the church is a volunteer organization that it represents both our greatest challenge and our greatest hope.

If we don't like one church, we can leave it for another. It takes a voluntary commitment to follow Jesus. You don't go into difficult and uncharted kingdom territory unless you are committed from the heart. So when reconciliation happens in the church, it will happen for the right reason. Because we always have the option to leave, when it happens we'll know that it's pure, that it's for real, that it's honest. And we'll know that a love for God has made it possible.

Our spiritual pilgrimage toward reconciliation must begin at the feet of Jesus as we look to him for purity, purpose and perseverance. Only there can we begin submitting ourselves to each other, black and white.

We'll need a solid foundation when we start to reach out to our racially different neighbor in hopes of hammering together the kind of house that God desires. The residue that blacks and whites carry is a heavy load. Its weight threatens the very structure of the house. Only the kingdom of God provides the rock-solid foundation on which we can build reconciled relationships. As the hymn goes, "All other ground is sinking sand."

12

Acts:
A Reconciliation Story

For he himself is our peace, who has made the two
[Jew and Gentile] one and has destroyed the barrier, the dividing
wall of hostility, by abolishing in his flesh the law. . . .
His purpose was to create in himself one new man
out of the two, thus making peace,
and in this one body to reconcile both of them to God through
the cross, by which he put to death their hostility.

EPHESIANS 2:14-16

O NE MOTIVATOR IN MY RECONCILIATION PILGRIMAGE AS A WHITE *person has been discovering comrades from the pages of the New Testament who wrestled with the racial separations of their day. These separations were not based on differences in skin color. One Webster's definition of race is "any group of people having the same ancestry, . . . activities, habits, [and] ideas." Like the Serbs and Croats or Palestinians and Jews or Tutsis and Hutus who separate and struggle today, the life of the early church recorded in the book of Acts was made up of distinct ethnic and cultural groups with histories of animosity and distrust. To Peter and Paul, destroying the "dividing wall" was more than good theology—it became practical as it was hammered out on the anvil of their own lives.*

The task of putting to death the hostility between minority Greek Jews, majority Hebrew Jews, Samaritan outcasts and heathen Gentiles was a central concern for the early church. It was not a sideshow to the drama of God's work. The story of how the gospel reconciled diverse people together into one faith and one church takes center stage in Acts. The way the first Christians broke down the walls of their day can teach timely, useful lessons to us as we face similar challenges today.

At the top of a mountain Jesus' eleven hand-picked followers stood eagerly before him, the exhilaration of his resurrection still pounding in their hearts. Their commander in chief sounded a final call to battle: "Go and make disciples of all nations" (Mt 28:19).

The implication of these simple words was radical: the gospel was not just for Israel, but for all people and races. If the eleven had been able to put the words together with Jesus' example, his meaning would have been crystal-clear. In three years Jesus had turned everything upside-down: he was ridiculed as "a Samaritan" because he went out of his way to interact with the despised half-breeds; he had healed Jews and Gentiles alike; the great commandment to "love your neighbor as yourself," he said, meant especially loving those who are different from you.

But Jesus wasn't surprised that his words had gone over his disciples' heads. There aren't many secrets when you've traveled and roomed together for three years. As Jesus handed over the mantle of leadership, he knew his loyal followers carried a lot of racial baggage on their rocky journey toward extending the faith beyond their native Israel. Because he had grown up in the same racially obsessed climate as they, Jesus understood that they were dealing with something deep inside themselves.

The Racial Residue of Jesus' Day

The eleven apostles carried racial residue from the deeply ingrained Jewish caste system. In this system there were three rungs on the racial ladder: Jews, Samaritans and Gentiles.

Highest on the ladder were Jews, God's chosen people with special status. Among Jews there were further separations. "Pure" Jews born in Palestine were better than foreign-born Jews. Jews of Greek descent were looked down on by Jews of Hebrew descent, and the two groups even worshiped in segregated synagogues.

The second major group, the Samaritans, came a long step down the ladder from the Jews. The bitterness between Jews and Samaritans was almost a thousand years old. Samaritans were regarded as half-breeds—Jews who had compromised the faith and intermarried with Gentiles. While they practiced many Jewish customs, including circumcision, their religion was regarded as a prostitute religion. The Samaritans had their own temple and only accepted the first five books of the Old Testament.

Most despised and lowest on the ladder were the uncircumcised Gentile heathens. For a Jew to talk, eat or associate in any way with a Gentile was strictly forbidden by Jewish law. Relations with Gentiles were governed by strict religious codes and social customs designed to guard Jewish purity. John Stott describes the Jew-Gentile separation as an "impassable gulf" that was contrary to God's intentions: "By choosing and blessing one family, he intended to bless all the families of the earth. . . . The tragedy was that Israel twisted the doctrine of election into one of favouritism, became filled with racial pride and hatred, despised Gentiles as 'dogs,' and developed traditions which kept them apart."[1]

Although three years with Jesus had changed the eleven apostles significantly, they were still native-born Jews who had grown up on the highest rung; racial residue still tainted them.

Days later, as Jesus prepared to depart, his disciples' residue of superiority prompted them to ask one last question: "Lord, are you at this time going to restore the kingdom to Israel?" (Acts 1:6).

By now Jesus must have been ready to say, "Read my lips." His answer reveals, once again, the deeper implications of their mission: "You will receive power when the Holy Spirit comes on you; and you will be my witnesses in Jerusalem, and in all Judea and Samaria, and to the ends of the earth" (Acts 1:8).

With the hindsight of history it's easy to wonder why the apostles didn't grasp these words. But come to think of it, haven't we had a hard time understanding today's equivalent? If Jesus had the pulpit in your church next Sunday, what would he say is your Samaria—the people in the remotest part of your city or county, those you might have to work hardest to meet?

The Great Commission raises important challenges for us today, just as it did for the disciples who first heard it. What work is required to overcome the mistrust, fear and bitterness that are the residue of years of racial separation? Does God call believers of different races to join in a common mission, or to fragment into separate churches? How do we bring Christ and culture together into a church called to be "one in mind and purpose"? In what ways is it wrong to be separate, and where can we affirm and celebrate our differences? Even if it is God's will to have one church, how do we break through these barriers?

Before Jesus' disciples understood just what their Master meant, they went through years of tackling difficult racial hurdles. How they did it suggests how we might tackle our hurdles today.

Unconscious Barriers

Not long after Pentecost came the first showdown between interracial antagonisms and the gospel of reconciliation. Great numbers were coming to the Lord in Jerusalem—three thousand repented following Peter's great sermon on the day of Pentecost alone. Powerful miracles were taking place. A dynamic Christian community was forming. But the hustle and bustle was still confined within Jerusalem's gates, and the good news was still marked "For Jews Only."

The first cultural tremor hit toward the top of the Jewish caste system, between Hebrew and Greek Jews in the church. Greek Jews complained that the native Jewish widows were being favored in the daily "meals on wheels" program (Acts 6:1). The probable cause of this injustice? The believers were together in a close-knit community during the week, but when the sabbath came, Hebrew and Greek Christians followed standard custom and went to separate synagogues to worship. This separation led to racial cliques and resulting shades of favoritism. The overlooking of the Greek widows was not intended, yet it was the inevitable result of racial separation.

Today's often-unconscious separation between black and white Christians also brings unfortunate outcomes. A 1990 survey by *Christianity Today* showed that minorities made up only 8 percent of the work force of twenty-four well-known Christian institutions (media, education, parachurch and mission agencies)—substantially behind the nationwide nonwhite work force of 15 percent. Christian institutions are half as likely to hire nonwhites as secular institutions—it should be the other way around. "The major obstacle that evangelical employees and minority leaders point to," said the report, "is the continuing lack of contact between evangelical organizations and minority believers."[2]

Like other Americans we Christians do not interact closely with people of other races in everyday spheres of life. The end result is that the needs and concerns of the minority are often overlooked as the majority pursues its priorities.

In Jerusalem when the oversight of Greek widows was pointed out to the apostles, they immediately recognized it as an injustice. They also recognized that their involvement in overseeing the details of daily church life had left them too little time for teaching and prayer; they were spread too thin and weren't doing a good job. Their solution found favor with the whole church: they appointed a group of seven people to oversee the food distribution.

Luke places great emphasis on this incident, pointing out the seriousness with which the church selected the seven: these persons were required to be "full of the Spirit and wisdom" (Acts 6:3), and the apostles laid hands on them to commission them for their responsibilities. A look beneath the surface shows that this episode was a turning point for the church.

On its face the appointment of the seven was nothing more than a smart administrative move. After all, they would simply be waiting tables. But the seven people chosen were all Greek Jews.

The apostles analyzed the problem not only as a misplacement of their priorities but also as a cultural conflict. They chose seven Greeks to ensure that the injustice would not happen again.

What lessons can we draw to help us surmount the unconscious racial barriers in Christian circles today?

First, minority complaints should be taken very seriously. It's not that what minority believers say is more important; but because they are minority, it's easier to overlook them. It's tempting to push difficult cultural issues under the rug. The apostles didn't do that. The Greek Christians were a minority in the church, but the apostles listened, recognized the wrong and acted.

If we at Voice of Calvary had only had a sprinkling of blacks instead of a majority, would we have heeded the pain that led to our racial reconciliation meetings? Unfortunately, there are very few settings in which black and white Christians come together to speak honestly to one another's lives and organizations. Still, there is hope. Leaders from groups such as the National Association of Evangelicals and its black counterpart, the National Black Evangelical Association, have gone a long way toward a dialogue on racial reconciliation. If one part of the body voices its pain, regardless of whether it comes from the minority or from the majority, we should all feel the pain.

Second, culture-conscious choices may be needed to correct injustice. Instead of hiding behind a spiritual platitude like "We don't see color," the apostles recognized that the injustice had occurred because of the majority culture's blinders. Why else were seven Greeks chosen to take over the responsibility? In making this culture-conscious choice the apostles bent over backward to restore trust with the Greek believers—trust that was vital to the growth of the Christian community in Jerusalem.

Sometimes justice means you do have to be very conscious of color. One common barrier within ministry organizations is their support-raising policies. For several years when I worked at Voice of Calvary Ministries, all staff were required to raise their salary support on their own. Eventually we realized that it was much easier for white staff to raise support than for black staff. Whites generally had access to more resources from family, friends and churches. What was relatively easy for me and many other whites was a frustrating obstacle for our black staff. As a result there were more white than black staff members. So the ministry made a commitment to raise extra money through its fundraising department solely for the support of black staff. And soon more black Christians were able to join the ministry team.

Some campus ministries have made attempts to remove barriers to minority involvement. Recognizing that today's college campuses are increasingly multiracial, these organizations have set up special funds to pay the salaries of black staff who are unable to raise their full support. More such efforts are needed to build trust and bring committed members of minorities into our Christian organizations.

Third, minorities need to be given a greater voice in the life of the church. The overlooking of the widows was only a symptom of a deeper problem. By creating a new leadership team, the apostles gave the Greek minority a greater stake in the life of the church. The choice of these Spirit-filled Greek brothers would ultimately have far-reaching effects on the church's direction.

As the early church's example shows, people who are indigenous to a culture can most readily articulate its needs and concerns. At Voice of Calvary Fellowship we are convinced that maintaining a strong interracial witness necessitates keeping an interracial leadership team. We choose our elders on the basis of their spiritual character, and we take care to ensure that the racial makeup doesn't tip too far either way. If you want to make a stronger witness for reconciliation, whether in your business, church or ministry, there is no more important step than bringing interracial dialogue and witness into the highest levels of your leadership.

Fourth, faithful responses to cultural injustice can lead to greater fruit for the gospel. Sprinkled throughout Acts are six summary statements about the church's growth. Each marks a landmark event, a turning point for the church. The first was Pentecost, after which Luke writes, "And the Lord added to their number daily those who were being saved" (2:47). The appointment of the seven Greeks was the second landmark event. To underline the church's faithful action Luke emphasizes its impact: "So the word of God spread. The number of disciples in Jerusalem increased rapidly" (6:7).

Samaritan Outcasts Too?

The seven Greeks did not take their new responsibility lightly. Backed by the church's confidence, these minority leaders began taking visionary steps that the apostles themselves, too hampered by their cultural blinders, did not have the foresight to take.

When we think of great New Testament evangelists, two dynamic leaders come to mind. First, Peter, the apostle to the Jews. Who can forget his great speech to the Jews gathered at Pentecost, when three thousand souls were saved? And then Paul, the apostle to the Gentiles, and his great missionary journeys. But neither of these men grasped the revolutionary implications of Jesus' phrase "all nations" as quickly as two less-known pioneers who began a string of events that burst the gospel out of Jerusalem.

These two, Stephen and Philip, were among the seven who had been appointed to oversee food distribution. Soon they took point positions into the new territory promised by Jesus in Acts 1:8. His gifts unleashed, Stephen went public, preaching and performing great signs. His bold speaking soon landed him in a trial before the Jewish society's highest council, the Sanhedrin. The charge? "We have heard him say that this Jesus of Nazareth will destroy [the temple] and change the customs Moses handed down to us" (6:14).

Stephen's powerful rebuttal prophetically signaled God's intention to move the gospel beyond Jewish tradition and make it accessible to any faithful people who would call upon God's name. His accusers, argued Stephen, might have the physical sign of God's chosen—circumcision—but they lacked the true sign—"circumcised" hearts and ears (7:51). Outraged by Stephen's speech, his hearers carried him out of Jerusalem and stoned him to death.

Following Stephen's death, writes Luke, "a great persecution broke out against the church at Jerusalem, and all except the apostles were scattered throughout Judea and Samaria" (8:1). But this persecution did much more good than harm. Echoing Jesus' command to take the gospel to Samaria, Luke continues, "Those who had been scattered preached the word wherever they went. Philip went down to a city in Samaria and proclaimed the Christ there" (8:4-5). The persecution was clearly God's way of extending the gospel beyond its Jewish walls.

While the apostles huddled up in Jerusalem, Philip steamed ahead into Samaria to preach Christ. Like Stephen, Philip had been emboldened by his new responsibility. In his wake people were healed. Unclean spirits were driven out. Crowds began forming to listen to his preaching, as word rapidly spread throughout the region.

It's difficult to overstress the significance of Philip's move into Samaria. The Jew-Samaritan split was a thousand years old.

A modern equivalent of Philip's bold step into Samaria might be a black Christian's moving into Bensonhurst, New York, to start a reconciliation ministry. Or for a white, moving into the heart of Detroit's inner city.

When Iowa farm boy Wayne Gordon graduated from Wheaton College and decided to move into Lawndale, one of Chicago's highest-crime neighborhoods, to start a ministry, everyone told him he was crazy. "What about the crime?" "You really expect to find a wife who will live with you there?" Wayne found a willing wife, Anne, and they've been in Lawndale for over twenty years, but at first it was hard for his friends to swallow.

Philip with Samaritans? The untouchables, the spat-upon "nigger Jews"? This too was hard for folks back home to swallow. It didn't take long for Philip's waves to ripple back to Jerusalem and the apostles who were gathered there (8:14).

"Can this be true?" they asked incredulously. "Well, the Samaritans are circumcised, but surely God won't give them the Holy Spirit, will he?"

Intensely concerned, the apostles dispatched Peter and John—the top-ranked apostles—to join Philip in Samaria and see things for themselves. John was an interesting choice; perhaps he was anxious to redeem himself for having urged Jesus to rain heaven's fire down on a Samaritan village that had refused them hospitality (Lk 9:54).

What Peter and John saw when they joined Philip in Samaria surely startled them. As they laid their hands on the Samaritans, these people were receiving the Holy Spirit! They stayed to preach, and hundreds of Samaritans gave their lives to Jesus. The gospel had reached across the great gap that separated Jews from Samaritans, to pull up and embrace the once-despised as brothers and sisters. The very people upon whom John had wanted heaven's fire to fall were now receiving new life.

Peter and John headed back to Jerusalem, but Philip plowed ahead, stretching the cultural boundaries of the church. God directed him to the Ethiopian eunuch, and with this man's conversion the gospel was headed to the "uttermost parts."

Again Luke makes a summary statement to highlight these landmark events, and now he includes Samaria within the purview of the gospel's expansion: "Then the church throughout Judea, Galilee and Samaria enjoyed a time of peace. It was strengthened; and encouraged by the Holy Spirit, it grew in numbers, living in the fear of the Lord" (9:31).

It was eager Greek believers, less handicapped because of their experience as a minority, who offered themselves as God's sledgehammers to begin breaking down the cultural walls that had restricted the church. More readily than the Hebrew majority, Stephen and Philip understood God's intentions to extend the gospel beyond one race. As part of a minority that suffered from the results of separation and prejudice, they had greater compassion for those who had been locked out and sensitivity to break through the barriers.

The crucial role Greek minority leaders played in liberating the gospel from Jerusalem shows the valuable contribution cultural diversity makes to Christian witness, expanding the possibilities for the gospel's growth. It widens the entire church's vision, helping those of us in the majority to take off our cultural blinders and recognize new opportunities and strategies for ministry. Bringing sensitivity and compassion for those who suffer, minorities teach us how to better approach people of other cultures.

It is crucial that the overlooked Stephens and Philips of our day gain a voice and a stake in our common mission. Just as the Greeks and Jews of the early church learned to do, we blacks and whites must recognize our need for one another. Without that partnership our ministry in the world is incomplete. Bill Pannell, professor of evangelism at Fuller Theological Seminary, warns, "Unless all of us are talking together, unless all of us are running together . . . learning to know and trust each other, it's going to be a very small team running a very big race. If that's the case, twenty-first century evangelism—and evangelicalism—will be the poorer for it."[3]

A Gentile, My Brother?

First the Greek barrier had been broken and then the Samaritan. Now came the greatest challenge of all. At the bottom of the ladder, apparently excluded from the promises of the gospel, were the Gentiles. Now, almost in spite of the church, God took matters into his own hands, stretching Peter beyond the limits of his understanding.

An angel was dispatched to a God-fearing Roman officer in Caesarea, Cornelius (Acts 10:1-8). The angel instructed Cornelius to send messengers to a Jew named Peter, staying at the home of Simon the tanner in the seaside town of Joppa.

As Cornelius's men approached Joppa, Peter was deep in prayer. In a trance he saw a sheet come down from the sky full of animals considered unclean under Jewish law. God spoke to Peter: "Kill and eat." This was God's invitation to a soul-food dinner: pork ribs, ham hocks and greens, and all the trimmings.

"Surely not, Lord!" protested Peter, who was devoutly antipork. "I have never eaten anything impure or unclean."

But God replied, "Do not call anything impure that God has made clean." Three times the soul-food invitation was made, and then Peter awoke (10:9-16). As he pondered this strange event, the men sent by Cornelius arrived, requesting that he come to Caesarea.

Still scratching his head, Peter headed to Caesarea. To accept this heathen Gentile's invitation was a big step for a dyed-in-the-wool Jew like Peter. Imagine what ran through his mind: *They're expecting me to say something. Which sermon should I pull out of the files? Wait, I don't have a Gentile sermon. Boy, I sure hope it's not dinnertime when I arrive. And how in the world am I going to explain all this to the guys back home?*

Upon meeting Cornelius, Peter—never one to pull punches—brought his anxiety into the open: "You are well aware that it is against our law for a Jew to associate with a Gentile or visit him. But God has shown me that I should not call any man impure or unclean" (v. 28). Cornelius explained about the angel's visit and then returned the ball to Peter's court: "Now we are all here in the presence of God to listen to everything the Lord has commanded you to tell us" (v. 33).

Suddenly all the strange puzzle pieces fit together in Peter's head: the sheet full of unfamiliar food coming down from heaven; the sudden visit; Cornelius's vision. The final words of Jesus on the mountaintop, "Go and make disciples of all nations"; the words of God on the rooftop, "Do not call anything impure that God has made clean." Through the layers of Peter's residue, a revolutionary idea broke to the surface: *This is my brother.*

This called for a new sermon, one that he hadn't rehearsed. "I now realize how true it is that God does not show favoritism but accepts men from every nation who fear him and do what is right," he began (vv. 34-35). Without waiting for Peter to finish his message, God filled Cornelius and his household with the Holy Spirit. Afterward, Peter stayed for a while—maybe he even took God up on his rooftop invitation and experienced soul food for the first time.

But soon trouble was brewing back in Jerusalem. Getting wind of what had happened, some of the Jewish believers became upset that Peter had sat down to supper with impure Gentile heathens. You can imagine the talk: "Samaritans, that's one thing. At least they're circumcised; at least they try to be like us. But Gentiles! Holy and unholy together? We're not meant to mix! God forbid!" The born-again Pharisees, Mosaic law manuals in hand, were chomping at the bit to carve Peter up. And when Peter returned from Caesarea, the opposition was ready.

A turbulent meeting ensued. As God's reluctant reconciler reported the startling events of the previous few days, there were no doubt gasps of horror and outrage. But as Peter described how the Holy Spirit fell on Cornelius, "as he had come on us at the beginning" (11:15), there were gasps of wonder. Then, finally, came the irrefutable conclusion: "If God gave them the same gift as he gave us, who believed in the Lord Jesus Christ, who was I to think that I could oppose God?" (v. 17). Everyone was awestruck: "When they heard this, they had no further objections and praised God, saying, 'So then, God has granted even the Gentiles repentance unto life'" (v. 18).

Luke attaches crucial importance to the disintegration of the Jew-Gentile barrier at Caesarea. The Cornelius story is recounted in full by Peter, and then it is referred to again in Acts 15 at the Jerusalem Council. Luke identifies Cornelius's conversion as another landmark event: "the word of God continued to increase and spread" (12:24). The last rung of the social ladder had been demolished, and now all—Hebrews, Greek Jews, Samaritans and Gentiles—stood together on level ground as heirs of God's kingdom.

By now the theology of reconciliation had been established, as described by Paul in Ephesians 3:6: "Through the gospel the Gentiles are heirs together with Israel, members together of one body, and sharers together in the promise in Christ Jesus." The church had overcome tensions between Hebrew and Greek Jews with the choosing of the seven. Then, led by the minority Greek pioneers Stephen and Philip, they had watched the gospel break through to the Samaritans. Finally, with God's irrepressible movement to Caesarea, they had seen that Jew and Gentile alike were children of God.

Tremendous obstacles had been overcome. And yet, it was just a beginning. It is one thing to regard someone as a child of God. It is quite another for him or her to become your comrade and peer. Jew and Gentile were equals before God, but not before one another. This was the next difficult hurdle for the early Christians—a story that we pick up in the next chapter.

Part 3

Commit

13

The Character
of a Reconciler

ONCE WE'VE SINCERELY ADMITTED THAT WE HAVE FALLEN SHORT *of God's will for black and white, and after we've put the problem before the only Physician who can heal us, we must move from conviction and passion to action. If you are ready to ask, "Where and how and with whom shall I live this commitment out?" you are ready for this final step in the reconciliation process, which Spencer and I call* commit. *Having a deep passion for something leads you to seek ways to make a difference. As you step out in action, God begins to develop Christlike character in you.*

This chapter continues the story of Acts. In their struggle for reconciliation, Peter and Paul reveal some key character traits that are needed by those with a passion to be reconcilers. The early church's eventual success in becoming one body—Jew, Greek, Samaritan and Gentile—proves that these are character traits worth struggling for.

The events through which God sledgehammered the gospel out of Jerusalem's walls to Samaria and then to the Gentiles through Cornelius's conversion opened a clear breach in the racial wall that separated Jews and Gentiles. As the Jewish Christians climbed over the crumbling brick and mortar of their racial prejudice, tough new challenges faced them on the other side. Jew and Gentile were together, but they were just starting to become acquainted.

While Greek Jews had pioneered the way, now two Hebrew Jews took point positions: Peter and Paul. As they navigated the unfamiliar terrain of Jew-Gentile relations, Peter and Paul discovered that it's one thing to regard a racial opposite like Cornelius as a child of God; it's quite another for him to become your equal. A great deal of mistrust and inequality, deposited over years of separation, had to be overcome.

Before he met Jesus, Peter had been a simple fisherman with a normal heavy dose of Jewish superiority. While Peter gave the Hebrew-dominated church's stamp of approval to the pioneering steps of the Greek minority, he was not the visionary behind these reconciling ventures. Before his conversion Paul had been a cream-of-the-crop zealot, a rabid protector of Jewish traditions. Says Paul of those days, "I was advancing in Judaism beyond many Jews of my own age and was extremely zealous for the traditions of my fathers" (Gal 1:14). Both of these men had far to go in developing the traits that would be greatly needed by the church.

The challenge of bringing Jew and Gentile into one faith had as much potential to split the two groups further apart as to bring them together. Peter and Paul had the difficult responsibility of keeping the reconciliation process on course. As you begin to enter the similarly challenging territory of black and white America, grab a notebook and take a few tips from Peter and Paul. First we'll follow Paul to the bustling commercial city of Antioch.

A Launching Pad for Missions

While the church in Jerusalem was the first headquarters for the expansion of the gospel, soon another city began to take a central role. Even after Cornelius's conversion, most of those scattered by the persecution still preached only to Jews. But a few believers, Greek and African Jews, took the multiracial nature of the church more seriously. Believers from Cyprus and Cyrene led the way north to the city of Antioch in Syria, where many Gentiles were saved.

When news of this ministry reached Jerusalem, the church dispatched Barnabas, a Greek-speaking Jew, to see it firsthand. Barnabas was excited; sensing the potential for what the church at Antioch could become, he went to Tarsus to get the best person he could find to help him: Paul.

From the beginning, unlike the Jerusalem church, Antioch was an intentional missionary church. No prodding was needed, no persecution necessary, no time wasted. In response to the leading of the Spirit, the fellowship sent Paul and Barnabas off on their first missionary journey, to Jew and Gentile alike (Acts 13:2-3).

Does Antioch's zeal for outreach have relevance to us today? Why did Paul and Barnabas choose this church as their base of operations? More important, why did God choose it?

The Antioch church broke new ground: it was the first true multiracial church, headed by strong multiracial leadership. Luke goes out of his way to emphasize the ethnic backgrounds of Antioch's leaders, probably to convince his readers of the power of this new religion. There was Barnabas, a Greek Jew; Simeon "called Niger," or Simon the Black, an African; Manaen, a Jewish aristocrat; Lucius of Cyrene, another African; and Paul, a Hebrew Jew from northern Tarsus. This multiracial fellowship became God's headquarters for expanding the frontiers of the gospel.

Certainly God can "strike straight blows with crooked sticks." This he did, time and again, moving the gospel beyond culture and race in spite of human reservations. But where a quiver of straighter, sharper arrows can be readily found, surely God can carry out his purposes more directly and with greater effect. God found a ready quiver at Antioch.

If we are not practiced in relating crossculturally at home, we will have difficulty being God's effective weapons to overcome cultural barriers abroad. Racial separation in the Western church is a liability as we take the gospel to other cultures and races, because the residue of our unreconciled barriers at home is carried abroad to the peoples we attempt to reach.

Unfortunately, other Christians around the world have their ungodly prejudices and separations too. Because Japan has colonized Korea several times, Koreans tend to bear a near-hatred for the Japanese (having grown up in Korea, sometimes I struggle with bitterness myself). If Jesus were to tell the good Samaritan story to Koreans, he would have a battered Korean saved by a compassionate traveling Japanese.

But these prejudices should come as no surprise, for we Americans, whom God used to bring the gospel to Korea and many other countries, have offered little evidence that our God is concerned about reconciliation. We infect believers abroad with the same diseases of division and separation that we have failed to cure at home.

As I witness the separations between white and black Christians, I see a gospel that is strong enough to save but often too weak to reconcile. And when we carry this disabled gospel abroad, it is still strong enough to save but too weak to reconcile. I wonder if some of the animosities in the hearts of Koreans would by now have been conquered to the glory of God if Americans had given flesh to their gospel through racial reconciliation both at home and abroad.

International Teams, a U.S. missions agency whose story is told in chapter eight, has worked in the Philippines for many years. The Filipinos who now lead the organization's outreach there have struggled with how to fit in white American workers who seem unwilling to follow. When the Filipino director visited the United States for a month in 1991, he spent a day with International Teams's urban director in Chicago, visiting sites of the ministry's partnership with black churches. For the first time, he told International Teams president Mark Dyer, he saw white Americans working under the authority of black Americans, accomplishing indigenous goals and objectives. Now, he said with excitement, he envisioned how whites could work with and serve the Filipino church.

The mission's witness of reconciliation in America gave credibility to its work around the world. It also made International Teams members better prepared to work under nationals in other countries. As we commit ourselves to create environments in which believers work out racial differences, these environments will become effective launching pads for mission, as Antioch was.

The Ripple Effect

Carried in new wineskins, Antioch's fresh ferment of reconciliation soon began to bubble out and shake the status quo in Jerusalem. The church's growing number of Gentile converts was threatening to Jewish Christians who still carried racial residue.

Peter had a hard time vanquishing his racial demons; during a visit to Antioch they proved to be alive and well, by Paul's account in Galatians 2:11-14. Ten years earlier Peter had accepted a Gentile, Cornelius, as his brother in Christ. Now Peter retreated in action from what he believed in theology.

There he was, eating soul food and kickin' it with his Gentile brothers and sisters. They were having a good time. Gospel music was playing, punctuated by frequent shouts of "Amen!" and "Sing it!" The pork ribs were sizzling on the barbecue. And Peter was caught up in the warm fellowship.

But then some other Jewish brothers crashed the party (we'll call them the Judaizers). They weren't too keen on Peter's cultural trespass, and Peter cracked under their pressure. "You're not one of them," the Judaizers might have said to Peter. "They're not like us. That isn't how you were brought up, eating that dirty pork. You don't want us to lose our precious customs, do you?" Peter didn't stand up to these folks. The demons of race whispered to him that they were right. How could he have let his guard down like that?

If Peter had hung with his newfound Gentile soul brothers, he would have lost some of his Jewish friends. But by choosing the Judaizers, Peter lost his soul brothers.

Sometimes reaching out to those who are racially different from us alienates and isolates us from "our own." For blacks, close relationships with whites can lead to the ultimate putdown: "So you think you're better than us, huh, being with those white folks? What are you, an Oreo?" Similarly, Spencer's college friend Dick, his lost roommate, was willing to go only so far in his friendship with Spencer. He was afraid of looking bad to his white friends.

Your choice to seek out new environments and relationships may feel uncomfortable. You may get some strange looks, and other people might even distance themselves from you. But remember, there will be others who will be encouraged by your actions.

In Raleigh, North Carolina, Freddy and Helen Johnson lived the high life, with three BMWs and careers that were moving swiftly up the corporate ladder. But Freddy and Helen felt a great emptiness inside that led them to sell their house and move "across the tracks," next to one of Raleigh's most neglected public housing projects. A few of their friends abandoned them. But many more have been motivated by Freddy and Helen's decision to admit their own lack of contact with their neighbors across town. Through their ministry, Building Together, Freddy and Helen have become a bridge between black and white, rich and poor. One couple's choice to reach out to their racially different neighbors has sent ripples into the farthest suburbs of Raleigh.

Our attitudes and actions have a ripple effect—either infecting or enhancing the behavior of others. In Peter's case even Barnabas—the one who always thought the best of everybody, the one who trusted the newly converted Paul when no one else would—got carried along with Peter and the Judaizers and began to separate himself too.

A Reconciler Confronts Racial Conflict

Paul realized that the new wineskin he and Barnabas had labored so hard to fashion was about to split open. Now there would be two churches, one for Jews and one for Gentiles.

Some must have urged, "Being together just doesn't work, but we're still one in Christ." Fortunately, this reasoning didn't carry much weight with Paul. The very credibility of the gospel's witness and power was at stake. No, this separation had to be dealt with immediately. In front of the entire church Paul directly confronted Peter's racism.

So often we're not willing to confront conflict and hurts. The fact that it was Paul, a privileged member of the dominant culture, who took a stand is particularly dramatic. Black people often wonder why they always have to be the bad guys who bring up racial issues. "How come white people never bring these problems up?" they ask.

During a meeting of American Christians at the Lausanne II conference in Manila in 1989, a discussion was held to lay out the priority issues facing the U.S. church in the coming decade. Elward Ellis, a black Christian leader, recalls sitting and waiting for the issue of racism to be mentioned. "I didn't want to mention it myself. But if nobody else would, I was going to."

Elward began to fidget in his seat. He had about given up hope when suddenly a white man stepped up to the microphone and spoke. "Racism is a sin that the American church needs to repent of," he said. "It needs to be a priority for us." The white speaker was Wayne Gordon, pastor of an inner-city Chicago church. Says Elward, "I was so relieved that someone else brought it up. I get so tired of being the bad guy." Sometimes we have to be the "bad guy" and rock the boat.

Did Paul's boldness do any good? Let's follow him to Acts 15 for the rest of the story. Again the setting is the Antioch church. Some visiting Judaizers were shocked to find Gentile believers who were not circumcised (v. 1). In their minds, becoming a Christian meant accepting Jewish customs too. They began to raise the battle cry "No Salvation Without Circumcision."

This challenge threatened Paul and Barnabas's entire ministry up to this point. They argued that circumcision was a cultural law that didn't fit in the new wineskin of grace. For Paul the question boiled down to culture versus Christ, and Christ must rule. His rebuttal to the Judaizers was "Circumcision is culture, not Christ."

Making the Choice for Unity
Let's take a close look at the choices facing the early Christians in this sharp conflict, because they're the same ones that confront blacks and

whites in the American church.

Our first choice is to disagree. Each side can stubbornly promote its own viewpoint. This usually results in a split along racial lines. Two separate churches. Two separate missions. Two separate cultures.

Even "agreeing to disagree," though it sounds more pleasant, has the same result. The "I'm OK, you're OK" approach is what blacks and whites most often settle for rather than confronting our conflict. We like to keep things safe and superficial, so we don't bring up differences. But this is living a quiet lie with the end result of de facto separation: "We operate the way we want, you operate the way you want."

Our second choice is compromise. One side can give in to the other for the sake of peace. But it's only when disagreements come into the light that truth and healing can come about. Tensions left unresolved usually surface in one way or another. Neither side learns from the other. Even when each side concedes something, we miss God's fullest blessing. We may want to offer, "We'll give you a little power over here if you keep quiet about that over there." But this tactic does not establish truth, and the church's witness to the full will of God is weakened.

Our final choice is to fight the conflict through to unity. Paul and Barnabas chose this last, most difficult road. Not content with the consequences of disagreement, they decided to fight for the unity that Paul holds up in 1 Corinthians 1:10: "I appeal to you . . . that all of you agree with one another so that there may be no divisions among you and that you may be perfectly united in mind and thought." Paul remembered when Peter broke fellowship with his soul-brothers at Antioch. He had witnessed the destructiveness of division. Left unresolved at the highest level, the difference of opinion regarding circumcision could have had disastrous consequences for the entire church.

To seek the road of unity requires real humility. In choosing this road Paul was handing over his ministry to be judged by someone else. Opening yourself to dialogue assumes that you are willing to change your position if you can be convinced that you're not doing what is best. It is often difficult for us whites to choose this road, because it might mean giving up the comfort of our position of dominance. But it is just as difficult for blacks, who might want to hold on to their anger and bitterness and may be reluctant to consider forgiving white people and giving them one more chance.

Unable to reach accord at Antioch but unwilling to accept division, Paul and Barnabas were dispatched to the mother church in Jerusalem to lay the issue of circumcision before the apostles and elders (Acts 15:2). When Paul and Barnabas arrived, they reported on their ministry among the Gentiles. When they finished, as Luke recounts, "some of the believers who belonged to the party of the Pharisees stood up and said, 'The Gentiles must be circumcised and required to obey the law of Moses'" (v. 5). The showdown had begun.

The Judaizers had some strong arguments. There was the Old Testament law: "Any uncircumcised male . . . will be cut off from his people; he has broken my covenant" (Gen 17:14). There were Jesus' words that he had come not to destroy the law but to fulfill it. And finally, the clincher: Jesus himself, the Son of God, was circumcised. These were persuasive arguments.

Then Peter rose from his seat to speak. Peter—a man of high ups and low downs—the outspoken disciple Jesus had nicknamed "Rock" for his leadership ability; the coward who had denied Jesus three times to save his own hide. The great apostle to the Jews; the reluctant reconciler with Cornelius. The bold preacher whose public sermons had landed him in jail; the fearful wimp who had retreated from fellowship with Gentiles at Antioch. Certainly Peter's words would be crucial to the decision. But what would he say? Everyone knew what had happened at Antioch. How had he resolved his confrontation with Paul? What would rule this time—his culture or his Christ?

Behind Peter's every word were the blood, sweat and tears of his long racial pilgrimage. He recounted the story of Cornelius's conversion, then closed with this powerful conclusion: "Now then, why do you try to test God by putting on the necks of the [Gentile] disciples a yoke that neither we nor our fathers have been able to bear? No! We believe it is through the grace of our Lord Jesus that we are saved, just as they are" (Acts 15:10-11).

Amazingly, Peter's words echo Paul's angry words of rebuke at Antioch (Gal 2:14-16). Though there he had been publicly humiliated, Peter here acknowledged his wrong. His speech before the council became a healing balm for the damage done at Antioch. His Christ triumphed over his culture.

Peter could have come up with a long list of reasons to counter Paul's rebuke at Antioch. "Who are you to confront me? I lived with Jesus for three years. He gave me the keys to the kingdom. I was there with James and John at his transfiguration, and when he healed Jairus. I saw him resurrected before any of the other apostles. I'm a pillar of the church. I'm the apostle to the Jews. Who are you, Paul, to tell me what to do? Back off!" But Peter accepted Paul as his peer, listened to him and accepted his correction.

We tend to sanitize our saints. But Peter was like we are, a frail jar of clay. Ten years had passed between the conversion of Cornelius at Caesarea and Peter's separation from the Gentile believers at Antioch. It took a lifetime for Peter to be cleansed of his racial residue. If even a great committed believer like Peter had to deal with heavy racial residue, should we expect our journey to be any different?

The Path to Corporate Reconciliation
The Jerusalem Council might have ended very differently if Paul had not confronted Peter. What ultimately mattered most in this historic gathering was not issues but relationships. Behind the scenes, honesty, forgiveness and healing between individuals are what make corporate unity possible. Peter's reconciliation with the Gentile friends he wronged at Antioch was what enabled him to be a spokesman for justice at the Jerusalem Council. Individual reconciliation creates the climate for corporate justice.

The two arguments had been made: "No salvation without circumcision" and "Circumcision is culture, not Christ." With the status of the gospel and Gentile-Jewish reconciliation hanging in the balance, now it was time to let the scale tip. The church's decision? Circumcision was cultural custom, not Christian command, and was not required for salvation.

The victory for grace alone was won. The gospel of Christ was to be not a sect of Judaism but an entirely new family. And what was the result of the Jerusalem Council's decision? Writes Luke, "So the churches were strengthened in the faith and grew daily in numbers" (Acts 16:5). The victory at the Jerusalem Council was another of the church's landmark events.

"If I give all I possess to the poor and surrender my body to the flames, but have not love, I gain nothing" (1 Cor 13:3). Over and over I have seen this principle prove true: we can take the "right" side on all the issues, but without an outpouring of greater love those gains are momentary and fleeting. Looking at the victory of the Jerusalem Council I can't help but think of many of our church meetings at Voice of Calvary over the years, including the 1983 racial reconciliation meetings. Each time what has brought us to a unified direction, even after many have given up hope, is individuals' courage and willingness to resolve their conflicts one to one.

We must take heed that even as we make necessary national and churchwide efforts to bridge the gulf between black and white Christians, those attempts not replace the more difficult work of building trust at a personal level between whites and blacks. Such relationships offer the most substantive hope for our race problem, just as the work behind the scenes at the Jerusalem Council was vital in achieving a great victory.

Bridges Get Stepped On

In their efforts at reconciliation Paul and Peter were often misunderstood by both Jew and Gentile. After Cornelius's conversion Peter went back to Jerusalem and faced the angry opposition of those who didn't understand. Later he took Paul's criticism at Antioch and admitted he was wrong. Paul stood up for the Gentiles at Antioch and saw Barnabas, his comrade, oppose him. When the Judaizers visited, Paul's ministry to the Gentiles was misunderstood and maligned. Later he was perceived as an enemy to Jewish customs. At any of these moments it would have been easy for Paul to give up on keeping unity between Jew and Gentile.

Standing between the races Peter and Paul took blows from both
sides. There was constant pressure to choose one over the other. But
Peter and Paul didn't take the line of least resistance. Each broke with
his upbringing and offered a greater vision to both Jew and Gentile.

You too will find that a passion for reconciliation will often put you
in difficult situations where you'll feel walked on by both sides. Take
heart—you're in good company.

A newcomer who walked into the church after the Jerusalem Council and saw the joy shared by Jew and Gentile might have raised hands
in praise: "See what happens when we come to Christ!" But the lesson
of Acts is that oneness in Christ doesn't happen overnight. Reconciliation has to be intentionally pursued. It is hard, faithful work that overcomes separation between the races. The way was pioneered by Spirit-
filled believers who had a very clear intent to break the gospel out of
its cultural walls.

Peter's and Paul's passion for reconciliation carried them through
the tough times and developed deep godliness within each of them.
Through such a process God takes us as rough stones and rubs and
rubs us until we become precious gems. Over many years God rubbed
away the residue of those first Christians—from Jesus' upside-down
example, his marching orders to go to "all nations," the choosing of
the seven minority Greek Jews, the persecution and scattering of the
church, the bringing of the gospel to Samaria and then to the Gentile
Cornelius at Caesarea, the building of a multiracial church at Antioch,
the difficult confrontations between Judaizers and Paul, to, finally, the
great victory at the Jerusalem Council.

The first Christians' faithful response to these challenges left a
powerful example for us to follow. God has not closed the book on
landmark events. What will future church historians say about us?
That we dared to reach across our most difficult divides and resolve
our most entrenched separations? That we dared to go where no
Christians of any race had gone before?

Our journey toward reconciliation between Christians of different
races will be much like that of our forerunners in Acts. The first Christians were Spirit-filled, just as we are. Yet the residue of their heritage

still infected them, just as ours does. God was patient with them, and we must be patient with one another. But through those who were ready and those who were not, God intentionally, relentlessly and forcefully propelled the gospel forth. Eventually he got their attention. And if that is the approach of the God of history, then we too must be intentional, relentless and forceful.

14

White Fear

FEAR IS ONE OF OUR MOST CONTROLLING EMOTIONS. THE FEAR OF *failure drives many of us to work hard. The fear of being hurt drives us to seek safe places for ourselves and our loved ones. Whether the fears are justified makes very little difference to people who are afraid. Their only concern at that moment is to feel safe. Their actions are controlled by that fear.*

White fear is one factor that keeps open the gap between black and white Christians in America. For me, this fear is demonstrated when at the sight of my black skin there is a flip of a power door lock, a nervous smile, a purse drawn tightly under an arm. And the ultimate sign of white fear is the conspicuous absence of white faces in my inner-city neighborhood. White fear must be overcome if we are to be successful in bridging the gulf between blacks and whites.

In the summer of 1991 in downtown Detroit, an incident was captured on videotape. Unlike the infamous Rodney King video, this one sent chilling shock waves of fear across white America. The film showed three whites being viciously attacked by a group of black females. As I watched the footage, what captured my attention was the intense anger of the black women. Their faces, distorted with anger and hate, were reminiscent of my father's description of the faces of the white policemen who beat him back in 1970. As one of the white women struggled to get up off the ground, a black woman took the time to come back and aim one last kick at her. The video confirmed in many white Americans' minds the violent anger that they suspected blacks feel for them.

Webster's defines *fear* as "a feeling of anxiety and agitation caused by the presence or nearness of danger, evil or pain." Fear is a God-given instinct necessary for the survival of the species. All forms of life have it in some form.

One night at a state park my family was visited by a hungry raccoon. Experience had told him that he could get food from people like us. But instinct told him to keep his distance. He would eat all the food we offered him, as long as we threw it a safe distance away from us. Even though I knew we would not harm him, my intentions made no difference to him. There was no way that his instincts would allow him to eat the food out of my hand. Such healthy fear is probably one of the reasons this raccoon had lived to get as big and fat as he was.

Like the raccoon (my daughter named it Bandit), people have many different kinds of fear. The difference between us and the animals is that we were also blessed with the capacity to reason. Reason is supposed to help us distinguish between real and imaginary fears. The problem is that we don't all reason from the same life experiences. After all the years I lived in Jackson's inner city, it is reasonable for me to feel safe living there. But for most people, who see the inner city only through the sensational reports of the news media, my neighborhood is a very unreasonable place to live.

Black Male Image: Fact or Fiction?
Another cause of white fear is our society's perception of black males. If you ask any woman, black or white, "Who would you least like to see approaching you on a dark street?" if she's honest, she is likely to reply, "A black male."

Does the black male deserve this image? The answer is yes and no. From a statistical standpoint, yes. Black men make up less than 8 percent of the population of the United States, but they commit nearly 40 percent of the country's homicides (90 percent of these crimes are against other black men). But the problem with judging from these statistics is that 90 percent of black men don't fit the negative image. It is disheartening when I pull up beside a white woman at a traffic light and she reaches over and locks her door. Why can't she tell I'm one of the good guys? And yet how is she to know that I'm not one of the 10 percent of black men who maybe should be feared?

Some blame the media for creating this negative image of black men. Of course there is some truth to this. When a white man commits a heinous crime, he is just another crazy man; when a black man commits the same crime, the story seems to be more newsworthy. Somehow it seems more dramatic to show a picture of a black teenager in handcuffs than a white teenager. Still, I don't want to come down too hard on the media because that shifts the responsibility to the wrong place. When white people lock their door because they see me, I am more angry at that 10 percent of my male group than I am at the media. Even so, the media could help by shining their lights on the 90 percent who are the "good guys."

Should Whites Fear Black Anger?

The anger acted out by the young women in Detroit was symbolic of the frustration all blacks feel. Even though most blacks were embarrassed and appalled by the videotaped beating, I daresay many got a little satisfaction from viewing the film. Even though most would never admit to it, they could almost feel the pleasure of that one last "for-the-road" kick.

But though blacks have much pent-up anger and frustration, the reality is that whites have very little to fear from the anger of blacks. Outside of a few highly publicized incidents, such as the beating in Detroit and the assaulting of truck driver Reginald Denny during the Los Angeles riots, whites are not often actually the victims of black anger. Yes, whites have been victims of black violence in burglaries and robberies, but not because they are white. Blacks are the victims of these crimes ten times more often than whites. If you have been a victim of a black crime, it is probably because you were seen as an easy target, not because of your skin color.

Black anger usually explodes in response to a specific event in which they believe they were treated unjustly. So the Detroit incident was highly unusual. This attack on white women was not in response to a specific racial incident.

Many Korean businesses were burned in South Central Los Angeles because blacks were angry at a Korean store owner who had shot a thirteen-year-old black girl in the head after her back was turned. Her crime was trying to shoplift a bottle of orange juice. The shooting was captured by a video camera, but the grocer was sentenced only to probation. Such incidents build up anger in blacks because they are certain that if the situation were reversed—for example, if a black grocer shot a white or Korean teenager—the punishment would be much more severe.

Suppose Bernard Goetz, or the Korean grocer, or the four policemen who beat Rodney King, or any other whites accused of a violent crime against blacks had to face all-black juries with black judges. And suppose they all received more severe sentences than blacks who committed crimes against whites did, even when the blacks' crimes were recorded on videotape. Then whites would have reason to be afraid of blacks. Instead, the situation in our society is usually the reverse.

Some whites are afraid that if blacks ever acquire the same power that whites have, we will do to them what they did to us. That blacks would actually make the lives of whites miserable for the sake of revenge is highly doubtful. Most black leaders urge blacks to cultivate positive relationships with whites. Even Louis Farrakhan, although he believes that the white race is evil, does not advocate black revenge. I believe whites who nurture the fear of revenge are wasting their emotional energy.

Capitalizing on White Fear

As I said earlier, fear is a very powerful emotion. Playing on whites' anger and fear seems to be working well for some politicians. Buzzwords like *affirmative action* and *quotas* make temperatures rise, and everyone has an opinion. Blacks and liberal whites feel that some type of affirmative action is necessary in order to battle the "white male club." "Left to their own devices," they say, "white males will not treat women and minorities justly." Conservative whites, on the other hand, usually insist that taking proactive steps that favor minorities is nothing but reverse discrimination, even when the goal is ensuring fairness. And a few conservative blacks are now saying that affirmative action harms blacks more than it helps. Both sides have good arguments. But as we have said throughout this book, it is overwhelming to address the complexities of America's race problem outside the confines of Christianity.

This is one reason I believe that affirmative action, in the long run, will not survive. It calls one person or group to make sacrifices for the good of another. So it asks people to live by a Christian principle though they lack the motivation necessary to make the sacrifice—love for Christ. Christianity is a voluntary enterprise. Looking to the interests of someone else works best when it is a *choice* one makes.

When I discuss these sensitive issues, therefore, I begin by addressing motives—Christian motives. I tend to take seriously the opinions of people like Supreme Court justice Clarence Thomas and writer Shelby Steele on the issue of affirmative action—not because they are Christians but because their approach seems to be unselfish. If they are being forthright, they oppose affirmative action not for selfish reasons but because they feel it is doing more harm to blacks than good. This I can respect.

I have a much harder time hearing the arguments of those who oppose affirmative action for selfish reasons. We blacks know all too well what it feels like to suffer discrimination, and we wish that on no one. But for every white male who has been turned away from a job because of affirmative-action policies, there are a hundred blacks and women who have benefited from it.

As we consider affirmative action, then, let's make sure that our motives are Christian. Trying to do the best thing for the people at the bottom of our social ladder is what Jesus was all about. If through our research and discussion we determine that affirmative action is, in the long run, harming blacks instead of helping them, it will be our Christian duty to advocate trashing it and replacing it with something that is helpful.

Fear of the Racist Label

White Christians who contemplate entering into deeper relationships with blacks often fear being labeled racists for saying what they think. Racists believe they are better because of their race. This part of interracial relations is probably one of the most sensitive. If a white person makes too great an effort to appear nonracist, his or her actions could be interpreted as paternalistic (paternalism is a disguised form of racism). And if a white brother comes across as if he knows more than his black counterparts, this could also be interpreted as racist. I have seen frustrated whites nearly ready to throw in the towel because they feel caught in this Catch-22 situation.

In our experience, the problem is usually not racism or paternalism but a lack of trust. It is true that some insincere blacks, motivated by selfishness and not really interested in a mutual give-and-take relationship, will throw these charges in the face of whites in order to maintain an advantage. If you find yourself in such situations, try to work harder at building trust. If this is unsuccessful, you will have to use your own judgment about whether to persevere or to move on.

Of course there will be failures along the way of reconciliation. They are to be expected. Just be careful not to make hasty judgments. Building trust takes time. And without trust, interracial relationships are doomed to fail. One of the best ways to win trust is to demonstrate a willingness to take the back seat, and I don't mean in a car.

Once this trust is established, there will be more give and take. Those on each side must be given freedom to speak their minds. Regardless of what Chris and Phil Reed say to me, I never think they are being racist. I truly believe they want what's best for me. So when they challenge me about my weaknesses, although it hurts deeply, I have to respect what they say. Because I know they love me, I can't simply disregard their observations and say to myself, *Oh, they're just racist,* or *It's a "black thang," and they can't understand.* And when I challenge them, they don't fear that I'm just trying to get back at white people.

A relationship in which either partner can't be held accountable—in which someone is given a blanket excuse to escape confrontation—is not healthy. If this is true with blacks and whites who are peers, it is even more so with whites in relation to black children.

Jawanza Kunjufu, an expert in building self-esteem in black children, spoke at the 1991 conference of the Christian Community Development Association. As you can tell by his name, Kunjufu is problack; he insists that more black men should be involved in teaching at the lower grade levels. One concerned white person asked, "Do you believe that whites can develop black children into high achievers?"

Given Kunjufu's problack emphasis, his answer surprised many people in the audience, including some of the blacks. "I believe that a teacher's expectation of the child is the most important aspect in developing children into high achievers," he said. "A white female with high expectations of her students will be more successful than a black male with low expectations."

In some inner-city ministries, white adults assist in teaching or tutoring black youngsters. If black children are to benefit from such crosscultural contacts, trust must first be established between the black and white adults in the ministry, so that the whites will feel free to exercise firmness with the children. And whites must have the mental toughness to do what is best for the children, not what feels good. Many times white adults are so appalled by the family situations black kids come from that they cannot bring themselves to expect excellence from the children. But if contact between white adults and black children is to be helpful, it must be loving but no-nonsense. I know of several situations in which whites have treated black children like pets, never expecting them to take responsibility for their own lives. Some might say it would have been better if these children had never met a white person. Children need trust and discipline, and black children are no exception.

A New Enemy

I am convinced that much of the racism and hate that formerly prompted whites to separate themselves from blacks has now grayed into fear, anger and resentment. And we blacks need to be able to recognize the difference, even though to us these emotions look and feel nearly the same.

Attempting to fight white racism and hatred left me feeling hopeless. But a battle against fear, anger and resentment, even though these are formidable foes, gives me much more reason to hope.

Over the years Christianity has not fared well when it comes to racial issues. From his jail cell in Birmingham, Alabama, Martin Luther King Jr. voiced his disappointment over this sad reality:

> I had the strange feeling when I was suddenly catapulted into leadership of the bus protest in Montgomery several years ago that we would have the support of the white Church. I felt that white ministers, priests, and rabbis of the South would be some of our strongest allies. Instead, some have been outright opponents, refusing to understand the freedom movement and misrepresenting its leaders. . . . But in spite of my shattered dreams of the past, I came to Birmingham with the hope that the white religious leadership of this community would see the justice of our cause. . . . But again I have been disappointed.[1]

In the struggle for integration and racial equality thirty years ago, black leaders turned to the church for support. But because of fear, the American evangelical community missed a critical opportunity to demonstrate to the world the power of our gospel. Integration had to be forced on much of the country through legislation, so that many hearts were left unaffected. The results of those unchanged hearts can be seen in our separate neighborhoods, schools and churches. This is why we believe in reconciliation rather than simply integration. The difference is spiritual.

As we look for allies in this new struggle, our only hope is the gospel. Will Christianity miss another crucial opportunity to display the love of God? Or will we Christians, white and black, face our fears and take our rightful place of leadership in showing the world how racial and ethnic peace can be won?

15

More Than Skin Deep

Love without truth lies,
and truth without love kills.

EBERHARD ARNOLD, CHURCH LEADER
AND FOUNDER OF THE HUTTERIAN SOCIETY

THE CHALLENGE BEFORE US AS WHITE CHRISTIANS IS TO TRAN-
scend our fear and, by doing so, to go deeper in God's upside-down kingdom.
But normally we venture into deep waters only with those who are like us.
How can blacks and whites go more than skin-deep, beneath the fear, anger,
guilt and pain, to develop real friendships? In this chapter I want to point out
some of the roadblocks that have to be removed if trust is to grow in interracial
relationships. Such relationships are possible—if we're willing to cut below the
surface of skin color and deal honestly with the content of our character.

Keeping believers together under the pressure of Hitler's rise to
power was no easy task for Eberhard Arnold, a wise veteran of battles
for church unity. The battle for togetherness, he believed, can be won
only by the one-two punch of truth and love.

Usually we err on one side or the other when we try to deal with racial problems. Truth without love kills relationships. Watch a TV talk-show debate on race and you're likely to see a shouting match between an angry white who is tired of hearing blacks complain and a frustrated black who is sick of hearing whites deny. "Racist!" they both yell. On the flip side, love without truth is a lie. We'll pat each other on the back, mask our differences with warm fuzzies, sing "red and yellow, black and white, we are precious in his sight," and praise the Lord that "we're all one in Christ." Charles King, who led racism seminars throughout America, started his work in churches because he believed people would listen there. But King found that white Christians wouldn't talk honestly about their racial attitudes in the pews and sanctuaries of the church. He stopped giving his seminars in churches.

Neither love nor truth alone takes us further than the color of our skin—one papers over our differences with the lie that race makes absolutely no difference, while the other allows race to make so much difference that we can't learn from each other.

Alone, truth is powerless to heal. And love alone is equally powerless. Brought together, however, they become spiritual dynamite that can break down walls.

In the summer of 1983, after a particularly emotional meeting between blacks and whites in Jackson, I didn't know how much more I could give to those relationships. Stripping away my racial blinders was painful. I needed to hear the passion of black people, to understand their scars, to have my superior attitudes unmasked. But these truths would have killed my relationships with black brothers and sisters if they hadn't grabbed me and held on. Their love enabled me to accept hard truths about myself.

Doing Surgery on Each Other

A doctor can't do open-heart surgery on you unless you're willing to get onto the operating table, allow him to cut beneath the skin and expose your most sensitive and vital organs to his healing knife. You do it only if you trust the surgeon.

"Racial reconciliation," maintained Tom Skinner, "is whites and blacks holding on to each other, not letting go, and doing surgery on each other." Reconciliation requires exposing our vital organs to the truth that we speak to each other. It's risky. If trust hasn't been built, the operation is destined to fail. But when we build trust and stay on the table to the end of the surgery, there is hope for healing in the most delicate and vital places of our racial residue.

There is a little voice in a black person's head that whispers words of skepticism about the motives of whites. *What's in it for her?* she wonders when a white person reaches out to her. Black people suspect that when the rubber meets the road, we'll retreat to our benefits and options. When the racial issue gets personally costly, white folks will go their own way. Because of this fear of getting burned, blacks avoid making themselves vulnerable.

A revealing public-television documentary called *The Color of Our Skin* tells the story of one class in the Defense Equal Opportunity Management Institute, the U.S. military's school to promote interracial understanding. In one small interracial group, soldiers meet every day for three months to discuss their racial attitudes. The black group leader, Evelyn Johnson, becomes fast friends with a white sailor, Kelly Anderson, who makes a special effort to develop rapport with minority-group members. While other classmates deny that racism still exists, Anderson boldly speaks to the entire school about the oppression of blacks. Later, group members are asked to choose the classmate they feel closest to, and Anderson and Johnson pick each other. But another black soldier warns Johnson that when things get hard, whites will turn their back on you. Johnson assures him that she is a good judge of character. She likes and trusts Anderson.

Several weeks later, however, in the midst of a heated discussion, the conversation gets around to a subject that brings Anderson's previously submerged prejudices to the surface. Anderson denies that he has advantages because he is white and responds defensively with a "We made it—why can't you?" attitude.

Johnson is stunned as Anderson's feelings of superiority surface. This other side to her white friend puts up a sudden wall of mistrust. When school closes, the two former friends awkwardly shake hands and say goodbye. "I felt like Anderson just left me stranded," Johnson reflects sadly. "I told one of the other blacks, 'I don't want you to tell me I told you so.' "

Trying to survive but afraid of getting burned, many blacks wear a mask around whites. A white person will often feel very warmly accepted by black people. Walk into any black church on Sunday morning, and the folks are likely to seat you at the front and go out of their way to make you feel welcome. "See how well we get along," you marvel.

But the basis of this comfort is an unspoken rule: Don't talk race. I've heard whites say about a black person, "John doesn't seem black." We label black people either "safe" or "dangerous." A black woman in New York City admits, "I have as many white friends as black, but my white friends and I don't talk about race, because when we do, we get testy."[1] As long as blacks stay on the "safe" topics, they're okay. But racial experiences and attitudes are marked "No Trespassing." If that is the price blacks must pay, we're asking them to be dishonest in order to be our friends.

In *The Content of Our Character*, Shelby Steele describes this interracial dynamic as "bargaining." Writing of Bill Cosby's popular TV show, he says bargaining

> may have something to do with the [white] public's gratitude at being offered a commodity so rare in our time; he tells his white viewers each week that they are okay, and that this black man is not going to challenge them. When a black bargains, he may invoke the gratitude factor and find himself cherished beyond the measure of his achievement; when he challenges, he may draw the dark projections of whites and become a source of irritation to them.[2]

At times in a discussion with a black friend, he and I have seen an issue differently, and he has said to me, "Well, it's a 'black thang'; of course you wouldn't understand." True, I can't understand fully. I'm not in their shoes. As a white I'll never face the same struggles. But that attitude puts up an immediate wall, implying that we can't learn from each other. It's as if I've been typecast in a role: "You are a representative of the white race and its undeniable record of wrong." I'm not Chris anymore, but "White Male." Rather than being respected for myself, I am locked into my corporate identity. My race becomes more important than our relationship.

In such situations it is vital for whites to understand the distrust and to keep working to win trust in spite of the wall. Meanwhile, blacks need to strive to keep opening up in spite of their fears of becoming vulnerable.

Being Honest About Cultural Differences

Throughout this book we have emphasized that interracial relationships must be approached as crosscultural challenges. If you were going to China to build relationships with Chinese, you'd learn the language, read up on Chinese history and do all you could to prepare yourself to cross the cultural barriers. You'd bend over backward to appreciate and learn from the cultural differences between North Americans and Chinese. You have to be willing to do the same in the arena of white and black.

Rather than being points of conflict, our cultural differences should become opportunities to learn from and enrich one another. My version of Woody Harrelson in the movie *White Men Can't Jump* would have to be "White Men Can't Sing, Clap and Rock at the Same Time." It took me a couple of church-choir practices to realize why I was so tired at the end: trying to adjust to the different musical style, I was singing nearly every song at the top of my lungs. (Joanie later taught me that yelling is not the way to get a good sound, but it sure felt like it at first.) On top of that, I had to learn how to rock back and forth with the other choir members, while still singing. But wait, that's not all. I had to clap, too, and still sing and rock! (After ten years I still can't consistently do all three.) And then I discovered that the clapping was on the wrong—whoops! I mean a different—beat. Whites clap on one and three, blacks on two and four.

Our black members have learned to enjoy singing songs from my culture too. And then there are the "in-between" songs—beautiful melodies written and recorded by whites that we sing with a special black gospel flavor. Each culture enriches the other.

It goes much deeper than a white person's learning how to rock, sing and clap at the same time. There are other cultural differences that took me a while to understand and affirm. I was raised to be controlled and polite, not expressing my opinions until I had them completely formed in my head. As I began to get involved at VOC, I noticed that blacks displayed a heatedness and an honesty that made me uncomfortable. At first I saw this as just another unspiritual dimension to black anger. But I began to appreciate that they were better at getting honest issues and emotions into the open.

To blacks, whites often look phony and insincere. It looks as if we're not giving our all. "Be for real!" they say. The white style, however, favors stroking each other and not letting things get out of control. We sacrifice some honesty in favor of keeping things respectable and polite.

Which is better: honesty that gets everything right on the table or affirmation that makes everybody feel good? Well . . . both! In fact, each style has a strength and a weakness. It would be healthy to develop a hybrid of the two that more closely reflects our biblical mandate to "speak the truth in love."

Dealing with Black Anger

Understanding black anger is one of the most difficult challenges for whites. In chapter seven Spencer talked about the bitterness most black people feel toward whites. Inability to endure that sharpness has led many whites to cut off their attempts at reconciliation.

My ears had an automatic off-switch when blacks started to raise their voices. My reasoning was, "This kind of anger is ungodly. So if you can't express your feelings better, I'm quitting this conversation." This reasoning began to develop into a justification for leaving certain relationships behind. After all, how could I be expected to build a relationship with someone who was so angry with me?

Over one late-night breakfast bar with Spencer, Nancy and Donna, I admitted my frustration with some angry statements I'd heard from blacks. Spencer and Nancy gently responded, referring to South Africa's then-insidious apartheid system: "But Chris, South African

whites say, 'We can't negotiate with blacks until they stop using violence.' But why are the blacks violent? Violence is not a spiritual
response, but it's a reaction to real sin and killing and injustice against
them. They're trying to get the whites' attention." They had a point.
Either the angry blacks were seeing racial ghosts, or they were react-
ing to some real problem.

I began looking beneath the anger to the hurt behind it. As I grew
to know black people more deeply, I realized that their anger came
from personal wounds—experiences in which they had suffered
wrong—and just plain weariness with being black in a white world.

It also helped to remember the many times I had disagreed with a
situation and had gone "to the top" to protest. I would tell myself
beforehand, "Okay, I'm not going to get angry. I'm going to be calm."
But at the first sign of disagreement, I would start raising my voice and
getting red in the face. But the other person would sit patiently and
watch me blow up. It was easy for him not to get angry, to be reasonable, patient, cool. Why? Because he had the power. It didn't take long
for me to get frustrated with someone who had power but who didn't
admit to a problem that was clearly visible to me.

Understanding anger as a response to wrong helped me to see how it
can be a very positive, even godly characteristic. "Man's anger does not
bring about the righteous life that God desires," says the Scripture (Jas
1:20). Human anger is quick-tempered, self-serving and vengeful. But
remember—God gets angry too! Says the prophet Nahum, "The LORD is
slow to anger and great in power . . . Who can withstand his indignation?
Who can endure his fierce anger?" (Nahum 1:3, 6). It's God's anger that
we must emulate, not the anger of human beings. God's anger is righteous indignation directed not at a person, but at sin and injustice. So if
God gets indignant, it must be okay for us as well. Like God's, our anger
must be tempered by mercy and aimed at injustice and sin.

But sometimes blacks use their anger as an ungodly weapon.
"White folks have hurt me all my life. Now I'm going to hurt them
back. I'm never going to reach out." Anger is used to keep whites at
arm's length, or as a defense to keep from being hurt. Black anger
holds great power over guilt-stricken whites. We may become overly

sensitive to any charge a black person makes.

At one time I supervised a black man who resisted any direction from me. There were times I called him on the carpet for being late to work or not getting an assignment done on time. Whenever I did this, he complained that I treated him differently from the white employees. His challenges caused me to do a lot of soul-searching. It's not easy to know your deep-down motives sometimes. But I concluded that I wasn't treating him more harshly. I was seeking excellence, while he was trying to use race to avoid accountability.

Black people need to receive truth from whites too. They need to be able to listen and not label us racist when we say that the vacuum of committed, skilled leadership in the inner city can no longer be blamed on white flight alone but also on "green flight"—the departure of black middle-class people who are seeking a better life. You need to allow us palefaces to exhort you in areas of spiritual and cultural weakness, just as you speak to our lives about racism. It's kingdom culture we're after, not blackness or whiteness.

Relationships of trust can't be built from a motivation of guilt. Ultimately a black and a white can't be peers if the white is operating out of guilt. Guilt harms our attempts to build long-term relationships. It can provide a burst of energy to win a hundred-yard dash but not the sustained endurance necessary to tackle a marathon. When things get difficult, we'll say, "Well, I tried and it didn't work. No use feeling guilty anymore."

One white person in our racial reconciliation meetings was the "amen corner" for all the negative feelings black people voiced. While there was certainly some genuineness to his allegiance, an undercurrent of guilt ran through many of his reactions and remarks. His statements just didn't seem genuine. Within a few years, this person had slowly drifted away from his black friends. Now he has retreated to an all-white world.

Persevering Through Pain

Lem Tucker, late president of VOC Ministries (he died of cancer in 1989), created a motto that he tried to live by: "He who has the greatest truth must also have the greatest love, which is the greatest proof." Because he was my boss and I am a hardheaded person, our discussions were often heated. My last memory of Lem is several days before he was admitted to the hospital. We had finished a long, difficult meeting, and I was demoralized and drained. Lem dropped in unannounced at my house. "I just came," he said, "to make sure everything is okay between us. I don't have all the answers, but our relationship is important to me, and I want you to know that." We talked for a few minutes, affirmed our commitment to one another and hugged. I knew that Lem and I were on the same road together, though as we journeyed we often argued about the best way to reach our destination.

One of the deepest qualities of love, says Paul in 1 Corinthians 13:7, is that it "always perseveres." You can't back away from that white sister when she disappoints you. You can't walk out on that black brother when he reveals his pent-up bitterness. We have to accept that sometimes we're going to disappoint each other, hurt each other, say the wrong thing. Blacks have to hold on and allow whites to be honest about where we're at. We shouldn't be penalized for not understanding and asking to be educated. Blacks shouldn't be penalized for taking off their survival masks. For sharing their scars. For not wanting to give up their culture.

If Donna and I kept tallies of the times we were wronged by the other, each of us could probably say, "I'm getting the short end of the stick." But because we've made vows for life, times of hurt and misunderstanding have become times of growth in our marriage. In the area of interracial relationships, the principles behind marriage vows have a powerful application. "In sickness and in health"—when we're happy with each other, and when we're disappointed and hurt. "For richer or poorer"—when I get my way, and when I give up for the sake of the other. "Till death do us part"—disappointments and hurts don't go unaddressed, because we're in it for life. Either we ignore problems and our relationship deteriorates, or we work them through to unity and our relationship grows.

Keeping racial scorecards will leave both sides thinking they're on the losing end. It's in the spirit of the marriage commitment that we need to heal our relationships. For there will be times of joy and victory but also disappointment and pain. The basic commitment of "in sickness and health," "for richer or poorer," "till death do us part" enables us to go into it for the long haul. For whites, this commitment is the only way we can earn the trust of our black brothers and sisters. For blacks, it's the only way to learn to trust us.

In our workshops Spencer often recounts his difficult experiences to help whites understand why black people get angry. His mother was present during one of these talks, and afterward she stood up and softly began recounting some of her most painful experiences at the hands of white people. There were those civil-rights days in Mendenhall, when every morning as she turned the car key, she wondered if the car might blow up. "But I'm not angry anymore," she said. Then there was the time her husband was nearly beaten to death by white patrolmen. "But still I'm not angry anymore," Mrs. Perkins repeated. Finally, she told us how as a girl, she and her family were hauled up to the Mississippi Delta's cotton fields, "like cattle," she said, to pick cotton on the plantations owned by whites. "But you know, I'm not angry anymore."

As Mrs. Perkins sat down, a white man, John Anderson, stood. His voice choked as he turned to Mrs. Perkins and spoke a personal confession, "My grandfather was one of those farm owners." John told about growing up in the Delta and accepting the wrongs as "the way things were." Many years later, as a middle-aged adult, he had read the book Black like Me, which opened his eyes. Eventually this white Mississippian found his way to an interracial Mississippi church, Voice of Calvary Fellowship, and devoted himself to a new relationship with black people.

Mrs. Perkins had every right to be angry. Over the years she has struggled with this anger. But through it all God has given her the grace to forgive. As is true of so many of my black brothers and sisters, God has transformed her anger into passion—a passion for whites to understand the pain and commit ourselves to reconciliation. John's confession said, "I do understand. I was part of the system that hurt you. At the time I didn't realize how hurtful it was. But now your passion for justice has become my passion too." By the grace of John's God, he, like many of my white brothers and sisters, has been able to strip off his blinders, receive forgiveness and join black Christians in a common mission.

In relationships of one-to-one trust is our hope for healing. Our most vital organs have been polluted with the residue of race. As we go more than skin-deep to do surgery on each other, we can become God's agents not only for the painful work of cutting and repairing but also for recovery and healing.

16

Soul Mates

THROUGHOUT THIS BOOK WE HAVE ENCOURAGED CHRISTIANS TO *create environments in which interracial relationships can develop and be nurtured. These intentional settings are a must if we are to learn understanding and if we are to witness to the unbelieving world a racial harmony that is achieved by the power of our gospel.*

But the more this happens, the more we will have to face a fear that is deeply rooted in our psyche. Some say it is our ultimate fear, and therefore reconciliation's greatest obstacle. Others maintain that until it becomes a "nonissue" we will not have passed the final test of our fragile racial harmony.

To be honest, from the time we began talking about writing this book, Chris and I wrestled with how or even whether we should bring up this issue. From a marketing perspective, I suppose bringing it into the open could be considered unwise. But because we are committed to calling forth groups of believers who can witness to the world the oneness found only in Christ, we are obliged to discuss the issues that will surely spring out of our newfound oneness.

Like me, she sang tenor in the choir, so on occasion she sat beside me. The first time I really noticed Nancy, the source of my impending travail, she was having an intense conversation with someone else about her experiences in Nicaragua. Since I had just spent three enlightening weeks in Kenya, her experience interested me. So we set up a time to compare notes.

As I got to know Nancy, I was overwhelmed by the depth of her character. She was a very intelligent woman, but her intelligence was cloaked in humility. Her servant attitude came not out of weakness but out of strength. This was an enigma to me, and I had to know more about it.

The quality that sparked me to think long-term was Nancy's gentle spirit. The more I talked to her, the more impressed I was and the more I struggled. This was a woman, it seemed, with whom I could easily spend the rest of my life. But there was one great barricade that read plainly, in big bold letters, DETOUR. Nancy is white.

I still remember a conversation I'd had several months earlier with Lem Tucker, then executive director of Voice of Calvary Ministries. We'd talked for hours about the vanishing black male role model and the importance of strong black families. We'd agreed that we black men needed to marry black women in order to build healthy black Christian families. Many interracial couples, we noted, are lured by the social taboo and consequently build their relationship on a shallow, sick physical attraction.

Conversations like this one were an ongoing part of life at VOC. If there was one thing that was consistent about VOC, it was that we didn't skirt tough issues.

Now I realized that if I pursued my relationship with Nancy, I would become a black man who was not doing his part for our race. How would I answer the charges that would surely follow—that I was just like other sick black men who wanted to have a white woman? I ached over this dilemma, wrestling with my conflicting ideals. Of course God was bigger than race, but what was my responsibility? I had been in love with several women before and had had thoughts of marrying more than one of them. But this time there was no doubt in my mind. Nancy was the one. She was my "soul mate."

Why would God do this to me? Why did she have to be white? Which of my ideals was most important?

It had been drilled into my family that God is no respecter of persons—that in the body of Christ there is neither Jew nor Greek. Asked what Jesus would say about interracial relationships, very few Christians would dare say that he would condemn them. Still, we have to live in the real world. We need strong black families. The black community is suffering from a lack of black male leadership.

Finally, there was the practical warning that came to me from more than one source, and this argument probably tugged at me harder than the others: "Any ministry you are involved in will suffer if you marry Nancy. Your relationship will turn off blacks and whites, Christians and non-Christians. You will compromise your credibility as a black leader." These were the conflicting realities that tore at me as I attached my heart and soul to Nancy.

As I look back now, I'm afraid that I acted selfishly and chose the individual happiness of marrying my "soul mate" over my responsibility to my race. To this day I have never resolved all these issues in my mind, and I will not dismiss them in an attempt to justify my actions. Some questions will always remain.

Sadly, some will conclude that my marriage to Nancy is a personal judgment on the quality and character of black women. Although this could not be further from the truth, I understand the emotions beneath this response. I will always have to live with the fact that my marriage says different things to different people.

Did I marry Nancy to make a statement on racial reconciliation? Definitely not. I married her because I couldn't bear the thought of not doing it.

Interracial marriage is considered by many to be the ultimate fear behind resistance to integration and racial reconciliation. And at times our marriage does get in the way of a meaningful discussion of the issues. If I had known that God was planning to lead me into this ministry of reconciliation, I don't think I would have considered interracial marriage a possibility.

But God has a way of equipping us with the tools necessary to carry out the mission he calls us to. And he sometimes uses even weaknesses like self-interest to cement our wills to his purpose.

Let me explain. It seems to me that many people accept Jesus Christ, expecting that God will then be on their side, sanctioning their causes and blessing their endeavors. A particularly strong incentive for seeking salvation is to escape from hell to the paradise of heaven. These are selfish motivations that are contrary to the kingdom principles Jesus taught. But God seems to allow them to get us started on the discipleship process. So in this case, he uses one of our most intense weaknesses, self-interest, for his good and ours. And I've found this to be true about my marriage to Nancy.

Making Race Personal

One of the principles we stress whenever we talk about racial reconciliation is the importance of one-to-one relationships. One-to-one relationships are crucial because of the way human beings are put together. When our family members, friends or loved ones are hurting, we hurt right along with them. The intensity of our pain is in direct proportion to the depth of our love. If we aren't close to them, their pain doesn't bother us as much. So the people who will be most committed to racial reconciliation are the people for whom it has become a personal issue. Deep crosscultural friendships help make reconciliation personal for us.

In 1991 Nancy's sister and brother-in-law adopted a beautiful black baby named Katherine. Their reason was simply that Katherine needed a home, and they could give her a stable one. Now their lives are forever bound to hers. Therefore, now when they see racial inequities, it is no longer in the abstract; they see little Katherine's face. Sometimes they have taken a stand if doing so improved Katherine's lot in life. I suppose someday Chris and Michael, Katherine's older white brothers, will have to defend her in the normal brotherly ways, but also because she is black. The more harmony this family can foster between the races, the richer Katherine's life will be. For them race will forever be personal.

My father, who sometimes catches me by surprise with his keen perceptions, made an interesting remark as we traveled in New Zealand to encourage racial reconciliation between the Maori and whites. "If you look for the people who have the greatest commitment to racial reconciliation," he said, "many of them are interracial couples. It is true here in New Zealand, and it's true in Australia. These couples have more passion about the issue because they don't want to be forced to choose sides. They want their children to be able to enjoy the best of both cultures." Interracial couples have more at stake. Their immediate worlds are deeply affected for good by racial harmony and affected negatively by racial strife.

Even in the secular world self-interest can give extra inspiration to the quest for racial harmony. After I read Shelby Steele's *The Content of our Character*, a passionate plea for racial understanding, I was not surprised to find in it a brief description of his family life what is undoubtedly a source of his passion: "We are the only black family in our suburban neighborhood, and even this claim to specialness is diminished by the fact that my wife is white."[1]

God in his wisdom takes our self-interest and uses it for his good purposes. White people don't necessarily have to think about race. But because Nancy is married to me and we have three biracial children who are black in the eyes of most of the world, she is very passionate and sensitive about race issues. Whenever our children are called the "N-word," Nancy will probably feel the pain more intensely than they do. This is as personal as it gets.

The same is true for Chris, Donna and other white brothers and sisters in our body. Their deep commitment to me and to other black members of our church makes them ache whenever they see us hurt by the racial callousness of our society. Likewise, when we blacks detect the pain of rejection from other blacks on the faces of our white brothers and sisters, we are moved to ease it.

This, I believe, is the point Paul was making when he said, "If one part [of the body] suffers, every part suffers with it; if one part is honored, every part rejoices with it" (1 Cor 12:26). When we become one family, the pain of each other's hurts and the joy of each other's triumphs become personal.

Hard Questions

In spite of the way God has used my relationship with Nancy for the good, I'm still convinced that the guts of racial reconciliation will have to be worked out between black men and white men, black women and white women. Gender is a wild card that can become confusing in the discussion of racial reconciliation.

Frightened Christians with nightmares of interracial marriages breaking out everywhere if we achieve greater racial harmony often ask Nancy and me, "Do you promote interracial marriages?" Our first inclination is to say no, even though our very presence contradicts that response. Our hesitation comes from a fear that people will be distracted by that issue.

For many educated, upwardly mobile black women, this issue is extremely volatile given the critical shortage of marriageable black men. For these women, the question of interracial marriage is much more than an abstract sociological discussion. It is personal.

If you combine all the black men who are in prison or on parole, figure in those who are gay, add those involved in the drug culture as users or sellers, then consider those who are undereducated and unable to hold down a decent job, it's all too clear that finding a desirable man is a challenge for black women. The last thing they figure they need is to lose some of the remaining men to white women.

Even though my four sisters love Nancy and me deeply, they sometimes complain to us about the unfairness of the situation. And some black women who have for years been diehard idealists—opposed in principle to interracial marriage—are beginning to wonder if interracial relationships could be a solution after all to the dearth of marriageable black men.

But there's another reason Nancy and I are inclined to say no, we don't promote interracial marriage. We have seen too many interracial romances that are unhealthy—two people who have come together because they were not supposed to, because they were turned on by the stereotypical taboos, because they were curious about each other or just to be rebellious and to make a statement. Spike Lee calls it "jungle fever." A good marriage can't be built on such a foundation.

Several times Nancy and I have been approached by starry-eyed young people who are involved in an interracial relationship. Their youthful passion can deafen them to wise counsel. We generally urge them to take their time—Nancy and I were both approaching thirty when we were married. But if the relationship is healthy, if both people know who they are, if the costs unique to the building of this particular house have all been counted (a very difficult calculation for two people in love)—then let those who know better than God judge this couple; we will simply ask God's blessing.

Family Issues

Nancy and I have been blessed. Our relationship was born and nurtured in the protective environment of an interracial church that is committed to racial reconciliation. We both come from families who take their Christianity seriously. At the beginning we weren't sure whether the Jesus in our family members would win out over the embarrassment of having a family member betray their race, but it didn't take long for their faith to shine through. The support and love we've received have been a blessing that we are unable to measure. And there's no question that our positive experience colors our answer to the question of interracial marriage.

Although I will probably always wrestle to reconcile my various ideals regarding interracial marriage, the human debate is not a quandary in the mind of God. The twelfth chapter of Numbers gives us a clear indication of how God views interracial relationships. "Miriam and Aaron began to talk against Moses because of his Cushite wife, for he had married a Cushite. 'Has the LORD spoken only through Moses?' they asked. 'Hasn't he also spoken through us?' And the LORD heard this" (vv. 1-2). Moses' leadership was being challenged because of his choice of a wife. In the minds of Miriam and Aaron, because Moses had married outside of his race, his commitment to his people—his credibility—was in question.

In the Bible, Cush is the name applied to the land we now call Ethiopia. The people of Ethiopia are black. So Moses had married a black woman, and the discussion between his brother Aaron and his sister

Miriam is still taking place today. But to God the nationality or color of Moses' wife was a nonissue. God rebuked and punished Miriam and Aaron for speaking against Moses; he affirmed Moses' leadership.

God doesn't put too much stock in any of the human traits we are so quick to take pride in or take offense at—traits we weren't responsible for getting in the first place. And so Moses, who had a biracial family, is one of the best role models and celebrated leaders in the Bible.

For Nancy's family, a secure, middle-class Mennonite clan from mostly white Pennsylvania Dutch country, race has now become a personal issue. For my father and mother, who have taught the biblical truths of racial reconciliation throughout the nation, my marriage to Nancy challenged the depth of their commitment to those truths— and the truth won out. We have heard sad stories from several interracial couples who have had to sacrifice the love of their families because of their marriage. We are extremely grateful not to have experienced this pain. I am not sure if I could serve the God of our parents if that God did not allow enough room in their hearts for us. So it makes Nancy and me proud to proclaim to the world that the God of our fathers and mothers is indeed the God of our own family. Yet the struggle to reconcile our ideals continues.

17

Unlikely Comrades

It's weird. But it's a good kinda weird.

CECIL MCKINLEY

T HE RICH RELATIONSHIPS WE ENJOY AT VOICE OF CALVARY ARE THE *fruit of many years of single-minded work to build friendships between blacks and whites. My friendship with Spencer began in a small group that formed after the racial reconciliation meetings. As we faced new challenges together, we found that God had much beyond black and white issues for us to learn from one another.*

God is a matchmaker of unlikely relationships. Only Jesus would take a Black Panther Zealot like Simon and an Uncle Tom tax collector like Matthew and make them brothers in the new family of his disciples. Only God can take centuries-long antagonists—the descendants of former slaves and former slaveowners—and make them comrades in the family of the kingdom.

In July of 1984 our small Bible-study group—half black and half white—sat in Spencer and Nancy's living room at 321 Valley Street and

bared our souls and our fears. We had been meeting every week for a
year. We had taken many steps together—weekly one-to-one meetings,
group retreats, pooling 5 percent of our income to help meet the
needs of our neighbors. And we had finished studying the Sermon on
the Mount.

Our common fear was that our next step in response to our study
might involve rearranging the very structure of our lives. Joanie
summed it up: "If God is calling us to give up more, and if we're willing
to, I'll do it . . . But do I have to give up my purple comforter too?" We all
doubled over laughing—we were scared and excited at the same time.

The unity in this room was in sharp contrast to the atmosphere of a
gathering in another room, only thirteen months earlier and a few
blocks away, where the racial reconciliation meetings had taken place.
That night I had wondered whether I had any future with black people at all.

God had brought me—each of us in the group, in fact—a mighty
long way since that night of despair. We had hung in with each other
long enough to see that beneath the bitterness, anger and fear, we
shared some dreams about being the people of God. Just knowing that
the group accepted me, in spite of my weaknesses, was healing. Our
focus embraced our racial diversity; we had chosen for ourselves the
name Antioch, the city in which the New Testament's first fully multiracial church was born. But our growing direction transcended the
race issue. A motley gang of unlikely comrades were trying to find a
way to follow Jesus together as we had never done before.

We approached the task of forming an intentional community as a
test of our faith in God. There were only so many times we individually could see ourselves falling short. If we were willing, uniting our
lives and pooling our resources could free up our time and money to
be used more creatively for the kingdom. Either we would take the risk
or we'd settle for less than what we knew was possible. Several times
we came up against this wall and backed away for lack of faith.

Finally, in December of 1985 we decided to look for a house to buy
and move into. Two weeks later, God made us put our money where
our mouth was when an ideal property came on the market: two large

houses on six acres of open land, right in the middle of our target neighborhood. By the end of the summer we were living in these two houses together and pooling our individual incomes in a common purse. We shared meals, renovated the houses and even freed one person up to do full-time youth ministry in the neighborhood.

In 1992 six adults (three black and three white) and four children celebrated six years of life together. Antioch's sixth year was also my eleventh year at Voice of Calvary. Looking back I saw how God had moved me one step at a time. From the comfortable womb of my culture I had come to a community in which I was part of a minority. But I hadn't really known these black people alongside whom I lived, worked and worshiped. Through the racial reconciliation meetings my blinders had been stripped away. I had begun to see the cost of reconciliation, that it required more work and commitment from me. Then God had provided another womb of belonging: Antioch. As blacks had become my friends, a strange thing had begun to happen. The more we trusted each other, the less race was an issue. Not only did I allow black people to speak to my life and weaknesses, but I had earned enough trust to speak to theirs.

Few Christians will ever attempt to form an intentional community, and certainly not everyone is called to it. But we can all experience this joy of seeing how, when we deal honestly with our racial differences, trust is built. And when we win the trust that says, "I know you have my best interest at heart," racial differences take a back seat to issues of character. On the other side of our racial residue is the richness of building up, edifying and encouraging each other.

Contending with Character

Some friends have become special comrades. "How good and pleasant it is when brothers live together in unity!" rejoiced David (Ps 133:1). Having experienced the deep joy of my camaraderie with Spencer, I've decided that David had more than friendship in mind. Except for Donna, I don't think I've ever been as united with another person as I am with Spencer. Dr. King dreamed that one day his children would be judged "not by the color of their skin but by the content of their character." This is what Spencer and I have experienced: true reconciliation, relating not on the basis of our race but on the basis of our character.

Before I knew Spencer, I feared his blackness. I know he would not have respected or trusted me if I hadn't worked through that fear. I wouldn't trust him if I thought he would throw race at me when we disagree. But he wouldn't dream of saying, "Chris, it's a 'black thang.' You wouldn't understand." As we have proved ourselves, character has become more important than race. We contend with each other's character and help each other be better disciples.

It's pretty hard to get us confused with each other in person. But our lives are so intertwined that often people, even close friends, will call me "Spencer" on the phone and refer to him as "Chris." We work together. Our children almost think they're brothers and sisters. We have traveled together throughout the country. Neither of us is a great speaker. But because relationships between black men and white men are the most difficult and the least seen, when we speak, our relationship shows that reconciliation is possible. You can dismiss an idea but not a demonstration.

There are many situations I couldn't have endured without Spencer. Once he was out of town, and I was going through some real pain in a situation. I couldn't sleep. I had headaches. I had to take long walks to hold myself together. Donna did her best to help, but because of the nature of the situation she couldn't get directly involved. Once Spencer got back in town, I was like a tag-team wrestler desperately stretching out my hand in exhaustion to send my teammate into the fray: "It's your turn to take the point. I can't go any longer; now you go and get 'em."

Our strengths and weaknesses complement each other. I'll go into a meeting vowing not to get mad, and lose my temper one minute after the opening prayer; Spencer is steady and composed. I am a superorganized pragmatist; Spencer is a visionary who misses meetings because he didn't write them on his calendar. I'm impatient with people; Spencer's strong opinions belie a softie who patiently hangs in with people who hurt him or who fall short. There are people I would have given up on long ago, but I can't, because Spencer keeps holding on to them.

Naturally, we have to put work into our friendship. I'm impatient, so I get more upset with Spencer than he does with me. I'm more ambitious; he's more humble. Sometimes he's too laid-back. But we know these things about each other and talk about them.

As long as we've worked together, Spencer and I have been committed to being a team of equals, to representing a new model of leadership based on unity and interracial witness. It's an unfamiliar concept, and often people in search of a "bottom line" look to Spencer. At one point in our working together, I began to feel as if we were more like Batman and Robin than Butch Cassidy and the Sundance Kid.

Why does he get all the credit and attention? I thought. *Don't they know that we're in this together, that each of us is indispensable?* It was pure ol' envy and jealousy.

It was difficult confessing to Donna how I felt. I was even more embarrassed when I admitted my feelings to Spencer. But we had to work it through. After we talked for an hour, we both acknowledged how smart God is. He seemed to have our sanctification well in hand: for Spencer, who doesn't warm up quickly to new people, God was opening the doors too fast; for me, more eager and ambitious, God was cracking the doors too slowly. He had both of us where we needed to be.

When you're devoted to a common direction, you can't have hidden agendas. You can't give mistrust or misunderstanding a foothold. Everything has to be on the table and dealt with.

I believe in racial reconciliation because of what camaraderie with blacks like Spencer has meant to my life. The biblical conviction that the breach between blacks and whites needed to be healed was the first seed. But what has watered and pruned the plant of reconciliation into maturity is the fact that black people have helped me become a better disciple of Christ.

I was a know-it-all spiritual infant when I arrived at VOC. Black people brought me down to earth. At VOC I saw a lived-out Christianity that attracted me to follow Jesus deeper. It's in a black neighborhood, at a black-led ministry, in an interracial church that I have learned the Bible. VOC gave me the greatest gift—my wife—and taught and showed me how to love her.

By their example, black people have discipled me. From Lem Tucker I learned integrity. From Sam Pollard I learned a passion for prayer. From Mr. and Mrs. Govan I learned compassion and encouragement. From Gloria Lotts I learned to love children. From Joanie Perkins I learned to get my real feelings out in the open. From Derek Perkins I learned how to be a discipler.

Yes, there are white people too—Donna, Nancy, Phil and Marcia Reed, Phil and Tressa Eide. These friends, too, give Voice of Calvary, and especially black people, much of the credit for their spiritual growth. And it is reciprocal. My black brothers and sisters would say the same about their relationships with me and other whites.

When the chips are down, VOC people have come through for me and my family. Before we were married, when Donna and her housemates were terrorized by a man who entered their home, VOC people gathered around her and helped her through it. When Donna's uncle died, the whole church stopped and prayed for us. When we first tried to conceive a child and couldn't, we felt deeply cared for and prayed for. Being far from our families is difficult. But Mr. and Mrs. Govan are like grandparents to us. Our son, Benjamin, has many "brothers" and "sisters," "aunts" and "uncles."

The funny thing is, racial reconciliation isn't just about what we miss in not solving a racial problem. The issue is what we miss about knowing God and about living out the gospel when we are not reconciled.

There is a great paradox here. While we are called to die to our selfish interests, it's not until we put our own interests at stake that we really begin to "prove neighbor" to our racial counterparts. When we become comrades, we have a personal stake in enriching each other's lives because they're so wrapped up together.

A Good Kinda Weird

We've been blessed and humbled to see that the rich quality of life we experience is a light to others. In the spring of 1990 Antioch decided to be a host family for an inmate on a community-service project for Prison Fellowship. We requested a black inmate, reasoning that such a person would feel more comfortable in our interracial home. Parents got the children primed for our coming guest, his room was readied, and we eagerly anticipated his arrival.

When our guest arrived, we were shocked. "I'm Cecil McKinley," he slowly drawled, in one of the thickest white Southern accents I'd ever heard. Cecil was from rural Sumrall, Mississippi. This fact did not win any points with our black members, who admit to bearing scars from childhoods spent in small Mississippi towns. When Cecil saw our rainbow-colored household, his eyes widened as if he were seeing a strange new species of animal. The adults exchanged nervous glances, summing up our predicament without a word being said: "Y'all, this is going to be a real long two weeks . . ."

For two weeks Cecil was immersed in our life. He ate with us at the dinner table, came to church and joined Donna and me in a "Kids' Night Out." He even came to VOC choir practice with us, holding one-year-old Jessica Pollard, her black fingers twined in his white fingers, as our choir members belted out black gospel songs. We began to enjoy Cecil's outgoing but gentle nature. His down-to-earth humor. His love for children. In a few short days, we won each other's friendship. Cecil was clearly a very special person.

Toward the end of the second week, Cecil ambled into the kitchen where several of us were doing dishes. "Ya know, I've been other places where people are around each other all the time, but they don't like each other. Y'all live together, and y'all really like each other." And then he summed it up: "Ya know, this place is pretty weird . . . but it's a good kinda weird!"

On his last night Cecil became uncharacteristically serious. "Ya know, Chris, these have been a strange two weeks. I can't help the way I was raised. There was certain things I was taught, ya know. And I can't change the way other folks think. But I learned something, and I'm never gonna be the same. I'm never gonna forget this place."

When we said goodbye to Cecil, I held back tears. In those two weeks a small-town Mississippi white boy who'd lived his entire life around black people had experienced his first true contact with them. Race had become a personal issue for Cecil. But it wasn't just Cecil who had changed. Our prejudices, too, had been confronted in the form of this "redneck" disciple of Christ who simply carried a truck-load of humble love in his heart. If Cecil, through some simple genuine contact, could begin to see some of the wrong of his upbringing, wasn't it possible that others could?

And Cecil didn't forget us—when he was released after seven years in prison, he asked to stay with us until he got back on his feet.

Cecil's down-home words carry a powerful punch of truth. As you begin to seek out black and white friendship, you'll see that it is indeed weird. Yes, it's strange and unusual, downright weird, for whites and blacks to be close friends and to actually enjoy it. Yes, it's weird for blacks and whites to talk about race, or even to dare to worship together. Yes, it's weird that Spencer and I are comrades. Yet there is an undeniably rich and unique joy to all that weirdness. It's a good kinda weird.

18

Kingdom Choices

The greater the risk we take, the more we forsake,
the greater God's kingdom we make.

N OT EVERYONE IS CALLED TO MAKE RACIAL RECONCILIATION A LIFE-*time commitment, as Spencer and I have. But regardless of where you live, worship or work, there are choices you can make to be a reconciler and show the world that your King plays by different rules. When you commit yourself to being a reconciler, you'll find yourself starting to go out of your way to walk on someone else's turf, taking more time to get to know someone at work, even stepping in to visit a church in an unfamiliar neighborhood. These are very simple choices, but you wouldn't expect "normal" people to make them, unless maybe they serve a God who calls his people to be "fools for Christ."*

The benefits we inherit simply for being born white in America are not earned or deserved. But once I accept that I have advantages, then what? I can't change the fact that my skin color benefits me. And it's not being white that's wrong.

Yet there are life choices we can control, intentional choices we can make as we seek to balance the inequities of an unjust society. Spencer and I call such decisions "kingdom choices." Kingdom choices let us put ourselves at God's disposal as his personal agents for accomplishing his will "on earth as it is in heaven."

I can't help the fact that I don't have to be intentional about affirming my whiteness. But I can educate myself in order to affirm blackness as well as whiteness. I can't change the fact that I didn't know the other race where I grew up. But I can decide who my friends are now. I can't change the fact that I was reared in churches where everybody looked like me. But I can choose what Christians influence my life now. I can't rub away what adults taught and demonstrated to me in my childhood. But I can raise my children to appreciate and understand people who are different. I can't help the fact that I have benefited from slavery and the oppression of blacks. But I can choose to use these benefits in a way that builds justice for everyone.

Jesus told a story about a master who left town for a while and gave each of his servants a different sum of money—talents is the biblical word—to use for his benefit. One servant was timid and fearful, and he buried his money so it wouldn't be lost or stolen. But the other servants were willing to risk what they had in order to gain even more and thus please their master.

Kingdom choices are our "talents"—our opportunities to invest in God's kingdom. To do nothing, to go with the flow or to be immobilized by guilt and fear is to bury what God has given you in the ground. It was risky for the two faithful servants to invest the money they had. Likewise, it's risky for us to put more time into loving our neighbor than gaining earthly riches, to forgive those who hurt us, to put the needs of others before our own, to believe that by serving we become great and that by giving up we receive. Living this way looks downright foolish to the world. But it's when we follow such "foolish" principles, Jesus said, that we build the kingdom on solid rock.

How can we most effectively use our kingdom choices for racial reconciliation? As I look at the lives of people who are committed to reconciliation, I see some common commitments.

Be Intentional

When Donna and I were first married, we lived in our own apartment, but I would often stay up late talking with friends who lived two doors away. Coming home one night, I was met by icy silence. Neither of us could sleep, so we aired our feelings. Donna said she needed more time together, while I didn't want to give up too much freedom. Eventually I saw that Donna was right. I still had a single person's mindset. A good marriage is hard work, and I wasn't doing my part to build it.

I learned to change my habits. I began to focus on initiating conversation each evening, asking Donna about her day and listening with interest as she recounted all the details. At first the changes felt awkward (and Donna will confirm that I have more growing to do!). But as I committed myself to change, what had felt stiff and difficult has gradually become a healthy habit and a source of blessing in our marriage.

Like building a good marriage, working toward racial reconciliation requires intentional change. Given a choice between initiating a conversation with a black or a white person, most of us will choose our racial cousin. We prefer to be comfortable, so we tend to mold our Christianity to fit the way we already live. But to "prove neighbor" we may have to go out of our way and do what feels less comfortable—just as the good Samaritan went out of his way to "prove neighbor" to a down-and-out Jew who was supposed to be his racial enemy.

Jesus was always challenging the normal, comfortable, habitual and convenient. For Jews in Jesus' day, it was normal to avoid Samaria when one was traveling from Galilee to Jerusalem. But Jesus intentionally went through Samaria. "Proving neighbor" takes Spirit-inspired work, energy and time. You may have to step out of your normal everyday existence to make it happen.

Many visitors to VOC, delighted to see blacks and whites worshiping and singing in a gospel choir together, gush, "What a wonderful place!" They want to jump right in without realizing the cost that's involved.

Elisabeth Elliot writes, "Personal sacrifice paves the way for God's miracles." Behind VOC's "miracle" of black and white there's a white brother who honestly admitted his discomfort with talking about race and sparked a discussion that helped everybody understand each other better. A black sister who patiently took the time to explain yet one more time how she fixes her hair. An elder who lost a friend because he lives on the "wrong" side of town. A talented choir director who encouraged one more white brother who doesn't know how to sing, rock and clap at the same time. A white brother who dared to question why a black person who wasn't biblically qualified should be in leadership. A black brother who boldly took a white brother aside to confront him about his paternalistic language. A white sister who was assaulted but didn't blame the whole black race. A black sister who, after her best white friend left town, befriended yet another pale-faced newcomer. A white sister who took the time to learn how to cook greens, cornbread and fried chicken and invited her black friends over for "Soul Food Night."

If you don't know about black people, begin to learn. Back in my high-school days, God planted a seed in me when I read *Roots.* If you can't name a black scientist or inventor, or if your concept of black history is, as Jawanza Kunjufu parodies, "one day in Africa, one day on the slave boat and four hundred years of slavery," then educate yourself. Go to a Christian Community Development Association conference and find out what ministries are doing in black communities. Find the black ministries that are working in your area and ask for a tour. Ask how you can serve and volunteer your skills. Start supporting them financially. Visit, or even become a member of, a black church. Start a conversation with a black classmate. If you don't have black students in your campus fellowship, seek out a black Christian student and try to become his or her friend. Hang out in the black student union. Attend an NAACP meeting. Reach out to a black person at work.

Although Phil Reed, the chair of our church's pastoral team, is white, he has taken the time to become an expert on black history. Phil is renowned for his hilarious Black History Month skits that show how difficult life would be if it weren't for black inventors and scientists. By the end of the skit, Phil's shoes are gone (in need of Jan Matzeliger's shoe machine), his car engine has overheated (without Elijah "the Real" McCoy's lubrication advances), he's had an auto accident (in the absence of Garrett Morgan's stoplight), and he's starved for peanut butter (no George Washington Carver).

One February a black teacher from a local elementary school visited our church. She was so impressed with Phil's skit that she came up to him after the service and asked if he would come to her school and do it for her class. Phil was a little intimidated to perform the skit outside of his home church. But he put aside his misgivings, went to the school and performed to an enthusiastic reception.

Afterward, another black teacher came up to him. Tears trickled down her cheeks. "I just can't believe," she said, "that a white person would take the time to learn about black people like you have."

Small Steps of Faithfulness

It's human nature to back away from an overwhelming task. So God's strategy is to take us one step at a time. "In his heart a man plans his course, but the LORD determines his steps" (Prov 16:9). If you have faith as a mustard seed, you can move mountains. Not necessarily all at once; sometimes a shovelful at a time.

Don't wait until you know exactly what to do. God's soldiers take initiative. They have confidence in their General, understand his plan, and step out in ways that are consistent with his overall purpose. In his Word, God has already charged us to love him and love our neighbor. Making kingdom choices toward reconciliation means taking small steps of faith into unfamiliar territory. God will show us when we're ready for a bigger battle.

Lowell Noble is not your typical mover and shaker. He doesn't stand out in a crowd. He is not a great speaker. But he has accomplished a great deal because of a lifetime of small, faithful steps.

In 1968 Lowell was an ordinary teacher, satisfied with his career. But the murder of Martin Luther King Jr. jarred him. "Through the trauma of that event, the Holy Spirit got to me," he says. "I began to wake early in the morning to read, think and write about the racial situation. It was like a second conversion in my life."

Not until a year later did he come upon the opportunity to channel his heartache into action. Spring Arbor College, a small, white liberal-arts school near Jackson, Michigan, had an opening for a sociology professor, and Lowell got the job. He dedicated himself to leading Spring Arbor students through the same "second conversion" he had experienced.

There was not always strong collegewide support for Lowell's convictions. But living and worshiping in a black community encouraged Lowell and his wife, Dixie, to stay faithful. Lowell began a friendship with John Perkins and invited John's input into his life and teaching. He began to take small groups of students on trips to visit poor communities. Several years later he brought small groups of Spring Arbor faculty, administrators (including the college president) and students to Mississippi workshops on ministry to the poor. Slowly, this experience and others began to affect the classroom teaching of Lowell's fellow faculty members, and even to redirect the college's mission. In the summer of 1992, after twenty-one years of Lowell and Dixie's steady efforts, Spring Arbor launched an urban ministry along with the first college-level curriculum to train students for Christian community development and racial reconciliation.

I suspect that Lowell overcame his opposition simply by outlasting it. As he proved faithful with small opportunities, God gave him a little more and then a little more. And in God's timing, a plan unfolded that Lowell could not have imagined in 1968, or even when he started at Spring Arbor.

Seek Out Some Unlikely Relationships

Going out of your way to initiate relationships with people of the other race can lead to some long-term payoffs for reconciliation.

One way of building racial bridges or "proving neighbor" is interracial church partnerships. Given our conspicuous lack of experience in bridge-building, many such partnerships begin rather clumsily. But that is a small price to pay for the benefits they can bring.

Sandy Hull and Al Brown are both pastors. Sandy is the pastor of a white middle-class Presbyterian church in St. Joseph, Missouri. Al pastors St. Francis Baptist Temple, a small inner-city black church in the same town. Their partnership began when Sandy's wife, Belinda, persuaded him to break his normal routine.

Now and then Sandy gets to take a Sunday off, and he and Belinda usually visit another Presbyterian church. One Sunday, though, because Belinda had recently made an eye-opening mission trip to Mississippi, she felt strongly that they should visit a black church. Sandy wanted to take it easy and get some rest; being the only white faces at a black church didn't seem exactly restful. But Belinda insisted.

They ended up attending Al Brown's church. As a result Sandy got to know Al, and eventually their two churches began cooperating in various worship services and projects. In the summer of 1991 Brookdale Presbyterian Church and St. Francis Temple sent members to participate in a joint work project in Jackson, Mississippi. In February of 1992 Spencer went to St. Joseph to speak at their joint missions conference. And in the summer of 1992 the Reverends Hull and Brown led a work team to Mississippi again.

The partnership is exposing members from each congregation to the culture and values of the other. But the relationship was able to take root only because Belinda had insisted that she and Sandy go out of their way to "prove neighbor."

Place Yourself Where You Can Learn
Throughout this book we've given many examples of steps people have taken to build relationships with their racially different neighbors. By far the most serious such step is to go and make your home among them.

For a time I was involved in recruiting new staff for VOC Ministries. We put out the red carpet for those who were considering becoming part of the ministry. They were impressed by the dynamic ministry programs. They loved the warmth of our church. They were won over by the people they met. But lurking in the shadows was the question that sooner or later had to be popped: "Are you willing to live in our neighborhood?"

Many times the response was as Mark says about the rich young ruler: "At this the man's face fell. He went away sad" (Mk 10:22).

"Do I have to live in an interracial neighborhood?" is not the right question. What we should wrestle with is "What does it say about us as Christians if blacks and whites aren't neighbors?"

No, not everyone is called to go. Whether you should stake a claim for the kingdom in a community others are running from, or in which you and your family are racially outnumbered, can be settled only between you and God. Some are called to be on the supply lines as investors and encouragers and prayer warriors. But the battle will not be won unless many more troops sign up for front-line duty.

"I can take risks for myself," many people contend. "But what about my family?" Our family's needs and wants make kingdom choices difficult at times. In an article titled "Is the 'Traditional' Family Biblical?" Rodney Clapp plays devil's advocate to the current Christian emphasis on family priorities. After taking a careful look at the words and lifestyle of Jesus and his disciples, Clapp concludes:

> In Jesus' eyes, however good family may be, it is not sacred. Family, like possessions, reputation, and religion itself, is clearly subordinated to the mission of the Kingdom of God. For the Christian, church is First Family. The biological family, though still valuable and esteemed, is Second Family. Husbands, wives, sons, and daughters are brothers and sisters in the church first and most importantly—secondly they are spouses, parents, or siblings to one another.[1]

When our family moved to Korea in 1966, my parents had never been overseas. They had grown up in comfortable homes. They had four children, and the youngest, my sister Liz, was only nine months old. My grandparents didn't agree with the move. Life was difficult and dangerous in Korea then—dirt roads, unsanitary conditions, a constant threat of attack from North Korea, an oppressive military government. But Mom and Dad went, and planted our family there for twelve years.

Because my parents took a risk and went to Korea, it wasn't difficult for me to go to Mississippi later. Because Mom loved unwed mothers and Amerasian kids, and because when that poor blind man came to the door my dad didn't turn him away, I have a love for the poor. My parents made our home a place of ministry. Dad discipled college students in his study. Chuckie, from a poor farm family, stayed with us during college. The woman who worked for our family was able to send her children to college with my parents' help. And so now my home is a place of ministry too.

Spencer's parents were pioneers in reaching out to whites. They made a conscious choice to invite whites to join them in their ministry in Mississippi and California. Because of that, Spencer is less bound by culture than many of his peers are. Like me, he is freer to venture out in the waters of race relations because they were navigated first by his parents.

Our parents' "foolish" choices were among the greatest gifts they could have given Spencer and me. As a child of risk-takers I can offer the encouragement, "Be foolish. Don't stop daring to be faithful." Our choices make it easier, or more difficult, for our children to invest their own lives in the risky principles of the kingdom. Each choice we make for the sake of the kingdom gives them something more to build on. The more we work through our racial residue as adults, the less of a challenge it will be for our children. They will be able to go further. Our choices will become a legacy for our children when they have to decide where they will live, who their friends will be, where to worship, what career to pursue.

Karen Myers lived ten years, through most of elementary and high school, in a low-income black neighborhood in Jackson. Her parents, Sarah and Herb (then a doctor at Voice of Calvary's health center), often wondered whether they were making the right decision. It was tough to let go of valued aspects of their white Pennsylvania Mennonite culture. In Herb and Sarah's hometown, tight-knit, stable families were the norm, while many of Karen's playmates on their West Jackson street came from single-parent homes.

But Karen has no regrets about her parents' choice to serve where they did. "West Jackson is home for me," she says.

Karen's testimony raises the question of just what we mean when we say we want "well-adjusted" children. Speaking of her schooling she says, "Yes, it's possible that I may have gotten a better education, academically, somewhere else. But I've been educated in more important ways—in serving God's kingdom."

If today we could learn how to take small steps toward different races and cultures, our children might be the real winners. Maybe crosscultural life won't be such an unknown to them as it is to many of us.

Giving Up to Gain

My parents discovered a secret that enabled them to give sixteen years to Korea. The missionary Jim Elliot let everybody in on it when he said, "He is no fool who gives what he cannot keep to gain what he cannot lose."

Amid the cornfields of Iowa there is a group of Christians who know the secret too. They will tell you that there is more to be gained than lost in taking the risk of "proving neighbor." These humble Iowans shine a bright light back on the path for others who wrestle with how to use their kingdom choices for racial reconciliation.

In 1978, the heart of a small-town Christian Reformed pastor in northwestern Iowa was pricked for needs beyond Rock Valley's close-knit Middle America world. But the hardworking Dutch farmers of his congregation felt little urgency to take up the Reverend Dan DeGroot's vision of breaking down racial and economic walls.

Dan couldn't get this thorn out of his side. At a conference he met John Perkins, and the white Iowan and black Mississippian shared their hearts. They dreamed up a crazy idea: asking a group of Iowans to give up a week's vacation, organize a team, go to Mississippi and work in a poor black neighborhood. At least that was what the Iowans thought they would do. But Dan hoped for more. His goal was to create an environment that would change his parishioners—where they would receive as much as they would give. Dan laid his trap, and the goodhearted Iowans took the bait.

Seven days of living and serving in a black community alongside VOC's staff turned on lights that months of carefully prepared sermons could not. "As the Iowans came home," says Dan, "they said, 'We realize there are communities that need the skills and resources we have!' They began to experience a real joy and blessedness in giving."

And there were deeper transformations. "I didn't feel badly toward blacks," says Pat VanderPol, one group member who now makes an annual trek to serve in Jackson. "But I initially came with an attitude of 'rescuing these poor people.' Listening to my new black friends changed that for me. We're not the rescuers. To be brothers and sisters means you help where we need you and we help where you need us."

Year after year these Iowans went to Mississippi. Eventually the spark spread and developed into a tristate compassion movement among white middle-class Christians, Justice For All. Now more than two hundred people travel each year to renovate gyms, repair schools and rebuild houses in seven states. The ministries they serve include a rural Indian school in New Mexico, a shelter for abused women and children in Appalachia and an outreach in black inner-city Chicago. In the process Justice For All has won the respect of those they go to serve and learn from.

"We've been blessed as much or more by what we have received as by what we've given," testifies Dan. "Before, our folks couldn't imagine people in homes where the floorboards were rotting away. But even in the midst of their poverty these people radiated a joy for living. At home, this joy of living for the Lord was hard to capture. They began to see different struggles and priorities."

Continues Dan, "Many of our group, upon hearing a black-history presentation on Sunday morning, exclaimed, 'I never knew that!' For all of us it meant a whole new understanding of Scripture."

Justice For All has created an environment in which people can begin to deal with the latent prejudices they carry. The greatest reward, says Dan, is that a bridge has been built for reconciliation. "To see our people bonding with others from different backgrounds, and now for those relationships to develop over the years, is a powerful reminder of the gospel."

Hebrews 11 is often called the Hall of Faith. It lists the most faithful of God's servants—Abraham, Noah, Moses, Rahab. I like to call that chapter "the Hall of Fools" because each person listed took risky steps of obedience that were foolish in the eyes of the world. The road of racial reconciliation, too, has its fools—people like Lowell and Dixie

Noble, Phil Reed, the Myers family and Dan DeGroot. They dared to take a foolish step that launched them on a journey whose richness they could never have imagined.

These fools for Christ show us a way for living out our kingdom choices. Being intentional. Taking small steps of faithfulness and risk. Seeking out some unlikely relationships. Putting themselves in an environment where they could learn. Believing that the more they gave up, the more they would gain. Would that we all could be such fools for Christ.

There is a raging river to cross. But praise God that he has laid a path of stones—our kingdom choices.

19

Friends & Yokefellows

THE APOSTLE PAUL DESCRIBES HIS RELATIONSHIP WITH THE BROTH-*ers and sisters at Philippi by using words like* comrade *and* yokefellow. *Both words characterize people whose lives are bound together for a common mission. "Yes, and I ask you, loyal yokefellow, help these women who have contended at my side in the cause of the gospel, along with Clement and the rest of my fellow workers, whose names are in the book of life" (Phil 4:3). A commitment to advancing the gospel—a cause much too big for a lone individual, no matter how heroic—was what "yoked" Paul to his fellow workers. It is also the cause of the gospel, a gospel of reconciliation, that supplies Chris and me with the fuel to cultivate and maintain our unlikely relationship.*

When I was a boy, I would sometimes go with my uncle into the woods to cut down young Y-shaped trees. After much cutting and trimming, he would attach one of these forked instruments to the neck of a cow. He called the device a yoke. Its purpose was to keep wayward cows from going through or over fences. This device was effective; it didn't even allow the cow to put its head through the fence to nibble at the proverbial greener grass on the other side.

Yokes have served several purposes throughout history, the most negative being for slavery. Slave traders and slave catchers came up with ingenious variations in order to more efficiently secure their merchandise. Thus was born the phrase "the yoke of oppression." But the most common use of the yoke was for joining two oxen for a task that is too big for a single animal. Yoked teams of oxen were used to accomplish feats like pulling oversized covered wagons westward into the mystery of uncharted lands. The bigger the task, the more yoked teams were necessary.

One of my favorite childhood stories featured Paul Bunyan and his humongous blue ox, Babe. Paul and Babe were legendary giants from early-American logging folklore. In one Paul Bunyan tale loggers were having trouble getting their logs to float down a particular river. The river just had too many crooks and curves in it. So in order to make life easier for his tiny friends, Paul, using a giant-sized yoke, hooked Babe up to the river. With much snorting and a great heave, Babe straightened out in a few seconds what nature had taken centuries to create.

If racial reconciliation is to be a reality, one giant ox hooked to one enormous yoke will not be enough. Instead, we'll need scores of life-size pairs of yoked-together blacks and whites pulling at the crooks and curves that are the nitty-gritty of race.

Many times Christians will attempt to take the easy way out by appealing to Jesus as if he were Babe the Blue Ox. Just let Jesus hook up to the situation and presto—race problems are a thing of the past. Such thinking ignores the typical ways God has worked throughout history. Even in Old Testament times God didn't always use miracles to get the children of Israel out of tight spots. Most of the time he let their ability to step out on his promises determine their fate. I have often wondered why God didn't just strike down the giant Goliath. Hadn't God promised to go into battle on Israel's behalf? And the big guy was making fun of the army of God. If David had not stepped forward, God probably would have let them be defeated by the Philistines. God wanted someone to have enough faith to step out and face the giant. It should not surprise us that it took the naive faith of a child to take God up on his promises. And the giant of race will be defeated only when Christians step out with the faith of a child and face it down.

Because interracial relationships are very unusual, just two people can offer a remarkably strong witness. Chris and I travel all over the country together, and I sometimes amuse myself by imagining what people in airports are thinking about us: *Are they athletes? FBI? Musicians? Gays?* All these lifestyles produce more interracial friendships than the church does.

In our workshops we encourage people to ask questions. We believe there is no such thing as a stupid question. If the idea is there, it had to come from somewhere. We welcome all kinds of questions from curious Christians who are wondering about the practicality of these rare relationships. One of the simplest questions put to us got to the heart of the matter: "Are you guys really friends?" asked a skeptical young teenager. I believe she was trying to get us to say whether we really liked each other or just put up with each other in order to make a point about racial reconciliation. It's no wonder such a question was asked, given that most parents are not raising their children in an atmosphere of interracial friendship.

Of course Chris and I like each other. That's not to say we don't find each other irritating at times. But, as in a marriage, we've learned to appreciate the gifts each of us brings to the relationship. Together we're stronger than either of us is alone. If our yoke was broken, each of us would lose half our power.

And it goes a step beyond that. We have made an intentional commitment to each other that goes beyond our comfort zones. Friendships are great, and we hope this book helps to spark many interracial friendships, but we also hope that those new relationships will develop into more than the typical fickle friendships that turn sour when one or the other's feelings get hurt. Cultivating any personal relationship takes effort. Throw race into the pot and the stakes are immediately raised. As in any game, when the stakes are higher, the agony of a defeat is more intense, but the thrill of victory is also much more meaningful.

Friends or Yokefellows

Several distinctions need to be made between friends and what Chris and I call yokefellows:

☐ Friendships can happen with very little effort; yokefellows are intentional.

☐ Friendships are built for the benefit of the friends; yokefellows come together for the benefit of the kingdom.

☐ Friends are drawn together by their common interests; yokefellows are drawn together by a common mission.

☐ Friends like each other; yokefellows respect each other.

☐ Friendships are based on compatible personalities; the yokefellow bond is based on gifts that are needed to realize the goal.

☐ Friendships are fueled by emotion; yokefellows are linked by commitment.

☐ Friends separated by a fight may never speak to each other again; yokefellows will cheer each other on until their goal is reached.

When we think about great friends in the Bible, Naomi and her daughter-in-law Ruth come to mind. Ruth swept away any doubts about her commitment to Naomi in one of the most beautiful speeches in the Bible. "Don't urge me to leave you or to turn back from you. Where you go I will go, and where you stay I will stay. Your people will be my people and your God my God. Where you die I will die, and there I will be buried. May the LORD deal with me, be it ever so severely, if anything but death separates you and me" (Ruth 1:16-17). Ruth's commitment was so intense that her speech is often recited or sung at weddings. Nancy and I used it in ours.

The most celebrated friendship in the Bible is that of David and Jonathan. For many of us their relationship evokes the memories of that special friendship of our youth. "Jonathan became one in spirit with David, and he loved him as himself" (1 Sam 18:1). David and Jonathan had one of those enviable friendships that happen almost without trying. They loved each other. This type of friendship is beautiful, and it would be great if everyone had at least one such friend.

It has been said that birds of a feather flock together. We take this to mean that people who are alike in their customs, interests and even skin color will naturally gravitate to each other. This helps to keep conflict at a minimum.

But when you face a crucial mission, a mission too large for one individual, you need to form a different type of relationship, one that would normally not have a basis for existence. Differences in personality, interests and life experiences then become gifts, assets that make your team more formidable. Compatibility with each other is not as crucial as ability to accomplish the task.

This is probably the most critical distinction between friends and yokefellows. Wars and sports tend to produce yokefellow-type camaraderie. Lifelong relationships are formed in the preparation and execution of battle plans. Ex-athletes speak of missing this camaraderie more than the games.

Though most friendships take work if they are to stay healthy, they don't have to have a reason outside themselves to exist. But yokefellows are headed in a common direction, toward a common goal. When one becomes good friends with a yokefellow, it's like adding icing to a cake.

Biblical Yokefellows

It surely was a wise man who said:

> Two are better than one,
>   because they have a good return for their work:
> If one falls down,
>   his friend can help him up.
> But pity the man who falls
>   and has no one to help him up! (Eccles 4:9-10)

If there ever were two people who were yoked together in this way, they were Paul and Barnabas. These men were yokefellows by orders of the Most High. Acts 13:2 tells us that God said to the believers at Antioch, "Set apart for me Barnabas and Saul [Paul] for the work to which I have called them." They were called out for an important mission that was much bigger than the two of them. Perhaps under normal circumstances Barnabas and Paul wouldn't even have been friends. But because they were both faithful to fulfilling God's call, their lives were bound together. In the three chapters following Acts 13:2, the Barnabas-and-Paul team is mentioned nearly twenty times.

The way Paul and Barnabas handled conflict reveals a crucial difference between friends and yokefellows. As we all know to our sadness, friendships can be severed over hurt feelings or unkind words spoken in anger. Normal friendships are not designed to withstand a high level of conflict. Too much conflict is not worth it. Yokefellows, on the other hand, have to learn to live with conflict. If their mission is to be accomplished, their capacity to love through differences must be great, and they must have a mature ability to forgive offenses. For Christians called to reconciliation, the way yokefellows handle conflict makes the witness of their gospel more powerful.

The two recorded disagreements between Paul and Barnabas were over principle and strategy that could have hindered their mission. The first conflict came when Peter visited Antioch and ate with the Gentiles but then withdrew when Jews from Jerusalem arrived. Paul seemed to expect more out of his yokefellow Barnabas than he did out of Peter: "The other Jews joined [Peter] in his hypocrisy, so that by their hypocrisy *even Barnabas* was led astray" (Gal 2:13, italics mine). But if Paul hadn't been able to forgive Barnabas, the mission of taking the gospel to the Gentiles would have been compromised.

Their second disagreement came over strategy. Barnabas, who was named for his gift of encouragement, wanted to take John Mark along on one of their grueling missionary trips. Because John Mark had deserted them on an earlier trip, Paul thought it unwise to take him again. "They had such a sharp disagreement that they parted company. Barnabas took Mark and sailed for Cyprus, but Paul chose Silas and left, commended by the brothers to the grace of the Lord" (Acts 15:39-40).

Although Paul's unwillingness to take a risk on John Mark caused him to part company with Barnabas, the separation created two teams of yokefellows, Barnabas and John Mark, and Paul and Silas. Paul and Barnabas were both still committed to the task of taking the gospel to the Gentiles. Their differences were not personal, so they could still cheer for each other. In Paul's final letter from prison in Rome, he tells Timothy to bring John Mark to him. "Get Mark and bring him with you, because he is helpful to me in my ministry" (2 Tim 4:11). Evidently Barnabas's patient discipleship of John Mark paid off, because somewhere Mark had won back Paul's confidence. Although it is not recorded that Paul and Barnabas ever teamed up again, in 1 Corinthians 9:6—well after their split—Paul refers to Barnabas as a laborer who deserves to receive his living from the gospel but who, like him, chooses not to. So Paul continued to cheer John Mark and Barnabas on, even from what was his final prison cell.

Modern-Day Yokefellows
Julie Ragland and Priscilla Perkins are yokefellows. Julie is from a white upper-middle-class family in Chattanooga, Tennessee. Priscilla—well, she's my sister. They are the best of friends, but more important, they have a common mission. They share a burning passion for the underprivileged children of northwest Pasadena. Together, they believe they can accomplish anything, and they have realized their dream of starting a Christian school. Both pursued extra education to prepare them for this task. Because their hearts are so united, it will be very difficult to keep the Harambee Preparatory School from being one of the best in the nation.

Says Julie, "Because we are such good friends, we are often asked by the children if we are sisters."

"You should see the expressions on their faces," Priscilla adds with a grin, "when we tell them yes."

My own experience tells me how children perceive Priscilla and Julie's partnership. Once when I was talking about my sisters with my son, Johnathan (then six), he decided to impress me by naming them. "Aunt Joanie, Aunt Deborah, Aunt Betty, Aunt Priscilla." As soon as my younger daughter, Jubilee (then three), heard the name Priscilla, she was not to be outdone. She quickly jumped in to add a name she was certain to be correct, "And Aunt Julie!"

Bob Sturkey and Ralph Gatti were business yokefellows for many years. Bob was a successful black dentist; Ralph, a white businessman who manufactured truck tops in Akron, Ohio. In the fall of 1986 Ralph attended a businessmen's retreat that had a very heavy focus on reconciliation, and some under-the-surface racism in his heart was revealed and dealt with. Ralph returned from the retreat determined to build an alliance with a black man.

"My purpose was twofold," Ralph recalls: "to demonstrate the power of the gospel in a personal relationship, and to hopefully gain a ministry partner."

Both of his goals were achieved. Over the next several months Bob's and Ralph's hearts were knitted together. "Since we're both businessmen," Bob says, "the affinity between us was natural. But we identified with each other not only in business but also in sports, music and a mutual concern for our community and how to go about working out our faith so that it makes a difference in our spheres of influence."

In 1988 the rapid growth of Ralph's business began to consume him, burning him out and lowering his spiritual vitality to dangerous levels. Bob sensed the need of his new friend. "Let me help you," Bob insisted. "I can arrange my schedule at the office to spend at least a couple days a week at your company. I'd like the opportunity, and I'll do it for nothing until we see what kind of results I get you."

Ralph agreed, and in January of 1989 Bob joined Ralph's company. Bob's task was to manage the company's growth and to help the business use its resources to make a difference and a witness to the glory of God. In March 1992 Bob left his dentistry practice and joined Ralph full-time for several years in the pursuit of their mission.

Glen Kehrein and Raleigh Washington yoked up for many years in inner-city Chicago, Glen as president of Circle Urban Ministries and Raleigh as pastor of Rock of Our Salvation Church. Glen, who hails from Wisconsin, attended Moody Bible Institute during the Chicago riots in the late 1960s. He saw the anger and pain on the faces of young blacks, and he wanted to do something to relieve it. Raleigh was a career military man on track to become a general. His career was cut short by white officers who were jealous of his success; he was railroaded out of the army only a few days before he would have qualified to receive full pension and benefits.

Glen thanks God that Raleigh never became a general. Raleigh thanks God that Glen didn't run away from the anger and pain of the inner city. Glen and Raleigh are an odd couple who yoked together for Christian community development in Chicago's Austin community. The task was much too big for either one of them. They needed each other. When Promise Keepers launched a national racial reconciliation work, Raleigh moved to Denver to direct the effort. As one worked grassroots, the other nationally, Glen and Raleigh continued to partner and expand God's kingdom.

If not for the gospel, Raleigh and Glen probably never would have become friends. But because the gifts, life experiences and even colors of both were needed to make an effective witness, their lives are yoked together.

Kathy Dudley is a white woman from the Appalachian hills of Virginia. Dolphus Weary is a black man who grew up in the cotton fields of Mississippi. Both grew up in extreme poverty and vowed to get as far away as possible from poverty once they had a chance. But, of course, God had other plans for their lives. Although they have disadvantaged backgrounds in common, their histories are not the reason they are yokefellows. A common passion for youth was the primary fuel in their relationship.

Kathy works among inner-city kids in Dallas, Texas. Dolphus works four hundred miles away, making life better among the rural poor of Mendenhall, Mississippi. Although they are separated by distance, Dolphus has been a mentor to Kathy and has played a key role in her understanding of the people she works with. "Much of our communication takes place over the phone," Kathy explains. Dolphus's long commitment to youth development has borne fruit in children who have grown into Christian lawyers, doctors, teachers, preachers and community leaders. (I'm grateful for the positive influence he had on my life.) Kathy's commitment is bearing the same type of fruit.

The Call to Reconciliation

Twenty years ago, I would have said that it was whites who were most reluctant to build crosscultural relationships. Now I'm not so sure. As the light of racial reconciliation dawns on Christians around the country, white Christians are beginning to ask, "Where are the black Christians who understand the importance of this ideal?" This is a very good question.

The old fight for racial equality did not require any give-and-take. It demanded change only from whites. But reconciliation is more costly; it demands change of us all.

I know many black Christians are weary, but this is not the same old fight to be accepted. It is not the same old fight to be included as an equal. This is a new struggle—another step on our journey to the kingdom of God. It is another step in living out the full meaning of the gospel. It's crucial that black Christians continue to step forward and partner with white Christians who share our vision.

I understand that black Christians are sick and tired of trying to prove themselves. I understand being sick and tired of being the only black in an all-white setting. I understand being sick and tired of always being the one to bring up the subject of race. I understand being sick and tired of always having to take the first step. I understand that many black Christians are, in the words of Fannie Lou Hammer, "sick and tired of being sick and tired."

But we must remember that "the race is not to the swift or the battle to the strong" (Eccles 9:11); instead, God says, "To him who overcomes and does my will to the end, I will give authority over the nations" (Rev 2:26). For the sake of loving our neighbors, we must be willing to go out of our way. For the sake of the gospel, we must be willing to persevere.

The cause of racial reconciliation needs yokefellows. Not for the good feelings that might follow, even though they will; not for the adventure, even though it is an exciting journey; not because it is a good thing to do, even though it is good; not solely for the sake of racial harmony—even though it will lead to that—but for the witness of the gospel. The cause of the gospel needs interracial teams who are willing to take the dangerous point position to penetrate the gray, unknown territories that have traditionally separated white and black Christians. They must be willing to face the spears and arrows that will surely fly from the hands and mouths of blacks and whites who don't want to leave the security of the familiar. These teams of yokefellows, male and female, must be willing to be scouts preparing the way for the army of God to follow.

The cause of the gospel also needs bodies of believers that are yoked together. White congregations and black congregations must go out of their way to reach out to each other, confronting together the ills of their towns and cities—causes too big for any one church to tackle alone. White and black congregations can offer their different gifts to the cause, giving witness to the power of the gospel and giving opportunity for racial healing to take place among their members.

The cause of racial reconciliation needs friends but, more important, it needs yokefellows. Souls bound together by the cause of Christ, living out an uncompromising gospel in which Jew and Gentile, male and female, black and white can all drink from the same cup. Do we believe that Christ's cup holds enough hope for us all?

20

Playing the Grace Card

T HIS CHAPTER HAS BEEN ADDED TO THE NEW EDITION OF *MORE*
Than Equals. *On the night of January 24, 1998, Spencer preached its con-*
tent in a message he and I delivered at Belhaven College in Jackson, Missis-
sippi. He described a powerful weapon that the two of us added to our
reconciliation arsenal in the final months of our partnership. Three days
later, he died of a heart attack at age forty-four.

It was winter 1970, and my mother had taken my seven siblings and
me to visit our father in the hospital after white law enforcement officers nearly beat him to death for his civil rights activities. My sister
Joanie, then fourteen years old, took one look at my battered father
and stormed out of the room repeating angrily, "I hate white people. I
will never like them!"

My mother tried to convince her that her attitude was not very
Christlike. But with my father lying bruised and swollen, I could tell
that even though my mother knew in her head the right things to say,

her heart was not in the words she spoke. Not that it would have mattered. My sister was having no part of those tired old words *love* and *forgiveness,* anyway. All of us siblings wanted those men to get what they deserved. To our knowledge, they never did.

Today, to the casual observer my sister looks as though she has reneged on her vow. She has white friends, attends an interracial church and functions well in a white environment. But all her life, like many African Americans, Joanie has had a safe, time-tested method for emotionally dealing with whites.

Color-Coding

There is a scene from the movie *Roots* that illustrates this method. Tom and his family (newly freed slaves) have befriended a poor white couple. Against tradition George and Mary treat their new black friends as equals. One night Tom is visited by white night riders and tied to a tree. He is about to be horsewhipped for being "uppity," when, in a backhanded way, George saves Tom's life by demanding that he be the one to do the whipping.

Afterward, Tom's young son sits in tears on the porch with Mary. Summoning all the hate and bitterness an eight-year-old can muster, he vents his feelings. "I hate white folks," he sobs bitterly. "And if I get the chance, I'll do to them what they did to my daddy."

"But what about me and George?" Mary asks. "We're white."

The boy looks up, as if surprised that Mary could say such a silly thing. "But you and George are different," he says. "You good white people."

This is precisely how many blacks deal with whites today. From a distance they are "white folks" and therefore suspect. Once we get to know them up close and personal, there is a chance that we may mentally remove them from the negative category.

Attempting to explain this procedure is risky. Besides being forced to generalize, which is always dangerous, many blacks feel that such revelation of our secrets in mixed company borders on treason. But there are also many African Americans who are growing tired of the mental tiptoeing that takes place in so much racial conversation. For us, it is time to move into deeper waters.

"You Know How White Folks Is"

There is an automatic mental procedure that takes place for many blacks upon meeting a white person. First a decision must be made as to whether or not we will give him or her the time of day. If so, then immediately the "Is he for real or phony?" antennas are raised, the "white superiority" sensors powered up, and the "racism" detector activated—all in an effort to analyze quickly any "vibes" and interpret any data, verbal or nonverbal, from the subject. All this is necessary to determine whether the white person deserves special consideration as an "individual," that is, a "good white person," or as a "typical" white person, who should be quickly relegated to the category known simply as "white folks," as in, "You know how white folks is."

Whether the label is deserved or undeserved, in the minds of most blacks, all white people are "white folks" until they prove themselves "different."

Granted, this is not scientific analysis taking place. It is part life experience, part self-preservation, and even part projection. I have questioned very intelligent black people who will admit that this "sizing up" of whites is often not very objective or accurate. But it takes place just the same.

Now, before whites get too indignant, you need to acknowledge that many of you do something very similar when you meet a black person. "Is this a run-of-the-mill black, or is he or she an exception that I can respect and treat like a peer?" I don't know how many times I have heard articulate, educated black people explain with disgust how often they sense that whites are surprised by their speech, intellect or accomplishments. I can't count the number of times that I have been told by whites that I am "different."

But I will not attempt to deal with white categorizing or explain to whites how to move from the "white folks" category in a black person's mind. This is not intended to be another hoop for whites to jump through. This is about black responsibility in the reconciliation process.

Obviously, this judging process is unfair to whites. But most blacks don't care about the fairness of it. A fairly convenient rationalization goes something like this: the incidences of blacks beating the system, placing unfair demands on whites, and whites getting the short end of the stick—whether this happens through the courts or through affirmative action—represents only a brief moment in history. And these minor inconveniences don't deposit even an ounce of weight toward balancing the cosmic scales of historical justice.

The problem is, for those who believe that God intends for all believers to be one family and that our faith should supersede our race, something seems not quite right in our attitudes about whites. Something has been conspicuously missing in our dialogue about racial justice and reconciliation. It is the one characteristic that sets our God and faith apart from all the other religions. It is our secret weapon and the major reason why Christians have the best shot at eventually making racial reconciliation a reality.

In the same way that white people don't like hearing or discussing the injustices of the past because of where the discussion may lead, likewise I am not all that excited about bringing up the subject of *Grace.*

There is a part of my consciousness that trembles because it has already calculated the consequences of allowing grace to take its rightful place in our reconciliation process. That part of me knows where I am heading with this, and that it will not go over very well with my homeys. Still, I know that is the truth according to the gospel of Jesus.

Irreconcilable Differences

For more than ten years Chris and I have preached the importance of relationships in achieving racial reconciliation. The reason we are so adamant is because most of what we have learned comes out of our own true-to-life relationship.

For what was not the first time nor is likely to be the last, Chris and I came to what seemed like insurmountable obstacles in our relationship. By the end of summer 1997 both of us held tightly to a long mental list of ways that each had been hurt or disappointed by the other.

We were close to settling for irreconcilable differences and going our separate ways.

But in order to demonstrate that we were good Christian boys, we sought the counsel of some dear friends who had earlier become our spiritual parents, John and Judy Alexander. In my mind, we were just going through the motions. The damage was already done. The pain was too great. It was just a matter of making it official.

Neither of us was prepared for the overwhelming simplicity, complete absurdity and illogical genius of God's amazing grace.

The brand of Christianity Chris and I feebly attempt to live by demands that we make a good-faith effort to follow when we feel God is leading. Trying to live up to that commitment allowed us to be bushwhacked by John and Judy Alexander and their ramblings about grace.

Yeah, yeah, I know all about grace, I thought. I could quote John 3:16 when I was knee-high to a duck. Grace is God's love demonstrated to us, even though we don't deserve it. Grace is the father, welcoming home his prodigal son, even though the boy really deserves punishment. The ultimate act of grace was God sending Jesus to die for our sins when we were the ones who were guilty, not him.

But in all of my forty-four years of evangelical teaching, I never understood until now that God intended for grace to be a way of life for his followers. Maybe I'm the only one who missed it, but judging by the way that we all get along, I don't think so. Sure, I knew that we're supposed to love one another as Christ loved us. But somehow it was much easier for me to swallow the lofty untested notion of dying for each other like Christ died for us rather than simply to give grace to brothers and sisters on a daily basis, the way God gives us grace. Okay, maybe I'm dense, but I just never got it.

At our relationship's weakest moment Chris and I saw, as clearly as anything we had ever seen before, that only by giving each other grace could we find healing and restoration. We could either hold on to our grievances and demand that all of our hurts be redressed, or we could follow God's example, give each other grace and trust God for the lack. We chose grace.

Unconditional Forgiveness

I have heard a well-known Christian black woman tell of the time when her grown daughter got into a fight with a white woman on an airplane. Although she taught her children all their lives to be nonviolent, a smile creeps across her face and a gleam of pleasure twinkles in her eyes as she describes how her daughter "gave that white woman a black eye." Although this woman believes wholeheartedly in the concept of racial reconciliation, there is still something deep down in her that feels like it's payback every time a white person gets the short end of the stick at the hands of someone black. And she is not alone, even among black Christians.

Because blacks have suffered unjustly at the hands of whites, somehow our brand of Christianity has accommodated us and allowed us to hang on to this particular category of unforgiveness. Sure, we say that we are willing to forgive, and we do. But that special dispensation is reserved for whites who prove that they are "worthy."

I stumbled across Philip Yancey's landmark book *What's So Amazing About Grace* during the time when Chris and I were discovering grace all over again. It was as if God was attacking me with grace from all angles. According to Yancey, "Grace is unfair, which is one of the hardest things about it. It is unreasonable to expect a woman to forgive the terrible things her father did to her just because he apologizes many years later. . . . Grace, however, is not about fairness."[1]

It is just as unreasonable for blacks to forgive whites for past and present mistreatment. But grace is not about being fair. We wouldn't dare demand fairness from God—at least I know I wouldn't. What's so amazing about grace is that God forgives us and embraces us with open arms even though we don't deserve it. What's new about grace, at least for me, is that because we are grateful for what God did for us, we allow him to do the same to others through us. This means that if I know this loving God who is so full of grace, then I will forgive and embrace those who, like me, don't deserve my grace and forgiveness.

Our willingness and ability to give grace or to forgive others is an accurate indicator of how well we truly know God.

As African Americans we have considered much of white Christianity illegitimate, and rightly so, because it accommodated itself so conveniently to racism. But lately I have been questioning our own brand of Christianity. What does our inability to forgive and embrace undeserving whites say about our knowledge of and intimacy with this God of grace?

When I was much younger and just beginning to wrestle with the concept of reconciliation, I was occasionally asked if I had forgiven the men who beat my father, or the white classmates who made my life hell while I was integrating the segregated school. At that time, my response always focused on the ones who had committed the offense. "They've never asked me to forgive them," I would say. End of discussion.

However, Jesus knew that the only sure way to peace on earth and peace of mind was for humans to practice forgiveness. His last words on the cross were spoken out loud so that we would have an example to follow. "Father, forgive them, for they do not know what they are doing" (Lk 23:34). Jesus forgave without ever being asked. For our own sakes, not for the offenders', we are expected to do the same.

Black Christians possessing a truly Christlike faith would not only be compelled but would also be willing and empowered to forgive specific white offenders. Moreover, we would have the faith and compassion to begin practicing forgiveness to the nameless white collective that we refer to as "white folks."

I believe that African Americans will easily grasp the implications and magnitude of totally and unconditionally forgiving "white folks." Some blacks will choose to find ways to justify themselves. But some will rise to the challenge.

My sister, who vowed never to like white people as a child, is just now beginning the process. In December of 1997 she participated in a first-of-its-kind gathering in Jackson. We brought together twenty-five black Christian leaders and twenty-five white Christian leaders for an intense, honest, off-the-record dialogue on racial reconciliation in our city. Everyone agreed that none of us had been involved in anything this honest.

Two days after the gathering, in a church small-group meeting my sister bravely shared through tears that she, for the first time in her life, had begun the process of forgiving "white folks."

For Joanie and many other African Americans, practicing forgiveness will mean beginning to dismantle the old "white folks" category and practicing the discipline of seeing whites as individuals. It will mean responding with Christlike compassion and kindness to whites who reach out a hand, instead of going through the process of determining whether or not they are "worthy." It will mean no longer being obsessed with the blindness of our white brothers and sisters at the expense of tolerating our own.

And finally, reconciliation will ultimately mean not only forgiving and tolerating, but fully embracing whites as brothers and sisters, all of us equally unworthy in the eyes of God.

No it ain't fair. But it's right. And God understands that there will be slip-ups and wrong turns, moments of anger and unforgiveness. But as we grow in our discipleship of grace, each day will bring more victories. And when we fail, our God, who is full of grace, is eager to forgive. The more I have come to know this quality in him, the dearer he becomes to me, and the more I want to demonstrate this quality to others.

But What About Justice?

I grew up in one of the most justice-oriented families in this country. My father has been called a modern-day prophet of justice. Two of his most popular books are entitled *Let Justice Roll Down* and *With Justice for All*. Nothing that I am learning about grace and forgiveness diminishes my belief in Christians working for justice, especially on behalf of the poor and oppressed. I know many tired soldiers who, like me, have fought for social justice most of their lives. Nothing in the Scriptures even hints that these men and women should soften their message.

But I know that some of them have carried an extra weight of resentment against people they considered oppressors and people of privilege who seem to care nothing about the poor. I recognize it in them because I feel it in myself. But what I have found and latched onto is a whole new way of looking at those who refuse to hear the message of justice.

Although we must continue to speak on behalf of those who are oppressed, my willingness to forgive oppressors is not dependent on how they respond. Being able to extend grace and to forgive people sets us free. We no longer need to spend precious emotional energy thinking about the day that they will get what they deserve. What tremendous freedom!

What I am learning about grace lifts a weight from my shoulders, which is nothing short of invigorating. When we can forgive and embrace those who refuse to listen to God's command to do justice, it allows them to hear God's judgement without feeling a personal judgement from us. Which, in the end, gives our message more integrity. Being able to give grace while preaching justice will make our witness even more effective.

Creating a Culture of Grace

"Daddy, come quick," shouted my daughter. "Someone stole the presents from under the Christmas tree."

At first I thought it was a joke that the children were playing on me. But I could see quickly that they were visibly upset. Apparently someone had come into our house while we slept, picked out some choice presents, removed the blanket that covers my favorite chair and used it to haul away about a dozen or so gifts that were to be given on Christmas morning.

To say that the children were angry would be an understatement. After my son, Johnathan, realized that among the gifts stolen were his brand new top-of-the-line sneakers, he stormed out of the house in tears.

I sat silently on my coverless chair, stunned and fuming. I had seen the children's Christmas special *How the Grinch Stole Christmas* dozens of times since childhood. But I never believed such a tale could come true. How do you forgive a person like this? How do I teach my children to practice forgiveness?

Because it is unnatural, we have to practice forgiveness, like any other discipline. According to Martin Luther King Jr., "Forgiveness is not just an occasional act; it is a permanent attitude."

Later that day I put the question to my son. "How should we as Christians respond to the person who tried to steal our Christmas?"

"Yeah, yeah, I know, Dad," he said. "Even though he doesn't deserve it, we're supposed to give him grace."

Sure, I knew the words that came out of his mouth were almost the complete opposite of what Johnathan was feeling in his heart. I knew because I felt the same way. But I also knew we had to start somewhere. And if, one step at a time, our discipleship as Christians could include giving each other grace, if our children could learn and practice forgiveness as well as they practice praise and worship, if we could literally create a counterculture of grace, then just maybe, as we all mature in our faith, our hearts could finally line up with our words.

And the world would have to take notice.

Afterword

By my side in a pulpit during a reconciliation conference in Jackson, Mississippi, Spencer passionately spoke the words from the previous chapter. It was the night of January 24, 1998, and it was the first and last time that he voiced that message of race and grace.

Three months earlier we had walked through the darkest passage of our long partnership. Our own powers to persevere were depleted. But somehow, as God's insane love got hold of us, we were able to release our list of grievances, forgive and make a new beginning. As Spencer said, "We chose grace."

The implications were profound. At one of our Antioch Community meetings Spencer suggested that we sing "Come Thou Fount of Every Blessing." When we came to the words *"Oh to grace how great a debtor, daily I'm constrained to be; Let Thy goodness, like a fetter, bind my wandering heart to Thee,"* I watched tears of joy stream down his face. In some ways Spencer was deeply internalizing God's unconditional love for the first time in his life.

As Antioch embraced the culture of grace, Spencer and I took our national ministry to a new level. In the years since the first edition of *More Than Equals*, we had launched a nationally focused organization, Reconcilers Fellowship, to promote racial reconciliation. Now we began to lay a foundation for a Jackson-based training center. Starting locally, in December 1997 we organized "50 Under 50, 50/50." Fifty

Jackson movers and shakers, twenty-five white and twenty-five black, gathered for a two-day, off-the-record, honest dialogue about race relations in the city. It led to some profound breakthroughs; in a transcendent moment of brokenness, tears flowed from both pastors and CEOs, politicians and journalists.

The next month brought to town the "College, Ethnicity, & Reconciliation" conference. We had spent months preparing for it but nearly canceled it because of the turmoil in our relationship. Partnering locally with us were historically black Tougaloo College and predominantly white Belhaven. National partners included InterVarsity Christian Fellowship and the Council for Christian Colleges & Universities.

Spencer and I sat and talked in our little office on the Antioch campus before I went over to the first day of the conference. Downtown, a few minutes away, three hundred college presidents, administrators, faculty and campus ministry staff were converging.

We were both pumped up and spoke of the event as a new plateau for our ministry, a coming together of a national network built over many years. It was time to push the envelope, to move the discussion beyond "Reconciliation 101." But then Spencer sighed. "This has been one of the most difficult weeks of my life," he said.

Earlier in January, he had torn an achilles tendon playing on the church basketball team. Doctors told him he might never play his beloved sport again. My daughter Talia was fascinated by his blue cast—"Uncle Spencer's blue leg" she called it. I had watched him struggle and grimace in the rain, his crutches sinking inches into the mud.

But his struggles were more than physical. Accompanying our partnership's new chapter of grace had been a painful letting go of certain self-images. After serving a year as president of Reconcilers Fellowship, Spencer had courageously asked me to take his place. It wasn't his niche, he had come to see. The two of us had unified around a profound leadership change, still "yokefellows" but with new roles. I took the helm of Reconcilers Fellowship and Spencer the pastoral leadership of Antioch.

Before we parted, we spoke of the Saturday night message we

would preach together at the conference. Spencer was eager to present new thoughts inspired by our recent experience of forgiveness and peace.

The conference began, and an atmosphere of unusual grace, depth and humor reigned the first two days. Our small staff, over its head once again, had prayed much for this gathering, and it seemed like God showed up.

Then, on Saturday morning, Spencer suddenly collapsed during a conference general session.

As he was rushed with Nancy to the hospital and I followed in a car with their son Johnathan, the three hundred conferees pleaded with God for his life. The doctors said it was a "hypoglycemic episode"; Spencer was a diabetic, and his blood sugar was too low. He checked out fine, and they discharged him from the hospital.

I assumed we wouldn't speak that night. But Spencer called me that afternoon. "Let's do it," he said. "Are you sure?" I asked. "Yeah. The only thing I'm afraid of is the embarrassment of facing three hundred people who watched me throw up four times this morning." Laughing together always kicked in at the right time.

That night Spencer hobbled down front to a standing ovation and sat on a stool to take the weight off his foot. Admitting to weariness he spoke haltingly, pausing to catch his breath. He and I called God's people to be just as radically committed to grace as we were to justice. Our emotions were tender and our spirits bold as we spoke about the miracle of healing God had done between us. I listen to that tape now, and I find even myself moved by words and emotions that seemed to come from beyond ourselves.

A joyful Voice of Calvary worship service ended the conference the next morning. The two of us stood jubilantly side by side, Spencer on his crutches, clapping with the music as our church choir burst out with a gospel version of the "Hallelujah Chorus." That evening we kicked back at the traditional Antioch Super Bowl party and reminisced about the conference's great success. Spencer was excited that Donna and I were going away the next day to a hotel to rest. It was his idea, a gift from Antioch.

It would be the last time I saw Spencer on this earth. Around 1:00 p.m. on January 27, at his home on our Antioch campus, he died suddenly of a heart attack. By the time I got to the hospital an hour later, I saw my yokefellow lying silently on a hospital stretcher.

Looking Back

The rolling piney-woods backroads of Mississippi have a distinct beauty during the cool winter months. I drove those roads alone a couple weeks after Spencer's death. I was on my way to a retreat center to let all the pain out. I never knew until Spencer died how many tears the body is capable of.

I thought of Nancy losing her beloved soulmate. Johnathan, Jubilee and April Joy, their daddy. John and Vera Mae, their treasured son. The Perkins siblings, their brother and leader.

I thought of our small church body that was so dear to Spencer for twenty-five years.

I thought of our national work together and Spencer's transcendent voice.

I thought of my own pain, which a friend summed up: "Chris, you have lost three limbs: one part yokefellow, one part vocation and one part community."

There was too much I could not understand. *"How unsearchable his judgments, and his paths beyond tracing out! 'Who has known the mind of the Lord?'"* (Rom 11:33-34). I remembered that Jesus too had asked "Why?" before his death.

That first night at the retreat center I felt the presence of One who meets us in our grief: *"Blessed are those who mourn, for they will be comforted"* (Mt 5:4). Walking under the vast sky full of stars, I felt intimately connected to eternity. God was more real, and closer, because Spencer was with him.

I sensed God saying, *"My word went out through you and Spencer, and it will not return unto me empty—it will accomplish what I desire."*

I knew something was happening. I thought of so many allies on the frontlines of this battle who weren't there when we penned *More Than Equals*.

In Jackson there was Mission Mississippi's city-wide work on relationships and partnerships, and the Amos Network's coalition of
churches addressing hard-core issues of education, housing and
employment.

Nationally there was Promise Keepers, a major influence in putting
racial reconciliation on the evangelical map. The Call to Renewal, an
outgrowth of *Sojourners* magazine, was weaving together evangelicals,
mainline Protestants, Pentecostals, Catholics and black churches
around attacking poverty. The exploding network of the Christian
Community Development Association had grown from thirty member
organizations in 1989 to over five hundred churches and ministries on
the inner-city frontline. Hope in the Cities, a national outreach of
Moral Re-Armament, was pioneering on a more secular, city-wide
level.

Most of all, I gained hope from a new generation of reconcilers
sprouting up among college students, with whom Spencer and I
invested so much of our energy.

At the close of a 1997 conference at Harvard University, we sat in a
pew at Memorial Chapel and listened as a rainbow coalition of Christian students rose one by one to confess their racial sins to each other
during a spontaneous ninety-minute prayer service.

A few days later two University of North Carolina students escorted
us through a gauntlet of fraternity houses where guys sat on couches
and didn't bother with brown bags as they downed vodka and beer
from the bottle. "It looks like the 'hood," commented Spencer. But the
Christians were eager for something deeper. We were on our way to
speak a message of racial reconciliation, and found a standing-room-
only crowd of one thousand students; two hundred more listened in
on closed-circuit TV.

At a chapel symposium at Belhaven College we stood before the
student body as young Mississippians rose to face each other and say
they wanted to overcome their pasts. One was ashamed of his all-white
private school upbringing, started by a church during racial integration in the 1970s. Another confessed residue from the verbal abuse
she experienced at a predominantly black public school. A black stu-

dent rose to say he had experienced the same thing from whites in his high school but challenged everybody to forgive and make a new beginning.

I also knew of dozens of other students moving into inner cities upon graduation, reaching out to their neighbors and building interracial community together. In my college years Christian students weren't asking these questions or making these challenges or daring to take the risky steps that Spencer and I encountered in pockets of students across the country.

When God's people, unknown to one another, in different places, begin to act upon the same radical and overlooked truth, it's a sure sign that he is up to something.

A New Chapter

It has been a year and a half now since Spencer's parting, a time that opened a new chapter in my life that was inconceivable before January 1998.

God can call things into existence, and he can call them to a close. Sometimes it is harder to do the latter than the former. With the agreement of all of Antioch's members, we dissolved our communal life in the fall of 1998. We had reached a plateau and had neither the vision nor the will to carry community forward. We also decided to close down Reconcilers Fellowship. I came to see how much Spencer's partnership and friendship meant to me, and I had no passion to move on without him. After a long period of prayer and discernment with friends, family and church, Donna and I sensed God moving our family into a period of refreshment and deepening in a new way.

Voice of Calvary continues as a congregation deeply committed to reconciliation. One of our strengths had always been having many leaders, both black and white, within the body. And unlike the old days Jackson now had many other leaders and organizations committed to reconciliation to carry that mission forward.

While Donna and I felt deep peace about our decision, leaving our home of nearly twenty years was heart-breaking. In December of 1998 we moved to Lincoln, Vermont (next door to my parents). I began a fellowship of reflection and writing associated with Boston University's Institute on Racial and Social Division and contemplated entering seminary in the year 2000.

As I reflect on the years since *More Than Equals* first came out, I am struck by the amazing changes that took place at Voice of Calvary. The turbulent meetings of 1983 brought our black members into full empowerment within the church. In fact, while race has never ceased to be an issue at Voice of Calvary, it is no longer one of the most pressing. Reconciliation became the ethos of church life, pervading the habits and lifestyle of a critical mass of members who are friends "in sickness and health." The church has faced great tests around issues including worship style, moral failure, the role of women in leadership and others common to local church life. But in the fifteen years following 1983 there were no further racial crises. Those willing to endure the pain can see great change happen.

Looking at the national church scene, however, leaves me with mixed feelings. The 1993 publication of *More Than Equals* coincided with a rising tide that saw "racial reconciliation" become popularized among white evangelicals in a way Spencer and I never dreamed of. Thirty years after white evangelicals stood on the sidelines while fellow black believers and their so-called "liberal" white allies suffered and gave their lives, tearful racial healing services stirred Christians from Jackson to Cincinnati, from Atlanta to Los Angeles. In one, the "Memphis Miracle" of 1994, twenty-one white Pentecostal denominations disbanded their association to pledge a united fellowship with leading black Pentecostal groups. Unprecedented numbers of new books on race were released by evangelical publishers in the 1990s. Hundreds of thousands of Christian men committed publicly to Promise Keepers' "sixth promise" of racial reconciliation. Spencer and I visited or knew of dozens of churches and Christian organizations taking reconciliation seriously for the first time.

But we knew that if old habits remained entrenched, "racial reconciliation" would become a cheap cliché and the new enthusiasm a temporary fad.

The jury is still out. The battle tactics for blacks gaining a foothold in the nation—antidiscrimination laws, huge corporate lawsuit settlements (such as Texaco and Denny's), affirmative action, greater educational opportunity—have no parallel whatsoever in the church. While critical masses of blacks are entering corridors of national power and influence (passing the gained cultural and social capital to their children), this is not the case with evangelical Christian institutions such as parachurch organizations, denominations, seminaries and Christian colleges.

Real increased progress in the church will lead to real increased togetherness with and empowerment of minorities—and that will lead to real increased conflict. For emphasis I repeat a quote from sociologist Orlando Patterson in the new introduction: *"If the integration of two groups legally and socially separated for more than 350 years does not produce friction, it is the surest sign that no meaningful change has taken place."*

Sometimes I wonder if white evangelicalism as it exists can accept and integrate Christians of color in a way that transforms the whole church. It is too ethnically isolated, has far less diversity than secular organizations and resigns minority leaders to loneliness, powerless roles and even ostracism from their own ethnic communities. I wish we could just start over with new wineskins. The successful integration of white evangelical institutions will not be felt as harmony and peace but as struggle and conflict. There's not enough mess in the church yet. When there is, then we'll know the church is gaining ground.

A New Twenty-first Century Church
But I am also convinced that authentic reconciliation will disturb more than what is sacred to white Christian institutions.

In spite of cries for "separate and equal" there is no serious black movement for a separate government or economy. While "black-owned" and "black-run" are appealing given the ordeal of joining the mainstream, until there is widespread integration at society's highest levels, the influence and power of African-Americans will be limited.

A black-owned and black-run church is seen entirely differently. The biggest defenders of maintaining black churches are black Christians, not white. And for good reason. Birthed of necessity in response to the outright racism of white Christians, black churches gave dignity, hope, community, leadership, cultural refuge and (later) political clout to blacks amid devastating oppression. They became the organizing base for one of the greatest nonviolent social revolutions in the history of the world. One 1999 poll showed that nearly half of African-Americans credit black churches the most for improved conditions among blacks. Black Christians are the first to declare sacred the resulting parallel church institutions, denominations, leadership, resources and agendas. What was meant for evil, black believers not only redeemed for good but formed into perhaps the most authentic expression of church in America and a stronghold for redeeming the soul of the nation.

Which makes the whole idea of "desegregating the church" very touchy ground and many black Christians very wary of the words "racial reconciliation."

In the years since writing *More Than Equals,* Spencer and I met just as much resistance to reconciliation in the black community as in the white. On one hand, I understand. The lip service without substantive change, the fear that "racial reconciliation" equals further white domination, the "been there, done that" weariness—they are tough realities.

But there is ultimately no room for retreating to ethnic isolation. Opposition has never been an excuse to stop pursuing God's high callings, a reconciled church surely being one of them.

In Spencer's final message, as an aside, he said, "I am becoming more and more uncomfortable with the brand of Christianity that accommodates our weaknesses as black people while speaking truth about the weaknesses of whites. Growth for us means no longer being obsessed with the blinders of our white brothers and sisters at the expense of tolerating our own. There are many of us who have been dealing with this issue of reconciliation who are tired of the tiptoeing that we do, not getting down to the real issues. I for one am tired of seeing white people get the most benefit out of this movement of reconciliation because they are being challenged all the time to deal with their racism, to step up to the plate. A lot of them are starting to do it. I want us as black people to be challenged just as much."

Spencer believed the time had come to radically change our thinking about being church.

For the first time in a long and acrid history, white and black Christians enjoy vast opportunity for meaningful and mutual relationship and partnership without penalty of death, intense persecution or economic devastation. Reconciliation is no longer reserved for martyrs, and we are in a place to pursue racial reconciliation on a basis of equality as never before.

But it *will* cost something. The black church is a national treasure—but not without its cracks. From God's perspective genuine treasures reside only in "jars of clay," their power made perfect in weakness, "lest anyone should boast." And where black Christianity is not good, where it is pure power and ego, that, just as in the white churches, will not be surrendered without a brawl. All Christians must now examine their sacred wineskins and determine whether they can hold the new wine of the gospel of reconciliation.

How we move forward is complex. As Martin Luther King Jr. stated, "Black people need to be integrated into power, not out of it." The whole church has much to lose if integration doesn't go both ways. While blacks and other minorities regularly join and influence the mainstream, it is a rare white person or institution that is willing to go the other way. While desegregating white institutions, at the same time whites must ask another question: "Where is God already at work among people of color, and how can we submit to and serve those efforts of the Spirit?" A new movement of white Christians joining black churches, working under minority leaders and allying with minority-led Christian institutions is one of the surest way to demonstrate they are serious. Maybe our young people will lead the way in that.

Beyond Reconciliation 101

In pushing reconciliation to the next level, we continue to get little help from the vast resources of white evangelicalism.

Ours was one of nearly fifty books on race released by evangelical

publishers in the 1990s, more than double the number in the previous
two decades. There is now a compelling body of literature that can
guide whites toward lifestyles of justice and reconciliation. I'm flabber-
gasted, amazed, thankful for this rising tide. But I still see a number of
huge gaps.

First, *a body of reconciliation theology with influence on the church at large
is nonexistent.* Not one broad theological work on race and ethnicity
has been written that has been taken seriously by the white evangelical community. The impact of racial justice and reconciliation upon
the primary formation point for our pastors—seminaries—is still
minuscule. This is a huge hole.

Second, *Christian racial reflection and scholarship lags far behind
national debate, trends and developments.* Our books don't address
emerging issues and trends discussed in the public square throughout
the 1990s such as new dynamics brought by the black middle class
explosion, the increasing importance of distinguishing between class
and race division, questions about using "race" as a concept (as
opposed to ethnicity) given its questionable biological and genetic origins, adherence to a binary "black-white" concept of race based on the
"one-drop" rule, the benefits of interracial marriage both socioeco-
nomically and as a measure of racial healing, the explosion in numbers of mixed-race children who refuse to choose one ethnicity over
another and their growing impact and voice, and expanding reconciliation concepts beyond black and white.

In contrast to a mountain of secular books and research, I found
not a single twentieth century survey of race and Christianity written
in sociology, history, economics or journalism by Christian or secular
publishers. The weight of the work is completely anecdotal.

Third, *"reconciliation" remains amorphously unquantified.* How do we
know if we're winning or losing? By increasing multiethnic churches,
interchurch partnerships, white Christian involvement in ethnic communities? Housing integration and interracial marriages among
Christians? Minority presence in parachurch leadership and staffing?
White funding of minority-led organizations? White Christian involvement in and attitudes toward social and political investment in racial

justice? What are the standards, and where is the data? The whole "level two" side of racial reconciliation, how it manifests itself in structures, institutions, impact on society and the whole life of the church, is still dismally uncharted territory.

Finally, *few black Christians have been reached—or compellingly addressed—by these books*. While emphasis on white responsibility alone was understandable in the 1960s and 1970s, thirty years of muddy water under the bridge should have led us by now to reassess the situation, ask new questions and issue new challenges. I have not found any of the Christian books on race wrestling with such issues as whether black Christians should have attended Louis Farrakhan's Million Man March, instances of knee-jerk defense of corrupt black politicians by black clergy who brand any criticism of such politicians as racist or "Uncle Tom," or gaps between black "haves" and "have-nots" (in general, the black affluent of Jackson were no better allies for the black poor of our neighborhood than wealthy whites). My friend Lowell Noble, a sociologist, is convinced that African-Americans now suffer more harm from materialism and individualism than from racism. These and other obstacles in the black community are not explained (or even defended) and rarely if ever challenged.

We need gutsy Christian voices in the national public square that risk insult to raise issues of complexity and self-critique *without diminishing white responsibility*.

Holy, Muddy Ground

As for me, I've begun writing a memoir of Spencer's and my extraordinary friendship and our "beloved community" in Mississippi. It is the story of our struggles and growth especially in the years since *More Than Equals*. And Donna and I with our children await God's next chapter of activism and contribution in the call of racial reconciliation.

How could Spencer and I have predicted fourteen years together? Most of those years our families lived down the hallway from each other in our Antioch house. We shared dinner every night around the oversized table that Donna and I built for Antioch the year after we were married. Early on, Spencer claimed a spot at the far end and stayed there. We worked together, our desks only a few feet apart most years.

It was a real stretch to mix us up. But our lives became so intertwined that countless times people called Spencer "Chris" and me "Spencer"; we stopped correcting them.

He patiently taught me how to fish Mississippi waters, different tactics for bream, catfish and bass. To barbecue—"No, no, the sauce goes on at the end so it doesn't burn." To forgive deeply. I schooled him in the ways of Koreans, introduced him to autumn in Vermont and taught him about organizing your life and using the most of what God gives you.

He was the same guy in public as at home. Even at fine restaurants he asked for ketchup with his steak.

Together we dared to believe black and white didn't have to settle for where the residue of our past left us. Paul's one new humanity out of two peoples (Eph 2:14) wasn't pie-in-the-sky. It was meant to be a living reality. We lived it and became transformed.

We drew out the best in each other. But we took each other off a pedestal early in our friendship. Our relationship stretched us each in the right places, uncomfortable and painful places. We got close enough to see each other's dark side. Sometimes I wished he would somehow disappear, that exit with honor could be found.

In the same day Spencer could stand over me in a rage and say, "I'll knock you out, boy!" and later slip me a simple letter asking forgiveness: "I'm sorry for all the mean stuff I said this morning." The same relationship surfaced in me the image of Christ in self-giving sacrifice and the ugliness of the evil in my own heart—sins of the prodigal son's "perfect" brother who is lost in jealousy and anger.

But because of grace even as our dark side is exposed, we can be redeemed.

My friend Glen Kehrein, coauthor of the book *Breaking Down Walls* and a reconciliation veteran, once said to me, "Chris, racial reconciliation is one of the best roads to humility that we can take because of the opportunity to die to self." If Glen is right, then racial reconciliation must be a very high calling in the eyes of a God whose Son, not long before his own death, said to his disciples, "Unless a kernel of wheat falls into the ground and dies, it remains only a single seed. But if it dies, it produces many seeds. The man who loves his life will lose it, while the man who hates his life in this world will keep it for eternal life" (Jn 12:24-25).

Yes, deep reconciliation will produce justice and new relationships between the races. Yes, this will lead Christians to become a bright light of hope in the public square. But I have become convinced that God is not very interested in the church healing the race problem. I believe it is more true that God is using race to heal the church.

You see, Jesus never promised that we would solve the race problem. In the beatitudes of his great Sermon on the Mount, when we "hunger and thirst for righteousness," Jesus doesn't promise we will see society changed—only that we will "be satisfied." When we become peacemakers, he doesn't promise we will win prizes from our peers—only that we will share in the privilege of being called sons and daughters of God. And when we are persecuted for the sake of reconciliation, Jesus doesn't promise we will win unbelievers in the process—only that our reward in heaven will be great.

No, Jesus never promised we would solve the race problem. But if we are faithful to pick up our cross and die to self for the sake of reconciliation, he does promise that we will be changed into his likeness.

Tears still come when I think of Spencer. I laugh deeply remembering things only he and I thought were funny. I still tremble looking down the road ahead without him. But I always thank God for allowing me and my yokefellow to end our race together at the tip of a new territory of grace.

For me a chapter came to a close with Spencer's union with God. But in the end the real "story" was not about us, or even race, but about God and his grace. And that story, God's story, is not finished. Our almighty loving God always has the final word.

Chris Rice

Notes

Introduction to the New Edition

[1]Orlando Patterson, *The Ordeal of Integration* (Washington, D.C.: Civitas/Counterpoint, 1997), pp. 15-16 (italics mine). A profound book offering a mountain of persuasive documentation, Patterson's work is a must read for understanding black-white relations at the end of the twentieth century. I am indebted to his scholarship and insights.

[2]The Gallup Poll Social Audit, *Black/White Relations in the United States* (Princeton, N.J.: Gallup Organization, 1997), p. 18 (italics mine).

[3]"The Good News About Black America," *Newsweek*, June 7, 1999, p. 40.

[4]Ibid.

[5]Patterson, *Ordeal of Integration*, p. 52 (italics mine).

[6]"Good News About Black America," p. 40.

[7]Patterson, *Ordeal of Integration*, p. 61.

[8]Charles C. Moskos and John Sibley Butler, *All That We Can Be: Black Leadership and Racial Integration the Army Way* (New York: Basic Books, 1996), p. 2.

[9]Gallup Poll, p. 15

[10]Patterson, *Ordeal of Integration*, p. 199.

[11]The following books are highly recommended for further understanding of Asian Americans and Latinos and their role in racial reconciliation: Justo Gonzalez, *Mañana: Christian Theology from a Hispanic Perspective* (Nashville: Abingdon, 1990); Virgil Elizondo, *The Future Is Mestizo: Life Where Cultures Meet* (New York: Meyer Stone, 1988); Andrew Sung Park, *Racial Conflict & Healing: An Asian-American Theological Perspective* (Maryknoll, N.Y.: Orbis, 1996); Jeanette Yep, ed., *Following Jesus Without Dishonoring Your Parents* (Downers Grove, Ill.: InterVarsity Press, 1998); Tom Lin, *Losing Face & Finding Grace: 12 Bible Studies for Asian-Americans* (Downers Grove, Ill.: InterVarsity Press, 1996).

Chapter 1: Race Fatigue

[1]Jonathan Kaufman, "The Color Line," *Boston Globe Magazine*, June 18, 1989, p. 21.

Chapter 4: Who Is My Neighbor?

[1]"Evangelicals and Racism: The Lausanne II Press Conference," *Transformation*, January 1990, p. 29.

Chapter 5: White Blinders

[1]Quoted in Steven Waldman, "Sports, Politics and Race," *Newsweek*, August 17, 1992, p. 35.

Chapter 7: Black Residue
[1]Walter Shapiro, "Unfinished Business," *Time*, August 7, 1989, p. 15.
[2]Shelby Steele, *The Content of Our Character* (New York: St. Martin's, 1990), p. 44.

Chapter 8: Silence Gives Consent
[1]Elie Wiesel, "Unanswerable Questions," *The Plough*, September 1986, p. 22.
[2]Lerone Bennett Jr., *Before the Mayflower: A History of Black America*, 5th ed. (Chicago: Johnson Publishing, 1982).

Chapter 9: A Little Respect
[1]Shelby Steele, *The Content of Our Character*, (New York: St. Martin's, 1990), pp. 68–69.

Chapter 10: From Anger & Guilt to Passion & Conviction
[1]Mary King, *Freedom Song* (New York: Morrow, 1987), p. 500.
[2]Nicholas Lehmann, *Promised Land* (New York: Knopf, 1991), pp. 177–78.

Chapter 11: Weapons for the Battle
[1]Ben Carson, *Think Big* (Grand Rapids, Mich.: Zondervan, 1992), p. 121.

Chapter 12: Acts: A Reconciliation Story
[1]John R. W. Stott, *The Message of Acts: The Spirit, the Church and the World* (Downers Grove, Ill.: InterVarsity Press, 1990), p. 185.
[2]Ken Sidey, "Evangelical Ministries Do Not Attract Blacks, Other Minorities," *Christianity Today*, February 5, 1990, pp. 41–42.
[3]William Pannell, "A New Generation of Olds?" *World Vision*, December 1989–January 1990, p. 29.

Chapter 14: White Fear
[1]Quoted in James Cone, *Martin and Malcolm and America* (Maryknoll, N.Y.: Orbis, 1991), p. 141.

Chapter 15: More Than Skin Deep
[1]Walter Shapiro, "Unfinished Business," *Time*, August 7, 1989, p. 13.
[2]Shelby Steele, *The Content of Our Character* (New York: St. Martin's, 1990), p. 12.

Chapter 16: Soul Mates
[1]Shelby Steele, *The Content of Our Character* (New York: St. Martin's, 1990), p. 21.

Chapter 18: Kingdom Choices
[1]Rodney Clapp, "Is the 'Traditional' Family Biblical?" *Christianity Today*, September 16, 1988, pp. 25–26.

Chapter 20. Playing the Grace Card
[1]Philip Yancey, *What's So Amazing About Grace* (Grand Rapids, Mich.: Zondervan, 1997), pp. 80–81.

Resources

*** Indicates a resource that is highly recommended*

National Networks
Call to Renewal
2401 15th Street NW
Washington, DC 20009
(202) 328-8842
<http://www.calltorenewal.com/>

A network of spiritual renewal and social justice weaving together Protestant evangelicals, mainline churches, Catholics, Pentecostals and black churches. Resources include *Sojourners* magazine, grassroots organizing, conferences and a study guide, *Crossing the Racial Divide*.

Christian Community Development Association
3827 W. Ogden Ave.
Chicago, IL 60623.
(773) 762-0994
<http://ccda.org/>

Founded in 1989, CCDA boasts five hundred organizational members —grassroots churches and ministries working interracially to redeem impoverished communities. Many CCDA organizations provide opportunities to serve and volunteer. Resources include an annual conference and *Restorer* newsletter.

Hope in the Cities
1103 Sunset Ave.
Richmond, VA 23221
(804) 358-1764
<http://hopeinthecities.org/>

An interracial, multifaith network fostering racial healing through honest conversations in many U.S. cities. Resources include an excellent handbook on facilitating city-wide interracial dialogue and partnership, and a video "Healing the Heart of America."

Classics
Baldwin, James. *The Fire Next Time.* New York: Dial Press, 1963. Autobiographical novel of the early 1960s racial crisis.

DuBois, W. E. B. *The Souls of Black Folk.* Chicago: A. C. McClurg, 1903. A great scholar and activist's classic work written as America entered the twentieth century.

Griffin, John Howard. *Black Like Me.* Boston: Houghton Mifflin, 1961. The gripping autobiographical story of a white man who had his skin darkened and traveled through the segregated South of the 1950s.

** Malcolm X and Alex Haley. *The Autobiography of Malcolm X.* New York: Grove, 1965. An unforgettable book with much uncomfortable truth.

Washington, Booker T. *Up from Slavery.* New York: A. L. Burt; Doubleday, Page, 1901. Autobiography of an ex-slave who became a great achiever and voice for black Americans.

Washington, James M., ed. *A Testament of Hope: The Essential Writings of Martin Luther King Jr.* San Francisco: Harper & Row, 1986. Speeches, writings and letters from America's prophet of reconciliation.

Christian Reconciliation
Alcorn, Randy. *The Dominion.* Sisters, Ore.: Multnomah, 1996. Novel about a black journalist and redneck homicide detective tracing a crime through a maze of inner-city violence and racial conflict.

Dawson, John. *Healing America's Wounds.* Ventura, Calif.: Regal, 1994. Why the sins of the past still matter, and how they infect the church today.

DeYoung, Curtiss. *Reconciliation: Our Greatest Challenge, Our Only Hope.* Valley Forge, Penn.: Judson Press, 1997. A holistic Christian approach addressing barriers of race, class and gender. Filled with vivid stories.

** Ortiz, Manuel. *One New People: Models for Developing a Multiethnic Church.*
Downers Grove, Ill.: InterVarsity Press, 1996. Distinctives, models and principles for building multiethnic churches. Invaluable for local churches.

Pannell, William E. *The Coming Race Wars? A Cry for Reconciliation.* Grand Rapids, Mich.: Zondervan, 1993. Call to a costly gospel amid America's increasingly multiracial society.

** Perkins, John M., ed. *Restoring At-Risk Communities.* Grand Rapids, Mich.:
Baker, 1995. Fifteen contributors active in faith-based community development share biblical foundations, principles and strategies.

Usry, Glenn, and Craig Keener. *Black Man's Religion.* Downers Grove, Ill.:
InterVarsity Press, 1996. Deeply researched analysis of religion and history
showing why racism is not inherent to Christianity.

** Washington, Raleigh, and Glen Kehrein. *Breaking Down Walls.* Chicago:
Moody Press, 1993. A black-white team sharing principles shaped by their
experience in an interracial church and ministry in inner-city Chicago.
Study guide also available.

** Yancey, Philip. *What's So Amazing About Grace?* Grand Rapids, Mich.:
Zondervan, 1997. If Christians took this book's message seriously, it would
rock the world.

Theological Works

Park, Andrew Sung. *Racial Conflict & Healing: An Asian-American Theological
Perspective.* Maryknoll, N.Y.: Orbis, 1996. A Korean-American's unique perspective, with many powerful insights on the general racial landscape.

———*The Wounded Heart of God: The Asian Concept of Han and the Christian Doctrine of Sin.* Nashville: Abingdon, 1993. Groundbreaking exploration of the
Korean concept of han, the deep scar upon oppression's victims.

** Volf, Miroslav. *Exclusion & Embrace: A Theological Exploration of Identity, Oth-
erness and Reconciliation.* Nashville: Abingdon, 1996. The most important
contemporary theological work on reconciliation.

*** *Word in Life Bible.* Nashville: Thomas Nelson, 1993. A Contemporary
English Version study Bible with references, articles and background information linking biblical texts and stories to racial and ethnic healing. A very
valuable resource for biblical study.

History/Biography

Berk, Stephen. *A Time to Heal.* Grand Rapids: Baker, 1997. Biography of John
Perkins, a major black leader of an unheralded but highly influential post-
civil rights movement to rally Christians across economic and racial lines.

Branch, Taylor. *Parting the Waters* (1988), and *Pillar of Fire* (1998). New York: Simon & Schuster. Two books (the first a Pulitzer Prize winner) chronicling the civil rights movement, placing its origins in the black church.

** Cone, James. *Martin and Malcolm and America: A Dream or a Nightmare.* Maryknoll, N.Y.: Orbis, 1991. A leading black theologian and scholar analyzes two of the twentieth century's most important black leaders in a classic debate of solutions.

Franklin, John Hope. *From Slavery to Freedom: A History of African Americans.* 7th edition. New York: McGraw Hill College Division, 1994. A classic survey.

Lincoln, C. Eric, and Lawrence Mamiya. *The Black Church in the African-American Experience.* Durham, N.C.: Duke University Press, 1990. The finest sociological study in this area.

** Marsh, Charles. *God's Long Summer: Stories of Faith and Civil Rights.* Princeton, N.J.: Princeton University Press, 1997. Extraordinary stories of five combatants on different sides of the Mississippi civil rights movement and how Christianity impacted their beliefs and actions.

McCray, Walter Arthur. *The Black Presence in the Bible: Discovering the Black and African Identity of Biblical Persons and Nations.* Chicago: Black Light Fellowship, 1990. A groundbreaking study.

Oates, Stephen. *Let the Trumpet Sound: The Life of Martin Luther King Jr.* New York: Harper & Row, 1982. A powerful and highly readable biography.

Personal Stories

** Freedman, Samuel. *Upon This Rock.* New York: HarperCollins, 1993. A moving, wonderfully written portrait of the life and miracles of a black church in Brooklyn.

Gordon, Wayne. *Real Hope in Chicago.* Grand Rapids, Mich.: Zondervan, 1995. The amazing story of Chicago's "Lawndale miracle"—how a church of blacks and whites transformed their decaying neighborhood.

Kadlecek, Jo, and Pamela Toussaint. *I Call You Friend.* Nashville: Broadman & Holman, 1999. The life stories of four women, two white and two black, and how they were woven together.

Lupton, Robert D. *Theirs Is the Kingdom.* San Francisco: Harper & Row, 1989. Stirring, honest stories of failure and success from a white urban activist in Atlanta.

** Perkins, John M. *Let Justice Roll Down.* Glendale, Calif.: Regal, 1982. The powerful autobiography of Spencer's father, who grew up in a sharecropping family facing racial violence and hate, left Mississippi, then returned after his conversion to pioneer in racial reconciliation and ministry among the poor.

** Raybon, Patricia. *My First White Friend: Confessions on Race, Love, and Forgiveness.* New York: Penguin, 1996. An elegant, personal African-American narrative of hope for healing the scars of race.

Weary, Dolphus. *I Ain't Comin' Back.* Wheaton, Ill.: Tyndale House, 1990. Growing up in rural poverty, vowing to leave Mississippi behind, Weary returns to his hometown to plant a church-based work of love and reconciliation.

Contemporary Racial Analysis

DuBois, Paul, and Johnathan Hutson. *Bridging the Racial Divide: A Report on Interracial Dialogue in America.* Brattleboro, Vt.: Center for Living Democracy, 1997. Success stories and principles for effective interracial dialogue.

Intergroup Relations in the United States: Programs and Organizations. This 1998 publication of the National Conference for Community and Justice (New York) is an annotated directory of over three hundred diverse organizations that focus on race and intergroup relations.

Kozol, Johnathan. *Savage Inequalities: Children in America's Schools.* New York: Crown, 1991; San Francisco: HarperPerennial, 1992. Heart-rending exposé of inequality in public education.

** Loury, Glenn. *One by One from the Inside Out: Essays and Reviews on Race and Responsibility in America.* New York: Free Press, 1995. One of the most important books of the 1990s for those who think seriously about race.

Moskos, Charles, and John Butler. *All That We Can Be: Black Leadership and Racial Integration the Army Way.* New York: BasicBooks, 1996. How the U.S. Army overcame 1970s racial division to achieve widespread integration by the 1990s, with lessons for civilian society.

** Patterson, Orlando. *The Ordeal of Integration.* Washington, D.C.: Civitas/Counterpoint, 1997. A profound book by a historical sociologist offering a mountain of persuasive documentation about both astounding racial progress and deep-seated remaining problems. A must read for understanding black-white relations at the end of the twentieth century.

** Steele, Shelby. *The Content of Our Character: A New Vision of Race in America.* New York: St. Martin's, 1990. Extremely honest and insightful dissection of the black psyche.

Video

** *Eyes on the Prize.* The compelling PBS series on the civil rights movement (available at many local libraries).

** *Roots.* This series, based on Alex Haley's best-selling book tracing his family from Africa to slavery to freedom, has impacted millions of Americans.

Study Guide

How to Use This Study Guide

The purpose of this study guide is to encourage group discussion of racial reconciliation using *More Than Equals* as a guide. This resource can be used as follows:

1. By an individual in his or her reading and processing of the book. While the material is geared toward groups, it can be adapted for personal reflection.

2. For studying the book with a friend or an associate, especially of a different ethnicity. This is a much better use of the material.

3. In a discussion group at church, on campus or in a peer group, organization or neighborhood. A newly formed group or an existing group such as a pastors' fellowship, interracial network or business group would find the greatest benefit from this study.

The primary focus of *More Than Equals* is black-white reconciliation. However, study guide questions can be adapted to other crossracial experiences and contexts as well. Modify them according to your needs.

Forming Your Group

People of different ethnicities, political views and life experiences often approach race very differently. The more diverse your group, the greater the possibility of growth. If your efforts to be ethnically mixed fall short, don't be discouraged. Start where you can, with those who are willing.

Narrowing Your Focus

You may want to narrow the group's focus to reconciliation in a specific shared context. In one study, ten students focused on their own relationships with one another. In another, a Chicago ministry divided its staff into small groups and discussed how to make reconciliation visible in the organization. In still another, one black and one white church each brought five leaders into a discussion group. The study became a launching pad for collaboration between their congregations.

Format & Time Frame

The study guide has five sections: *Beginning—Race & My World, Admit—Facing the Truth, Submit—Embracing a New Beginning with God & Others, Commit—Transforming Our World,* and *Wrap Up.* Your study can be condensed into a month or extended over several months. Pick and choose the pieces that seem most important for your group. If you have a limited time frame, the sessions and questions that are bulleted (• •) are essential.

Ground Rules

Choose race as your topic and often everybody's walking on eggshells. Adopt ground rules: "Beginning—Race & My World" offers some suggestions.

Meeting Tips

☐ Start every meeting by briefly reviewing your group's purpose and ground rules (see the next section).

☐ The study guide is built upon chapter material. The more people read the assigned chapters, the better your discussion will be.

☐ Don't be enslaved to the questions. When you hit one that captivates the group, stick with it. *The process your group goes through together is just as important as what you discuss.*

☐ Leave at least ten minutes at the end for prayer. One way to do this is to have everyone pray for someone in the group, such as the person on their right. Prayer binds the group and keeps it focused on God's truth and will for the group.

Like the book, this study guide is not a formula. Hopefully the Holy Spirit will shake up your agenda along the way. Don't resist—that's when real transformation begins.

Remember, sessions and questions marked with two bullets are highly recommended.

BEGINNING "Race & My World"

• • *Session One*

Before beginning the book study, your group should talk about its purpose, commitments and ground rules.

1. Agree on your group's purpose. Read the following out loud. Use it as a starting point to discuss and agree on your group's purpose.

The purpose of this group is to seek and to speak the truth in love about racial reconciliation. The apostle Paul pleaded for Christians to "keep the unity of the Spirit through the bond of peace," calling us to "become mature, attaining to the whole measure of the fullness of Christ" (Eph 4:1-16). In verse 15 lies a key to this unity and maturity: speaking the truth to each other in love. Speaking the truth in love is not only being honest about our personal thoughts and feelings but seeking and speaking what we believe is God's truth. Truth seekers are willing to be changed by what they discover. We are to speak "in love," seeking the best interest of the other, in the hope of helping each other become mature in the fullness of Christ. "Love without truth is a lie; truth without love kills."

2. *Agree on your commitment to the group.* Talk honestly about your expectations for regular attendance and reading of the book. *More Than Equals* holds out a process of reconciliation. The best groups become a continuing conversation, each session building upon the previous discussions and experiences. Missing meetings will deprive you of the benefit of the growth process.

3. *Agree on ground rules.* The following ground rules have proven extremely helpful. Read them over and adopt what seems best for your group. Write down your shared ground rules and have someone read them at the beginning of every meeting.

In this group we commit to:

☐ Focus on what is right, not who is right.

☐ Make it safe to bring up anything. We give each other permission to ask honest questions.

☐ Protect confidentiality.

☐ Give each other the benefit of the doubt. We assume everyone is here because they have chosen to grow.

☐ Not take ourselves too seriously.

•• Session Two: Personal Stories & Expectations

Step one: Take ten minutes to reflect quietly on the five questions below.

Step two: Beginning with the first question, have each member of the group respond. Have everyone respond before moving to the next question. Listen carefully to the person to your right. You will pray for them at the end.

1. What is your first memory of when race was an issue?

2. What is your most vivid negative personal experience regarding race?

3. What is your most vivid positive personal experience regarding race?

4. What is one thing in your world that is different from your parents' world in terms of race?

5. What one thing do you most hope for as a result of this study?

Step three: Have each person pray for the person to their right.

Optional Action Idea

Spend the first fifteen minutes of each meeting with a new person telling their story until everyone in the group has done so. This can be a profound experience of understanding what makes a person "tick" and will enrich the group's dialogue.

ADMIT "Facing the Truth"

"When I heard these things, I sat down and wept. For some days I mourned and fasted and prayed before the God of heaven. . . . 'I confess the sins we Israelites, including myself and my father's house, have committed against you.'"

—Nehemiah 1:4, 6

Introduction & Chapter 1: Race Fatigue

What do you think is meant by the title of this book, *More Than Equals*?

•• On a scale of one to ten with ten being excellent, what score would you give race relations in America today? What about in the church? Give the reason for your score.

•• The authors contend that integration was once the dominant national ideal for race relations, but now a higher ideal of reconciliation is needed. How do the two ideals differ?

•• *Personal Reflection*

What signs do you see of race fatigue, nationally and/or in your own world? Have you ever felt it? When and how?

Chapter 2: Foot Soldier

How does Spencer's experience in this chapter compare to yours?

•• Spencer concluded that "I could not allow my anger and bitterness to defeat me. If I was to be a follower of Christ, I would have to try to be like him—to keep on forgiving." What is the significance of this statement, and how does it impact your understanding of racial reconciliation?

•• *Personal Reflection*

Much of this chapter focuses on the influence of Spencer's parents. How would you describe your parents' racial attitudes and choices? How did those influence you?

Chapter 3: At the Crossroads

•• List some tensions and issues of the 1983 reconciliation meetings at Voice of Calvary (VOC). Do any resound with your own experience and understanding? Which are unfamiliar to you?

List outcomes of the racial reconciliation meetings. In your view, what were the strengths and weaknesses of the meetings? Do you think the meetings were a step forward or backward, and why?

•• Despite a high level of racial integration at VOC before the 1983 meetings, a racial explosion occurred. What might be some differences between being racially integrated and racially reconciled?

•• *Personal Reflection*

Think back. Have you ever been in a context where there was a real opportunity for racial interaction or partnership, but you didn't act? In hindsight, what actions could you have taken, and why didn't you?

Chapter 4: Who Is My Neighbor?

•• Have one group member read the story of the good Samaritan out loud (Lk 10:27-37). Discuss the following:

☐ What do you think of when you think *neighbor*? How does Jesus' definition compare to yours?

☐ In terms of racial reconciliation, where do you see yourself in this story: as the person who was assaulted and ignored, the person who passed him by or the person who went out of his way to help?

If Christians were to live out this neighbor principle in our lives and churches, what would be different?

Is loving our racially different neighbor optional or a nonnegotiable of the gospel?

Read and discuss the quote from Vinay Samuel on page 67.

•• *Personal Reflection*

What kind of person would Jesus use as neighbor if he was speaking to you?

According to Spencer, Matthew 6:14-15 makes it clear that our forgiveness from God hinges on our willingness to forgive others. Discuss the implications of a call to unconditional forgiveness of others. How would the racial climate be different in the world if this principle was practiced? How would your world be different (don't think just in terms of race).

Chapter 5: White Blinders

•• This chapter argues that attitudes, practices and systems that uphold white advantages are protected by often-unconscious white blinders. Compare and contrast your understanding of racism to blinders. How does the concept of white blinders impact your understanding of the race problem?

In what ways, if any, do you think that the issue of race is fundamentally different for a white and a black person?

"If a person is born white in America, the chances are good he or she is wearing racial blinders." Do you agree or disagree?

•• *Personal Reflection*

What did you think and feel about the "reconciliation inventory" (pp. 78-79), and how did you score? Honestly evaluate the impact of another ethnic group upon you and your world.

Chapter 6: School Daze

•• Compare the racial dynamics of Spencer's experience with Dick with his experience integrating the white school in Mendenhall. Discuss their different effects on Spencer. Was Spencer's retreat into his all-black world justified?

•• *Personal Reflection*

Spencer's experience of frequently being the only African-American in settings during high school and college and otherwise is not uncommon. Have you ever been the ethnic minority in a situation or setting? What did you learn from your experience?

Chapter 7: Black Residue

Discuss how black anger and self-doubt may each have played a role in the 1983 reconciliation meetings.

Spencer contends that anger is present in nearly all African-Americans. Why were Spencer and the blacks of Mendenhall angry? Do you understand why black people as a group are angry?

•• In the authors' understanding, racial reconciliation is not just about whites changing. Obstacles in both the white community and in minority groups need to be honestly faced for the sake of the gospel. Discuss how this is different from other approaches to racial solutions familiar to you.

"It is easy to remain angry with a faceless white race. It is much harder to direct that anger at a particular white brother or sister who has a name and a face." What are the implications of this principle as a hopeful step toward racial reconciliation?

Chapter 8: Silence Gives Consent

•• According to Mark Dyer of International Teams, "We excluded blacks not by design, but by not going out of our way to build relationships. We were going out and seeking whites to join our organization, but not blacks. . . . Our financial structures, literature, locations, networks, and even style of worship often create barriers to non-Anglo involvement with us in ministry." Using the International Teams story as a case study:

1. What were the specific institutional blinders at the organization?
2. What advantages and disadvantages did these blinders result in?

Pick one area of society (e. g., banking, public education, law), and imagine that these kinds of institutional and social blinders are pervasive. Brainstorm what the unconscious systems, patterns, preferences and attitudes might look like in that arena and play out their negative impact on a particular ethnic group.

One definition of *racism* is as follows: "For one ethnic group to think they are better than another ethnic group, and to act on that belief by segregating, discriminating, or eliminating the other group(s)." A second definition makes a distinction between prejudice and power, defining *racism* as "prejudice plus power."

1. Choose one definition for the sake of discussion, and discuss how "silence gives consent" to racism.

2. Can blacks be racist? If so, how are black and white racism different? If not, what is the nature and name of racial wrongs committed by ethnic minorities?

Consider the stories of Mark Dyer, Kay Muller and Nehemiah, and the institutions they impacted. What similar steps and journeys were involved with each of them in moving from where they were to their ultimate actions and choices?

•• *Personal Reflection*

This chapter, in fact the entire book, is not so much concerned with overt racism. Its focus is unconscious attitudes, systems, preferences, practices—the social and institutional blinders—which do not intentionally exclude, harm and discriminate but nevertheless have the same result. Do an honest examination of your life and circles of influence for how silence may be giving consent to social and institutional blinders. What do you "see"?

Chapter 9: A Little Respect

•• Use the chapter's example of the Maori and white New Zealanders as your starting point to discuss the following: "If a society is less productive, we assume it must be inferior. Never mind that its people love and care for each other more than we do. . . . What is superior: a culture that values technological advancement or one that values relationships? The people who accumulate wealth and power, or the Maori who give it away?" (pp. 122-23). What is normally used as the standard by which a culture is measured? What should be the standard? Are all cultures equal?

•• What is the difference between appropriate ethnic pride and ethnocentrism? When is making cultural value judgments wrong or harmful? When is it right and useful? (You may want to distinguish between issues of cultural preference and issues of truth.)

Spencer writes, "Many blacks feel that the only setting in which they can be fully respected is among other blacks" (p. 127). Someone once said, "When minorities want to be in their own group, it's called ethnic pride. When whites do that, black people march." Is there a double standard, or is there a different need among ethnic minorities for ethnic-specific groups to ensure that their concerns and needs are addressed?

•• *Before Moving On*
Admitting means coming to terms with painful truth we don't like to face. These questions are to assist you, in the presence of a loving and gracious God who cares passionately about justice and truth, to honestly examine yourself and the obstacles you face in racial reconciliation.

Which of the following four terms best characterizes your life's path thus far in terms of racial reconciliation: racially integrated, isolated, separated, or reconciled?

From Your Perspective
What specifically about other ethnic groups makes you wonder if reconciliation can really happen?

Is there anything in your world said behind closed doors and thought behind closed mouths that is not admitted in public?

What do you think other races think and say? (Remember, even if you disagree with a generalization made about your group, if others believe it is true, then for the sake of reconciliation it needs to be addressed.)

Is there one thing you wish others could understand about you or your racial group?

As a voluntary act of love for God, examine your attitudes, experiences, lifestyle choices, theology, family, blinders, residue and "silent consent." In the light of the gospel of reconciliation, is there anything you need to "admit"?

What conditions do people often put on offering forgiveness and on doing justice? What conditions does God put on them? When it comes to racial reconciliation, what would it mean to be committed to both unconditional forgiveness and unconditional justice?

SUBMIT "Embracing a New Beginning with God & Others"
"See what this godly sorrow has produced in you: what earnestness, what eagerness to clear yourselves, what indignation, what alarm, what longing, what concern, what readiness to see justice done."
—2 Corinthians 7:11

Chapter 10: From Anger & Guilt to Passion & Conviction
Spencer and Chris experienced the racial reconciliation meetings of 1983

"totally differently." How was this true? What lessons do you draw from that difference?

•• Compare and contrast SNCC's racial crisis and VOC's. List the similarities of tension leading to each crisis. Contrast the conclusions. How was SNCC's worldview different from VOC's? What principles and strengths did VOC draw from their Christianity that enabled them to not only endure but become stronger?

Chris writes, "The gulf between black and white can be crossed only on a bridge built by the hands of God. . . . Without God at the center, there is no basis for reconciliation." This is a bold statement. What does it mean to put God at the center of reconciliation, and why do you think Chris and Spencer believe this so deeply?

•• *Personal Reflection*
Describe how Spencer and Chris each found growth and hope in the aftermath of the crisis. Do you draw any lessons that offer you hope?

Chapter 11: Weapons for the Battle

•• What are some resources and distinctives of Christian faith that should offer Christians an advantage in taking leadership in racial healing?

•• *Personal Reflection*
Which of the weapons do you need to call on the most at this stage of your reconciliation process?

Chapter 12: Acts: A Reconciliation Story

Make a list of barriers, baggage and residue that existed between ethnic groups in the days of the early Christians. What stands out to you the most in looking at the struggles of the early church?

•• Summarize the four lessons drawn from the story in Acts 6 (pp. 156-58). Which one stands out to you and why?

•• *Before Moving On*
Which "weapon" from chapter eleven ("Weapons for the Battle") best describes where you are today? Why?

1. I need to confess, forgive and be forgiven.

2. I need to internalize this purpose as my own.

3. I need to persevere through the pain of racial reconciliation.

4. I don't see how this issue applies to me.

Writes Chris: "At best, we want to wipe away the pain that race causes; at the least, it's tempting to look for a quick fix to rid ourselves of our pangs of guilt. But God is taking us through a process, and it's important not to try to find shortcuts." In your prayer together, ask God to take you through the journey he desires for you, in his timing and in his own way.

COMMIT "Transforming Our World"
"Therefore, I urge you, brothers, in view of God's mercy, to offer your bodies as living sacrifices, holy and pleasing to God—this is your spiritual act of worship. Do not conform any longer to the pattern of this world, but be transformed by the renewing of your mind."
—Romans 12:1-2

Chapter 13: The Character of a Reconciler
Multiethnic Antioch, not Jerusalem, became the headquarters for taking the gospel to the world. In light of the examples from this chapter and chapter twelve, and the vast tribal, ethnic and racial tensions in the world, what benefits does a multiethnic base bring to Christian ministry in the world?
•• Read Galatians 5:22-23 and list the nine fruits of the Spirit. First, using Peter's story over the last two chapters, make a list of ways in which Peter likely matured in specific fruits as a result of his reconciliation journey. Second, discuss the benefits of spiritual growth for you and the church in pursuing reconciliation.

Thinking back over the Acts story in the last two chapters, where was it positive to "see color," and where was color-consciousness harmful? What lessons do you draw?
•• How might a church or other group committed to being multiethnic look and act compared to one that is homogeneous?
•• *Personal Reflection*
Consider the confrontation between Paul and Peter in Galatians 2. What in your world may need to be confronted publicly out of a commitment to reconciliation?

Peter and Paul were often misunderstood by both Jews and Gentiles. They were walked on from both sides and pressured to choose one side over another. Their choices often alienated them from "their own." How might a commitment to reconciliation lead to the same consequences for you?

Chapter 14: White Fear
•• Pick two or three of the following situations and discuss whether the fear is reasonable or prejudicial. Discuss the differences between the two fears. (There isn't necessarily a "right" answer in each case. Change the ethnicity of the characters and see how it influences your perspective.)
☐ Jim is walking down an empty downtown street at night. A black youth approaches, and Jim notices his heart is pounding.
☐ A security guard in a clothing store notices he pays much more attention to black shoppers than to others.
☐ Duane lives in the suburbs, and he's driving through an urban, high-crime,

mostly black neighborhood. He is very low on gas when he see a convenience store ahead. But he passes it, praying he can make it out of this neighborhood before stopping.

☐ The black student union is holding a dialogue titled "Confronting Racism." A black acquaintance invites Susan (who is white) to come, and Susan finds herself looking for an excuse not to go.

☐ Meredith pulls up next to a car with a black man inside. She discreetly hits the power lock button on her doors.

☐ Rich (who is white) is on an elevator alone. It stops, the door opens, and a black man, professionally dressed, steps on. The door shuts, and Rich finds himself feeling nervous.

☐ In the last six months, three black families have moved onto the street in David's all-white, middle-class neighborhood. David is starting to wonder what the effect will be on his property's value and the thought hits, *I wonder if it's time to sell.*

Spencer writes, "I am convinced that much of the racism and hate that formerly prompted whites to separate themselves from blacks has now grayed into fear, anger and resentment. And we blacks need to be able to recognize the difference, even though to us these emotions look and feel nearly the same." How would this new climate affect the challenge of reconciliation differently from the old climate?

•• *Personal Reflection*

Can you identify any fear inside yourself? What do you think is its source?

Chapter 15: More Than Skin Deep

"Love without truth lies, and truth without love kills." How do you see this principle reflected in Spencer's and Chris' journeys? How does the principle apply to race relations?

•• Chris uses the phrase "kingdom culture" and contrasts it to blackness and whiteness. How is "kingdom culture" different? In what specific ways might a commitment to putting kingdom culture first speak to and influence our own ethnic culture?

•• *Personal Reflection*

Chris contends that every culture needs the vision of those outside of their culture to see their group weaknesses clearly. At this point in your reconciliation "surgery," what could a person of another race do to further your growth process?

Chapter 16: Soul Mates

•• Describe Spencer's dilemma as to whether or not he should marry Nancy. Which were legitimate issues, and which were not?

Why do you think interracial dating and marriage has been so vehemently opposed even by many Christians? Why has so much energy been invested in opposing it by racists throughout history?

•• *Personal Reflection*

How might we combat the fact that empathy tends to flow along racial lines? Spencer writes, "The people who will be most committed to racial reconciliation are the people for whom it has become a personal issue." How could you make racial reconciliation more of a personal issue for you? Your church?

Chapter 17: Unlikely Comrades

•• Spencer and Chris found they had much more to learn from each other than racial reconciliation. How did Spencer and Chris enrich one another's lives in ways unrelated to race?

•• *Personal Reflection*

Chris writes, "We had hung in with each other long enough to see that beneath the bitterness, anger and fear, we shared some dreams about being the people of God."

1. What dreams do black and white Christians share?

2. What might an area of common mission be for Christians of different races in your context?

3. What work will be necessary to reach the point where you can work as a team?

Chapter 18: Kingdom Choices

•• Read the story of the good Samaritan out loud (Lk 10:27-37).

1. Discuss ways in which the actions of the good Samaritan were not "normal," uncomfortable, inconvenient and costly.

2. Discuss kingdom choices in the area of racial reconciliation that would be not "normal," uncomfortable, inconvenient and costly.

3. Discuss the outcomes for the kingdom of the good Samaritan's actions and your own.

This book contends that racial reconciliation is about intentionally going out of our way for the sake of the gospel. Racial solutions are often approached as adding "more color" to the circles and institutions we already travel in and control. What would it look like, instead, to go out of our way, seek where God is already at work among our neighbors and serve their leadership, institutions and efforts in areas where you identify a common mission?

•• *Personal Reflection*

What kingdom choices could you or your group make for the sake of reconciliation that would provide a clear and compelling contrast to "normal" race relations in your setting?

Chapter 19: Friends & Yokefellows
Spencer writes of partnership with Chris, "If our yoke was broken, each of us would lose half our power." In what ways does this become true in a yokefellow partnership?

•• *Personal Reflection*
"The cause of the gospel needs interracial teams who are willing to take the dangerous point position to penetrate the gray, unknown territories that have traditionally separated white and black Christians." As you look across the nation and world, your city, and the mission field of the church, what missions are compelling enough to put an interracial yokefellow commitment together for? Dream together about some "unknown territories" you see and some specific interracial partnerships that, if formed, could begin to penetrate them.

Chapter 20: Playing the Grace Card
•• In the eyes of the world, what must whites do to be "worthy" of embrace by blacks? What must blacks do to be "worthy" of white embrace? How do God's eyes of grace see things differently, and what are the implications for racial reconciliation?

According to Philip Yancey, "Grace is unfair, which is one of the hardest things about it." What are some specific "unfair" steps that Christians of different ethnicities can take on behalf of another ethnicity?

Discuss this quote from Spencer: "My willingness to forgive oppressors is not dependent on how they respond. . . . When we can forgive and embrace those who refuse to listen to God's command to do justice, it allows them to hear God's judgment without feeling a personal judgment from us. Which, in the end, gives our message more integrity. Being able to give grace while preaching justice will make our witness even more effective."

WRAP UP
•• *Session One*
1. On a scale of one to ten with ten being excellent, what score would you give race relations in America today? What about in the church? Give the reasons for your scores. How do your scores compare to those you gave at the beginning of the book study?

2. What impacted you the most from the book? What have you learned?

3. What one thing has been most impressed upon you through this study

that could change the way you live out Christianity?

4. What opportunities do you see now that you've overlooked in the past?

5. What might you have to sacrifice as the price of a true commitment to be a reconciler?

•• *Session Two: Before the Meeting*

1. Determine your focus. The goal is for your group to come to a shared understanding of what racial reconciliation looks like in your specific context—whether your church, city, organization, campus or other setting. (As an example, "Sunnyside Christian Church" will be used as the shared context. Substitute your church, campus, organization or other setting where "Sunnyside Christian Church" is mentioned.)

2. Advance preparation. Develop a survey sheet with the following questions and pass it out several days in advance. (Assure people that their answers will be anonymous.) It should be completed by each group member before the brainstorming meeting and brought to the meeting.

☐ List three or four words that honestly describe your perception of the level of commitment to reconciliation and the state of race relations at Sunnyside Christian Church.

☐ Name one or two strengths that you perceive at Sunnyside Christian Church in terms of racial reconciliation. Name one or two weaknesses or barriers you perceive.

☐ Name a different ethnic group from your own and list one or two strengths that you perceive that group might bring to the reconciliation process as it affects Sunnyside Christian Church. Second, name two weaknesses or barriers you perceive in that ethnic group that are obstacles to reconciliation at Sunnyside Christian Church.

•• *The Meeting*

1. Summarize individual feedback: 30 minutes. Gather the survey sheets and have someone read through them out loud, quickly and anonymously. Have another group member use a flipchart to list responses for each of the survey questions. (Don't attempt to be exhaustive; go for the big picture. If an area is mentioned more than once, check it each time it's mentioned again.)

2. Small-group discussion: 1 hour. Break into groups of no more than five or six. Each group should be as ethnically diverse as possible. Have one volunteer in each group facilitate and another record your key discussion points. Discuss the following:

☐ If the people of Sunnyside Christian Church were to achieve genuine racial reconciliation and healing, how would it look and feel? How would it be different from the current reality?

☐ What are the barriers to moving toward this new reality?

☐ What are some assets and opportunities available to us in moving toward this new reality?

☐ What are the most important next action steps?

☐ What are assets that you bring and would be willing to engage in extending reconciliation?

☐ What other key individuals or groups must be engaged in this process?

3. Large group: 30 minutes. Have one person from each small group summarize their discussion with the large group. Have someone list group results on a flipchart.

4. Next steps: 30 minutes. What are the most important next steps in moving toward racial reconciliation at Sunnyside Christian Church?